I Laughed, I Cried

Viv Groskop is an arts writer and stand-up comedian. She has written for *The Guardian*, *Observer*, *Daily Telegraph*, and *The Times* and appears regularly on TV's *Sky news* and BBC Radio 4. She has twice been shortlisted for PPA Columnist of the Year, is a Funny Women Finalist and winner of Spontaneity Shop's Maestro Impro. She lives in London. This is her first book.

I Laughed, I Cried

. . . .

*How one woman took on stand-up
and (almost) ruined her life*

Viv Groskop

Copyright © Viv Groskop 2013

The right of Viv Groskop to be identified as
the author of this work has been asserted in accordance with the
Copyright, Designs and Patents Act 1988.

This edition first published in Great Britain in 2013 by
Orion Books
an imprint of the Orion Publishing Group Ltd
Orion House, 5 Upper St Martin's Lane,
London WC2H 9EA
An Hachette UK Company

1 3 5 7 9 10 8 6 4 2

A CIP catalogue record for this book is available
from the British Library.

ISBN: 9781 4091 2784 0

Typeset by Input Data Services Ltd, Bridgwater, Somerset

Printed and bound by CPI Group (UK) Ltd, Croydon, CRO 4YY

The Orion Publishing Group's policy is to use papers that
are natural, renewable and recyclable and made from wood
grown in sustainable forests. The logging and manufacturing
processes are expected to conform to the environmental
regulations of the country of origin.

Every effort has been made to fulfil requirements with regard to
reproducing copyright material. The author and publisher will be
glad to rectify any omissions at the earliest opportunity.

This is a work of non-fiction, and the events it recounts are true.
The views expressed in this book are the author's.

www.orionbooks.co.uk

For S.P.T.

Contents

Author's Note

Between 28 August and 5 December 2011 I performed a hundred gigs over a hundred consecutive days. The following is a true account of that period, based on notes taken at the time. The gigs took place in the chronological order here. All references to people and places are real. I experienced everything in this story exactly as I describe it. It is all told from my point of view and, if there are errors, they are entirely mine. I decided not to give specific names to gigs (unless they're very well established, like King Gong at the Comedy Store) because open mic shows come and go and many of those described here no longer exist. Where names are anonymous or details obscured, this has been done in an attempt to protect the guilty.

THE WARM-UP

July 2011

The back room of a pub in Stockwell, south London. Close to 11 p.m. 'Please welcome to the stage . . . ' Oh no, it's me. Sometimes they don't tell you where you are in the running order. I know I must be on soon as there are only a few slots left. But it still somehow comes as a shock. As I register my name being called, the adrenaline kicks in. For a good few seconds I can't breathe.

I'm sitting near the back and I have to push through the crowd to get to the stage. Cheers, clapping, whoops of support. The applause dies down. It's just me, a microphone and whatever I thought I was going to say. And – oh, yes – a massive white torture light shining in my face and blinding me. There's the feeling, suddenly, that I have worn the wrong underwear: these pants are too tight and they are cutting into me. Not that anyone else knows this. I try not to let the information about the pants show on my face.

The audience, at least, is relaxed. Amateur comedy nights can be excruciatingly uneven. That is painful for everyone attending. But tonight has been one of the better ones. I'm here with a couple of friends. They are having a good time. I am having a good time. A lot of new comics I really like have been on tonight. The crowd has been warm and welcoming to everyone. No deranged hecklers. No major interruptions. No epic drunkenness.

1

I'm feeling happy and relaxed. My underwear felt comfortable until I got on stage.

I have done maybe twenty gigs in the past year or so, so it's not as if I'm as nervous as I was the first time I did this. That time the brightness of the spotlight surprised me so much that I stood up there with my hand shielding my eyes. I forgot all my jokes and had to fish a Post-it note out of my pocket halfway through my routine and then could not read my own writing. This is not going to happen tonight. No. I am marginally better prepared now. But I'm still not quite used to it either.

I have seen enough stand-up to know that it can descend into disaster in a split second. That's what audiences go to live comedy for: the element of danger. It could so easily go so wrong. You can feel the relief in the room when the crowd senses that someone is in control and knows what they're doing. I know I can be that person. But only if I get lucky. Very often I am not that person. I am the opposite of that person.

A tingle of nerves bubbles up. Can I remember the next bit after the bit I'm saying now? Yes, it's there. Thank goodness. My memory is functioning. I allow myself to feel excited and actually enjoy what is happening. I love looking at the people in the audience, not that I can really see them. From the stage, the audience is in pitch-black darkness. But I can make out a few faces in the shadows in front of me. There's an overweight man who looks like a roadie in the front row. He sits with his legs wide open, a pint in one hand trailing off to the side. As he laughs, his stomach wobbles and his drink sloshes out of the glass. He has lots of pale, white skin, a large reddish beard and a Metallica T-shirt. He's not interested in looking at me (which is good because he has the face of a serial killer) but he is listening intently and laughing a lot. I can feel that he likes me. Or at least doesn't mind me. I like him back.

To the other side are two girls dressed in what look like matching outfits: baggy T-shirts, leggings, slouchy boots. They are clinging onto each other, long hair everywhere, because they are obviously slightly drunk. They do want to look at me – or, rather, they want to stare and grin gormlessly. There's a pause before one of the punchlines and one of them hiccups loudly and giggles at herself. They're content. And bemused by the posh lady (I'm pretty sure that's how they see me) telling jokes about her husband and kids and hip hop lyrics and whatever other stupid things I am saying. I beam contentment right back at them.

I have some new things I want to say: some jokes I have not put into this routine before. I have no idea whether they are funny or not as I've never said them out loud to anyone. 'You know Tinie Tempah? Or "the short-arse with anger management issues", as I like to call him? But don't say that to his face. That would be da disrespect.' (Giggling. This works.) 'Jessie J's Guide to Dating: do it like a brother, do it like a dude. But please use contraception otherwise it's rude.' (It's from a lyric. Not everyone gets it.) 'Sorry that I have come here looking like this. Unfortunately this is what I look like.' (Everyone gets it.) The people I can see like the new bits. Metallica man has a wheezy, chokey chuckle. The two girls are infectious. They create more laughs because people are laughing at how silly they sound when they laugh.

I know there's a section coming up where I can build up to some even bigger laughs and go out on a high. Sometimes I get nervous about it all going flat as I get to the last bit. But tonight I just feel like I'm meant to be here, these things are meant to be funny and we're all just having a laugh. Everything comes out perfectly without me even having to think about it. Or, rather, it comes out perfectly because I'm not letting myself think about it.

If this were a drug then it would have to be made illegal

because it's completely corrupting. It takes all the willpower I can muster to force myself to tell the last joke of my five minutes because I feel as though I could stay up here all night and they would keep laughing. But I come to the words: 'That's my time.'

As I slot the microphone back into the stand, I can almost feel an inner force not wanting to let go of it and wanting to stay on stage. There are only two things stopping me. First, you're not allowed to do longer than five minutes if you're new. You embarrass yourself by making the compère stop you if you overrun. Second, I don't have any more jokes. Much as there's a part of me trying to stay here, there's a voice inside me that's stronger. 'Quit while you're ahead.'

Applause, cheers, whoops of support. I step out of the spotlight back into the darkness and disappear into the shadows at the back of the room. Someone else is talking on stage now but I can't really hear them. My heart is pounding. This is the best moment. When you're still up there talking and trying to remember the next bit, your brain is too focused to allow you to register how good you feel. It's not until you step off the stage than you can really take it in. I lean against the wall at the back of the room, drunk with happiness. I had a good gig. My friend Ruth leans over and whispers, 'You won't let it go to your head, will you?' Blimey. I didn't think it was that good.

The next morning

'Wow, Mum! You're the winner! You're the winner!' At last night's gig the audience voted for their favourite. That comic was awarded a trophy. The trophy is sitting next to my bed. Two small bodies are smothering me. They are arguing about who is going to look after *the trophy and where the trophy is going to be kept. 'Mummy's the winner! Mummy's the winner!'*

The trophy is awarded every week. Sometimes the audience votes for the person who really was the best, a person you can imagine having some sort of distant future as a stand-up comedian. Sometimes they vote for the person who was only funny because they were so awful, a person you cannot imagine with a distant future or any kind of future in the entertainment industry or any other industry or in civilised society generally. This trophy is awarded fifty-two times a year. That's a lot of new comics that the audience has liked. Most of those fifty-two will have given up comedy within twelve months.

Still, this morning I am not thinking about the fact that the trophy is not an Academy award. Or that it may have been given to me because I am not funny, I am simply laughable. I am thinking that I am a winner and that I can do this. As far as the children, Will, seven, and Vera, five, are concerned, I am now Michael McIntyre. Or I am at least as good as anyone on Britain's Got Talent. *Possibly better. Because I have got a trophy and they haven't. The children show no awareness whatsoever that the trophy is three inches tall, made of plastic and weighs as much as a sugar cube. As far as they are concerned, it is the Olympic Medal of Comedy. And now riches, fame and greatness await us all.*

I can't pretend I'm entirely unimpressed by the trophy myself. Regardless of how the vote went at the end, I knew that I had had a good gig. When you know, you know. I would never have started doing any of this if I didn't think I could sort of manage it. But until last night I had not really, truly believed that I could make it work. It's Simon, my husband, who says what I'm thinking. 'You won the trophy. What if you can actually do this?'

Twelve hours later

The basement of a pub in central London, near Tottenham Court Road. Early evening. I wouldn't usually do two gigs in the same week, let alone two nights in a row. But somehow it has worked out this way. I am with two friends: Sam, a novelist, and Sarah, an editor. I am excited to tell them about the trophy. In fact I nearly brought the trophy with me.

We get drinks and go downstairs to check out the performance space because I haven't done this gig before. As we turn the broken handle of the rickety door into the room, I gulp. It is a bit of a different vibe to the night before. There is no stage, no spotlight, no red velvet curtain. There is a dark basement with a low ceiling filled with mismatched chairs, some of them broken. It is a narrow, dank place with no natural light. This would be a good place to imprison someone you had kidnapped. The carpet is patchy and sticky. The stench of air freshener and rarely used coffee machine fail to mask the unmistakable smell of sewage.

I have asked Sarah and Sam to come to this gig because it is in central London and I knew it would be easy to get to. It is the first time they have seen me do comedy. As we all pull our sweaters up over our faces to block out the stink, I realise that this was a terrible error. You should never judge a gig's suitability merely according to its location. You should only judge it by experience. I try not to think about this and focus on the memory of the trophy.

The clock ticks nearer to the supposed 8 p.m. start, but the room is not filling up at all. In fact my two friends are the only audience members. I get a sinking feeling. To my great distress, Sam and Sarah have handed over a crisp £5 note each, lips pursed but warding off my offer to pay for their tickets. (By comparison, last night's well-attended gig was free.) I wince inwardly and attempt to wash down mounting waves of self-loathing with Diet Coke. I think £5 is probably too much to pay for a gig where there's no one else in the audience and you're going to be sitting through ten amateur comedians. We should be paying them.

The three of us go and sit in the second row as the only audience. All the other comics are standing at the back of the room. Once it becomes evident that no one else is coming, the gig kicks off. There is no discussion with the promoter and the MC about whether the night will go ahead, it is just assumed that it will. Sam and Sarah look mildly disgusted (that'll be the sewage), but also supportive, hopeful and optimistic. I am thinking that any moment now the sewage smell will clear, some more audience members will turn up and this will be a fun night.

None of these things happen. It is high summer, very hot. The later it gets, the hotter it gets and the more the room smells of shit. By the third act we are watching with our shirts completely pulled over our mouths. I'm fourth in the running order. There's nothing I can do except make light of the situation, run through my lame jokes and get through my five minutes as quickly as possible before I can go back to my seat and pull my shirt back over my nose again. Every feeling I experience is the opposite to what I had felt last night. I don't know what I'm doing. I don't know why I'm here. If last night I had to be virtually dragged off the stage, tonight you need a cattle prod to get me up there.

Sam and Sarah try hard to force out some laughs when the microphone is in my hand, but they can see that I'm dying inside. With the whiff of a thousand cesspools bearing down upon us, not much is funny. By the time the next act comes on, Sam is looking at me daggers. She is not a person who suffers fools gladly. This is a serious convention of fools. And they have convened in a sewage works. I am including myself in this.

I do not know how or why it is that we manage to stay to the end but somehow we do. Possibly we are so incredulous that we have ended up in this awful situation that we become physically unable to leave. At one point there is an act who performs some kind of rat-catcher skit dressed as a pest-controller, reading it all from a clipboard. We are now laughing hysterically and cannot make eye contact with each other because it has turned into the weirdest night ever. By the time the last act comes on (even more depressingly, he is quite good and should not have to do this), we have turned our clothes into permanent face masks.

At the end, hanging onto each other because we are laughing so much (but not for the right reasons at all), we stagger back upstairs, away from the smell and away from the rat-catcher man. I buy drinks for Sam and Sarah, look them in the eye and say, 'How can I ever pay you back for this?' Sam looks at me, struggling to mask the pity in her eyes. 'Basically you can't.' It is funny and we are making a joke of it. But, really, it's not funny at all. Because they both know that I have spent a lot of time preparing for this and this is what I would like to do. And it's pretty tragic. We have just had a depressing, wasted and stinking evening. I manage to make light of it. Inside I am dying.

On the way home, I cry on the train. The shame, the embarrassment. Why do I want to do this? When I get home I see one of the children has put the trophy in the middle of the mantelpiece. It looks small. It looks pathetic. It looks how I feel. I can't have another gig like that. Not in front of friends. Not in front of anyone. I either need to take this seriously. Or give up.

One month later

I am sitting in the kitchen at my friend Dawn's house on a late September morning. Six of us, friends since we were eighteen, have been at a twenty-year university reunion the night before. The remains of bacon sandwiches, half-drunk cups of coffee and crumpled newspapers are strewn across the table. Pretty much everyone is hung-over apart from me. I wasn't drinking because I was performing stand-up as part of the event last night and therefore was the designated driver.

Everyone's faces are frozen with that morning-after, half-panicked contemplation of what can be remembered of the night before. Bad things happen when people who are nearly forty go back to a place where they were once eighteen. People were drinking port from the bottle at 2 a.m. One of my friends had to be tied to a chair because she kept trying to lean 'seductively' out of a second-floor window. There was one excruciating moment when someone tried to start a 'disco' in the room where we were 'partying' by playing music on an iPod, turning the lights out and switching an Anglepoise lamp on and off repeatedly. There were some middle-aged attempts at dancing. It was at this point that I announced that the designated driver was tired and going home; anyone who wanted a lift would have to untie themselves from their chair and get ready to go.

In my sober state I have become a conversational target for Dawn's mother, Rosemary, a formidable, practical woman, who has come round for Sunday lunch. Rosemary is a force of nature. No one else is really up to holding a conversation with her. She is berating me for leaving early: I should be staying for lunch and I am not. I am getting ready to leave. 'I would love to stay. But I have to get to a gig in Brighton,' I explain.

As soon as the words come out, I realise that I should have lied. I should have said: 'I need to get home to cook dinner for my family', or: 'I need to get home to read my children the next chapter of Little House on the Prairie, or: 'I need to get home to embroider my husband's name lovingly onto a pillowcase'.

9

Rosemary raises her eyebrows. We are near St Neots in Cambridgeshire. Brighton is easily two hours away. She knows I have three children pretty much the same age as her daughter's. My youngest child is only just one year old. Brighton? A 'gig'? What is a woman of my age doing driving to Brighton for a 'gig' when I have already just spent the weekend away from my husband and children at a reunion? She looks at me, half quizzically, half accusingly. 'A gig?' She says the word as if I have just said I want to become a prostitute. 'What sort of gig?'

'I've started doing stand-up comedy, Rosemary.' A startled reaction. 'Stand-up comedy? Like Michael McIntyre?' Her eyes start to pop slightly. The expression on her face is not unlike that of Dame Maggie Smith when she learns of the invention of the telephone in Downton Abbey. 'It's not exactly Michael McIntyre,' I reply, as a picture of Michael McIntyre's £3 million McMansion pops up in my mind's eye, 'But yes. Sort of.'

'Where do you do that?' 'Everywhere I can. But mostly in London.' 'Do people think you're funny?' 'Sometimes they do. Sometimes they don't.' 'But Michael McIntyre is funny all the time.' 'Yes. I'm sure it appears that way.' 'Do they pay you?' 'Sometimes. Mostly not. It takes a long time to get good enough to be paid decent money in comedy.' Another raised eyebrow. I am waiting for her to say, 'Michael McIntyre seems to earn good money', but she does not say this. Instead she asks what people always ask: 'What's your schtick?'

I hate this question. It's a perfectly reasonable question. After all, what sort of comedy are we talking about here? Observational? One-liners? Dirty jokes? But I don't really know yet how to describe what it is that I try to do on stage and so it's hard to say. 'Charming oddball, apparently.' This is how a friend of a friend who reviews comedy has characterised my act. I don't really like it but according to him this is how I come across.

I am relieved not to have to get into what my material is, because I have not yet worked out how to characterise that either. Amusing wordplay about the trials of middle-class life? That sounds terrible. Jokes about motherhood and marriage? Even worse. Intentionally bad rapping about suburbia and feminism? Seal the exits.

Rosemary looks at me sceptically. 'What does your husband think of all this?' 'Oh, Simon's really supportive ... He's really into it.' Rosemary narrows her eyes. What I'm telling her is all very well, if what I am describing were some new madcap hobby. We've all had one of those. Goodness knows, Rosemary's husband once spent several years building a moat around the house with his bare hands. (This actually happened.) But it doesn't seem to explain the fact that I've already been away from my family for one night, performed comedy last night and am now about to drive another two hundred miles to perform comedy again tonight. That seems a bit excessive for a hobby. The beady eye again. 'So why Brighton tonight? So soon after last night?'

I have not really been telling anyone what I'm trying to do with my life at the moment as I'm only in the first week of trying to do it. But sod it. Maybe I should start now. A deep breath. I look Rosemary in the eye. 'I'm doing a hundred gigs in a hundred nights. Today is day eight. I've done seven gigs. Tonight is number eight. If I miss tonight's gig then I'll be behind by one gig. That's why I have to go. Otherwise I'd cancel it and stay for lunch. Obviously.' She looks at me disbelievingly. 'A hundred gigs in a hundred nights?' she repeats, checking to see if she understood what I said and whether I am serious. 'Yes,' I say, solemnly.

Rosemary bursts out laughing. I have never seen her laugh like this before. By the looks of it, neither has anyone else. She laughs for a very long time, stopping only to just about catch her breath and prevent herself from falling off her chair. I look on, coolly, secretly pleased. So far my efforts at comedy have proved a bit hit and miss. But if I can make Rosemary nearly fall off her chair then I must be getting somewhere. 'I'm sorry,' she says, gasping for air, suddenly worried that she has offended me, 'it's just ... why would you do that?'

'I know it's not a very sensible thing to do. And I sort of wish I had never started it. But I got the idea into my head that I needed to do it in order to find out if I am any good at comedy. I needed to know in the shortest time possible whether there's any point in me going on ... and now I've set myself this challenge and I'm stuck with it. I'm keeping a record of my progress, a diary. So that I can work out whether I am improving or not.' (So far this process is not very scientific. I type stream-of-consciousness rants into my iPhone on the way back from gigs and write down the sometimes hilarious and sometimes horrible things other comics have said to me. Typical exchange: new comic: 'How long you been going?' Me: 'I started two years ago but I've had some time off because I had a baby last year.' He: 'I'm not saying it's a competition or anything. But I'm a single parent of a four-year-old boy and I have done two hundred and fifty gigs in eleven months.' Me: 'Oh. Okay.')

Rosemary is both intrigued and horrified. 'But you must be out every night.' 'Yes. I will be. For just over three months.' 'What about the children? What about your husband?' 'They're really into the idea,' I lie, 'they know it's an extreme device to make myself do something I really need to do.' I shrug. 'Simon and the children don't mind. Really. And it's only three months.' 'Heavens. A hundred gigs in a hundred nights. Good luck to you, dear.' She chuckles to herself again. 'It seems mad to me, though. Quite mad.' Sideshow over, she turns to unload the dishwasher.

I pick up my car keys and go to get my stuff. It's a long way to Brighton and I have to drop in and see the children and Simon

12

on the way. The truth is, I am not entirely sure why I am doing it. And Simon and the children do mind. It's only been a week. And they are starting to mind quite a bit.

SHOWTIME

A Diary of a Hundred Gigs
in a Hundred Nights

1: Gigs 1 to 5:

'What on earth were you doing up there?'

Day 1, Gig 1: Kingston-upon-Thames

Surprisingly lovely open mic indie music night in a wine bar by the river. This is a night where anyone can do anything they want: play the guitar, perform poetry, rap. High praise from fellow performer under-18s beatboxing champion Mr Soundbytz. (Catchphrase: 'Soundbytz is gonna munch ya.') 'We've had lots of comics down here and they're usually awful. You're not. You're actually funny.' Not easy to get laughs in a room that hasn't been warmed up by a compère and when the act on before you is a mournful country and western singer. My sister, who came with me for moral support: 'I don't know why you do these things. I suppose you were quite funny, though. Or, at least, they seemed to like you.' Eight out of ten. If they're all like this, this will be a breeze.

Day 2, cancelled gig: Stockwell

Well, this is a bad omen on only the second night. Gig cancelled as I realised I had failed to book myself onto the list. Some sort of email cock-up. My fault. At least I realised before I got there. Managed to get onto the list at Islington at the last minute. I am realising that the logistics of getting a gig every night are going to be one of the most stressful things about this experiment.

Day 2, Gig 2: Islington

Survivable to easy. Convivial gig. No major incidents. Strange, melancholy MC who claims to be Argentinian but that may be a sort of Javier Bardem character act. I later find out that he genuinely is Argentinian. This is somehow even more frightening. Six and a half out of ten. One mark knocked off for weird MC.

Day 3, Gig 3: King's Cross

Wow. I can do this. Captured the attention of the whole room. Felt like I was flying. Felt like I could do anything. As I come off stage, MC whispers: 'You f***king smashed it.' This is what comedy people say when someone does well: 'You smashed it.' 'You stormed it.' 'You took the roof off.' No one has ever said this to me before. Ninety-nine out of ten. Floated the whole way home. I have found my vocation. If every gig is like this ... then I'm in heaven.

Day 4, Gig 4: Soho

Just. Unspeakably. Awful. Unavoidable return to sewage venue (where I had vowed never to return). Couldn't get a gig anywhere else tonight so had no choice but to force myself to go back. Attacked by another comic, a crazed gin and tonic-drinking girl who told me that my material was 'just the same as everyone else is doing'. Biggest laugh of the night: 'My name is Viv Groskop.' I know I have a stupid name but what is that about? Told by MC that I resembled Theresa May. Never wearing pearl necklace again (too dangerous for heckles generally anyway). Almost beaten up in pub by cross girl (not the same as gin and tonic girl) whom I accidentally hit with my large handbag. Cried in front of barman because no cash for Diet Coke. Abysmal evening. Zero out of ten. If every gig is like this, I give up now.

Day 5, Gig 5: Islington

With Bee Gees lookalike MC. Initially, cheering. Loads of friends in the audience. Died on my arse. My friend Alex: 'As soon as you started, I wondered what on earth you were doing up there.' You do not want anyone to be thinking that. Three out of ten. Want to give up. Strangely sanguine about having a bad gig, though. Expected to feel worse. Breakthrough? Or I'm just becoming delusional?

*

On the morning of Saturday, 27 August 2011, my baby son Jack, our third child, woke up to find he had turned one year old. I made him a cake in the shape of a number one. His brother Will gave him some Smarties. His sister Vera ceremoniously handed over her favourite soft toy, a mouse called Mouse. (She later took it back again.) On that day I stopped breastfeeding after a year of lactating, cried for about half an hour and had a quiet evening at home. The following day I started my mission: a hundred gigs, a hundred nights. No more Mummy. It was showtime.

This is not something I had ever imagined I would do. Ten years ago I would not have predicted it. Even a few months before it started, I would not have predicted it. Ten hours before I started it, Simon, my husband of eleven years, still did not fully anticipate that I would actually go ahead with it. When I first told him about the idea of gigging every night for just over three months, one hundred nights consecutively without a break, he just looked at me blankly and said, 'Why would you do this to us?' But we all have things we wish we had done with our lives.

This was mine. As a child, I wanted to be a comedian or a writer. In my twenties I became a journalist. I like being a journalist. I am perfectly happy being a journalist. But the older I get, the more often I find myself thinking, 'Really? Is this it? Is this how my life was meant to turn out?' I could feel my fortieth birthday in 2013 ticking away somewhere in the future like a time bomb.

I had always dreamed of being a stand-up comic, but only in the way that you might dream of walking on the moon. You might love the idea and read obsessively about other people doing it. But you never imagine doing it yourself. It was only after I hit my mid-thirties that I realised that there are some things in life which you can just do if you want to. No one is stopping you. Walking on the moon requires long-term planning and large amounts of cash. Stand-up just requires balls. And some basic organisational skills. (Which is why there are not that many women in stand-up comedy. They lack the basic organisational skills. Ho ho.)

It is stupidly easy to become a stand-up comedian. You just do it. You can be pretty much anywhere in the world any night of the week and be within a twenty-mile radius of an open mic gig. In London there are sometimes as many as ten of these a night. Any idiot can get up and talk into the microphone. One night, after doing a comedy workshop with some other people who had never gigged before, I became one of those idiots. Getting up there and getting through your five minutes is scary but not impossible. Doing it repeatedly and getting good at it? That's a whole other thing.

I eventually became fixated on the idea of doing a hundred gigs in a hundred nights for practical reasons. First, it was the basic number that always came up whenever anyone who knew anything talked about comedy. I had taken a comedy workshop taught by a comedy tutor called Logan Murray, a stand-up comedian who has developed a following among new comics. He used to be in a double act called Bib and Bob, with Jerry Sadowitz. Now he coaches people towards their first gig and helps lots of more established acts refresh their material. Some of the people he has taught have done well – like Andi Osho and Rhod Gilbert. Murray says: 'You need to do a hundred gigs before you even know whether you want to be a stand-up.' He also cited a hundred gigs as the minimum marker for getting paid; before that point you couldn't really hope to be paid. Before I started this extreme experiment I had done a few dozen gigs in two years and earned £10.

During the time I should have been out doing gigs, I spent a lot of time reading Logan's book, *Teach Yourself Stand-Up Comedy*. I think I thought that if I read it enough times, I would somehow become a stand-up comedian without actually having to do any stand-up comedy. This was not working. In the book, the comedian Richard Herring (affable, shambolic, was once one half of Lee and Herring with Stewart Lee) says this: 'There is a chance that you are not as funny as you hope. There is always time to improve and no one steps up on stage and is just brilliant straightaway.' That's comforting to read. Then he adds: 'But don't keep plugging away at this job if it really is not working for you. I would set a time limit of, say, five years. If you find that audiences still don't like you and promoters don't want to book you, then it could be time to think about doing something else.' FIVE YEARS? I am nearly forty. In five years' time I could be dead. I do not have five years.

If you read any interview with any stand-up comedian it will tell you the same thing. You have to do stupid amounts of gigs for stupid amounts of time (and, generally, no money) before you get any good and certainly before anyone like an agent, a manager or a television producer notices you and helps you towards some kind of career. Sarah Millican (cake-obsessed Northerner, biggest DVD sales ever for a female comedian) says that in her early career she gigged every night possible and took a slot wherever it was offered, no matter how inconvenient it was to get to. This is what you have to do to progress. There is no other way.

At the kind of gigs where you can get on the bill when you're new, the gig is free and the pub just agrees to put on a comedy night because they want to boost their drinks sales. Sometimes the pub will pay a small fee to someone to organise some comedy. One or two of the acts might see a bit of this money. It's unlikely, though. Basically, you are doing unpaid work experience and you have to be bloody grateful for it. You won't get on the bill at better, well-attended gigs unless you have been around for a while and people know you. As a new comic, you need to try out your jokes and get used to performing. Winning comedy competitions – or at least getting into a semi-final or a final – is a big help. But to win those, you need experience.

You quickly realise that you are in a catch-22: you are not good enough to get in front of a real comedy audience, but unless you can get in front of a real comedy audience you will never get good enough. This is where the open mic gigs on the amateur circuit come in. These are gigs where you can book in advance to perform or where you can take your chances by turning up on the night: you may or may not get on the bill. In London some of them are well established and have been running for years – Lion's Den Comedy Car Crash, Comedy Virgins, King Gong at the Comedy Store. (It is an unwritten rule that they are always called horrible, scary names, like this. And Comedy Bin. Touching Cloth is another.)

Then there are the big gigs which everyone on the amateur circuit is always trying to get in on: Up The Creek in Greenwich,

Downstairs at the King's Head in Crouch End and Comedy Cafe in Shoreditch. The five-minute spots at these places are all booked months in advance. You're more or less guaranteed a full house at these gigs and that's what all new comics are chasing: a room packed full of punters. Because they are long-standing venues and properly promoted, they pull in reliably big crowds. Plus, you have the chance to be on the bill with more established acts, one or more of whom might be getting paid for their spot. You can learn from these people and pick their brains. You can ask them to watch your act and give you feedback. Also, if the promoter likes you, they might ask you back to do an 'open spot' (unpaid) at a more professional night they run. Or if you're really good, they might book you straight in for a 'paid ten' (a ten-minute spot paid anything from £10 to £100 or a split of the takings on the door). Comedians who have been on the telly will do 'paid twenties' (twenty-minute spots) on Friday and Saturday nights, running between gigs in central London to make as much money as possible. Sometimes they'll do five in a night. You don't get to do this until you have been doing comedy for many years.

For the amateurs there are dozens more 'bringer' gigs. These are open mic nights where you are guaranteed a spot if you bring one or more audience members. Then there are nights where most of the acts are unpaid but they are booked and chosen by a promoter. Some of them will book you unseen if you send an email. Others want to see a video of you performing. Others want you to come to their night first and talk to you. Mostly they want you to bring audience to their gigs. It might sound crazy that you have to be selected and vetted for 'work' which you're not even being paid for, but these gigs are basically providing a rehearsal space for new comics. And there are so many new comics out there that promoters can pick and choose who performs. On Facebook there's a group called Comedy Collective for information about open mic gigs in London. The number of members – now almost two thousand – has doubled in a year.

If 99 per cent of all of this is unpaid, 100 per cent of it operates according to unwritten rules. Some of the gigs will only book acts once every six months. Others have waiting lists. Others have promoters who have their favourite type of comedy and if your comedy is not that, then you are going to wait a long time to get a slot. Maybe forever. This is why lots of comics set up their own gigs. In fact most of the amateur circuit open mic gigs are now run by comics for comics. At these gigs on a good night there will be between ten and twenty people in the room (fewer if the room smells of sewage). Ten of these will be comics and the other ten will be their friends (or possibly other comics, having a night off from gigging). If you're lucky maybe three or four people will be genuine punters. If there are more than twenty or thirty people in the room, then truly that is a red-letter day. As you can imagine it's not ideal, doing these kinds of gigs, but while you're waiting for your once-every-six-months slot in front of eighty people at Downstairs at the King's Head, it's all there is.

It's because of all this that before attempting to do a hundred gigs in a hundred nights I have not really done that many. Doing a gig in front of four hundred people at a fundraiser at Leicester Square Theatre is stressful. (I did this when I had only done about a dozen gigs in total. I was completely unprepared and it was horrific.) Doing a gig in front of twelve neurotic comics, two of their friends, a tramp and three Italian tourists who don't speak any English is far, far more stressful. But unless you do the gigs with the tramps and the Italians (sorry, Italians, it's not your fault, I picked you arbitrarily and there are probably more

Swedes around these days anyway), then you will never be good enough to do the big gigs. You will never really be good enough to do anything.

Knowing all this, for the first two years after I discovered comedy I spent a lot of time avoiding tramps and Italians by not doing that many comedy gigs at all because I was scared. Instead, I devoted all my time to thinking about Richard Herring's advice. Five years seemed like such a long time and I couldn't imagine putting everything else in my life aside and just doing comedy for that amount of time. Then, just as I was thinking that I needed to give up any thought of doing comedy properly, I happened across a maxim about changing your life: that in order for anything new and radical to happen you have to practise a new habit every day consecutively for ninety days. It struck me that that is a much more manageable period of time.

There is a lot of controversy in the rehab industry about where this idea came from and whether you have to stick to it in order to succeed. The 'ninety days' thing is used in Alcoholics Anonymous as a basic minimum requirement. Some people in the movement think you should attend ninety meetings in ninety days. The idea first came up in an article in the Alcoholics Anonymous newsletter *Grapevine* in 1959: 'Surely you can spare ninety days from your life? They might prove to be the most useful days in your entire lifetime. You may learn whether or not you're an alcoholic. And that's a good thing to know.' That is a good thing to know. But I am not really interested in whether I am an alcoholic. (That's not true. I'm not in AA but I know that I am mildly alcoholic, which accounts for my interest in such things.) What I want to learn is whether I'm a stand-up comedian. That would be a good thing for me to know. If I could spare ninety days from my life, would I have the answer?

Somewhere between Logan Murray's hundred gigs, Richard

Herring's five years and AA's ninety days, I settled on this idea. The thought of devoting my life to comedy for five years was daunting. What if I did a hundred gigs in a hundred days as a compromise? That would be close enough, surely? After that I would definitely know if I wanted to be a comedian. And I would also have a pretty good idea of whether I'd be good enough to be one too.

I had form on this score. I like extremity. When I was on my university year abroad in St Petersburg, I learned Russian by banning all contact with English speakers (including my own parents) for six months. In my mid-twenties I used to smoke forty cigarettes a day. I decided I wanted to stop and gave up from one day to the next. When I was in my mid-thirties I took an A level to prove that A levels are not as easy as some people say they are. When I have fixed my mind on something, I do it.

So I set up the hundred gigs. I thought if I planned it all on a computer spreadsheet, it would be too easy to delete if I started to lose heart. So I took a piece of paper and wrote a hundred consecutive dates on it. I started booking gigs and filling in each date. From the point of view of securing the gigs themselves, it looked as if it would be possible. But it was not going to be easy. There were plenty of open mic gigs on Mondays and Tuesdays where I could more or less guarantee that I could turn up unannounced and get a spot, even if it sometimes meant I had to bring an audience member in order to be allowed to perform (which was a pain but I could do it). Every other night of the week I would have to pre-book. Fridays and Saturdays were going to be the biggest problem because they are the nights when people want to pay to see comedians off the telly. There aren't so many open mic gigs on those nights. But maybe I could find a way around it. I convinced myself that I'd be able to get on somewhere every night if I really pushed it. This was the purpose of doing a hundred gigs in a hundred nights: to force myself into getting the stage time.

I made some rules. First, I would try to gig every night, but if that was impossible and I had to miss a night then I would double up the night after. I had seen other comics do this: you ask to go on first at one gig and go on last at another. Doing three gigs in a night is 'tripling up'. It's one way of getting extra stage time. It's not something you would want to do every night – it's exhausting – but it was the only way I could guarantee the experiment would work if I got ill or if gigs were cancelled. I would also try and get as many daytime gigs as possible (I had an inkling that these existed here and there), so that I could take some nights off. And I would try to gig as widely as possible, so that I wouldn't just be doing London gigs. I needed to work (at journalism) and earn money during the day to make this whole experiment affordable, but if I could feasibly travel anywhere to gig, then I would. Gigs outside London are sometimes regarded as a better testing ground. The audiences can be harsher. It's not just comics and their friends like it can be in London; it's proper punters.

Second, I would record video footage of every gig and watch it back at the end of every night or first thing the next morning. I needed to know if the good gigs were as good as I imagined and if the bad gigs were as awful as they seemed. Third, I would keep a diary of the gigs in note form on my phone. I knew that my memory was unreliable. I inflated both the good gigs and the bad gigs over time, making them seem better and worse in my mind than they actually were. If I had a record of how I felt at the time, it would give me a better sense of whether I should go on with this whole business or not.

Fourth, and finally, at the end of the experiment I would add

27

up how many gigs were good and how many gigs were bad. If the bad outweighed the good, according to Richard Herring's rules, I was officially rubbish and should spare the world from any more of my performances. And I would have done it in three months instead of five years.

I decided I would get Jack's first birthday out of the way before I started, because what sort of person starts an experiment like this before their baby has even turned one? I realise this slightly overlooks the fact that a person with three children, one of them still a baby, is not much better. But I am the person who quit smoking forty a day overnight. I can do this thing. This is my mission. I would let Jack have his birthday and then I would start. Before he was one year and one week old, I'd done five gigs.

2: Gigs 6 to 14:

'Got a lot of friends in, have you?'

Day 6, Gig 6: Greenwich

Unspeakably lovely gig! Joy of joys. One of the most hilarious and bizarre nights of my life. Totally unexpected.

Day 7, Gig 7: Cambridge

Crowd of 100+ for college reunion. Former classmate: 'Quite funny, I suppose. For a woman.'

Day 8, Gig 8: Brighton

One of those magical nights that makes it all worthwhile. Smooth performance, big laughs, happy audience. Beautiful ancient hippy man smiling beatifically in the front row. He made my night. Big love for the Tinie Tempah line, which has stayed in and now works. Big love for the sequinned cardigan. Brighton's my crowd. I can do this. I can do this. I can do this.

Day 9, Gig 9: Stockwell

What should have been my triumphant return to the place where I last won the trophy for being the comedian of the week turned out to be a total car crash. Middling. Uncomfortable. Tired. Trying too hard. Shame. Am I now getting worse, not better? Three out of ten. Don't miss breastfeeding but breasts slightly twitchy. Ignored them. Unlike the punter in the front row who STARED at them with menace throughout my entire set. Or maybe I imagined it.

Day 10, Gig 10: Sheffield

The first of a handful of daytime gigs I have managed to wangle. This one involved travelling up to Sheffield to perform to a mother and baby group. This is a new thing in comedy that a few people have been trying to get off the ground: you book the back room of a pub during the day, invite a load of new mothers who would otherwise be sitting at home going quietly mad and you try to perform stand-up comedy to them. It's like Baby Scream Cinema (special screenings when you're allowed to take your baby), only with stand-up instead of a film. Hugely nerve-wracking. Packed crowd. Barely heard over the wailing and screaming. I swear there were lulls when everything did go suddenly quiet and you could hear babies suckling. Appreciative audience, though. Never was it more true that the audience was just glad to get out of the house and would laugh at anything. A challenging but enjoyable experience. Sheffield is a bloody long way to go for a gig, however. Spent longer on the train than I did in Sheffield. Highlight of day: Marks and Spencer sushi on the way home. Rock and roll.

Day 10, Gig 11: Highbury

Middle-of-the-road gig. Tired. First attempt to do two gigs in one day. Met nice comics, though. Sometimes if you can just see one person you really like it makes the whole thing worthwhile. The nice people are, however, not always there. Salt and vinegar crisps on way home. Big sense of achievement from first 'double'. Now I'm one gig ahead. In your face, 100 days. In your face.

Day 11, Gig 12: Clapham

Fairly dead night but nice MC and nice comics. So excited to gig somewhere closer to home than usual (a lot of the gigs are in north and central London and I live in south-west London) so that I can be home before 11 p.m. Exhaustion setting in. Got Simon to watch a load of the footage back so he can gauge my progress. Simon's Video Verdict: 'I think you come across as quite odd.'

Day 12, Gig 13: Kentish Town

Too many acts. Friend said of one of the other comics (a woman in her early twenties who has done dozens of gigs and takes herself seriously as a comedian): 'Is she actually mentally ill?' I have asked myself the same question of this woman many times. And then worried that people also ask it of me. Same friend, later, after witnessing the death of several acts, including one who was visibly shaking, went green in the face and had sweat pouring off him: 'I say this completely without any agenda. Why would anyone want to do this?'

Day 13, Gig 14: Soho

Horrible atmosphere. Wrong-footed as idiot MC Dr Death (not his real name, just what he looks like) told me I was going on second, but he meant second after him. Toxic loon. Because I was taken totally by surprise about when I was supposed to go on stage, I started messily and never really recovered. Crazy guy!

Crazy way of counting! Annoyingly no footage of this shambolic gig because I did not realise when I was going on stage so I could not press 'Record' in time. One out of ten. Rubbish waste of time.

*

People always want to know what my husband thinks of the fact that I go out at night and do stand-up. In some ways, this is a weird question. This is not Jane Austen's England. Women are allowed to go out at night. In other ways, it's completely understandable. What is it like when you're in a relationship with someone and you suddenly want to do something very different with your life? Something that involves them having to be at home on their own in the evenings more and do a lot more childcare.

Simon and I met through friends in 1998. I was twenty-five, he was thirty-three. We got married within eighteen months. By the time we had been married for ten years, we had three children. There were two reasons why I was able even to consider doing this experiment. First, significantly, I am freelance and self-employed. So as long as I can keep up the day job, I can manage it. Two, far more significantly, my husband is the most tolerant and supportive man in the universe. (He genuinely is. Though he also told me to write this.) Without him, I could not have done any of it.

I knew that physically doing the gigs wasn't going to be easy. It was going to be exhausting and a logistical nightmare. But that was just one side of things; the other was how I would cope with all the emotional fallout. I was going to have to face head-on how I really felt about going out and leaving Simon and the children to do my own thing every single night, without any immediate reward, financial or professional. I was going to have to face up to my own regrets about the fact that I hadn't had the guts to do this before. And I was going to have to accept all the doubts I had about it being risky, selfish and delusional. When probably it was all of those things.

At the start, Simon and the children were sceptical about the experiment but bemused. 'Mummy, how many gigs have you done now?' Will asked in the first few days until he got bored. They didn't believe that I would do a hundred gigs no matter what. Initially maybe I didn't either. The truth was, I had no idea whether significant change is possible once you get past a certain point in your life. Was it just too late? Was I too old? Was I really serious about getting through all of it, especially when Jack was so little? And what was the real reason behind me doing this? Was it really that I was trying to chase some dream of something I had wanted in my childhood? Or was there something else going on?

The selfishness was a concern. I am never quite convinced of the wisdom of *Dragons' Den* type people who launch mad businesses on a hunch and then gamble their mortgage on it and borrow from all their friends to make it work. That often seems selfish. And yet those people are frequently lauded as 'great entrepreneurs'. Surely what I was doing was not as bad or mad as doing that? Everyone knows it's very hard to achieve anything in life without being single-minded. But it's also incredibly difficult to make a start at something like this before you have any proof that it will work. It's much easier to defend it once you have become incredibly successful. Suddenly everyone thinks it was all worth it. But that's just hindsight.

What bothered me was the in-between bit. It was not clear to me how you cope when you are in the middle of all that. How do you know when productive, future-invested focus is turning into obsessive delusion? This is a particularly pertinent question on the stand-up comedy circuit, which is populated in equal measure on the one hand with determined, talented individuals who want to try and get somewhere, and on the other hand with paranoid, sociopathic nutters who believe that someone will magically appear and propel them to riches, fame and greatness.

But it's a question for anyone, really. How much effort should you put into something, especially when there is a cost to your personal life? We all want to balance work and life outside work. But, realistically, how can you do that? Especially when so many people need to be able to retrain or reinvent themselves because there's no such thing as a job for life any more and the recession means lots of jobs are being made redundant. I wanted to see for myself what the cost might be, before just assuming that it wouldn't be worth it. (Which I slightly worried it wouldn't.)

Simon was not keen on me doing the hundred gigs. But he was not going to oppose it either. I think he understood that it was something I was going to have to get out of my system. Ever since I had started stand-up comedy, Simon had been a great support when things were going well; it was not so easy for him to understand why I kept on with it when things went badly. But he helped me to keep a sense of humour because he knew how much it mattered to me. When I came home from my first comedy workshop, which I did before I did my first gig, he looked at me and said, 'This is the most relaxed I have seen you in five years.' That is no small thing. (In fact it is worryingly large. How neurotic have I been for the past five years?) Plus, we were both aware that I had another motivation: I lost two work contracts in the recession in 2009. I sensed that the work I was doing was not going to be around for ever. In that kind of climate it made sense to be doing the thing I really wanted to do anyway.

I had also had the smallest of indications that I might be getting somewhere. A few months before the 'trophy' gig, I had performed at the Royal Vauxhall Tavern with some comics from

BBC Radio 4 and with Isy Suttie from Channel 4's *Peep Show* (she plays Dobby). This was a big deal for me. They had a big crowd in and, unlike most of the free gigs I had done up until then, you had to pay to get in. So it was already about a million times more professional than most of the things I had ever done.

Still, the one thing I was not expecting was to get paid. When I came off stage – having done a decent set, big laughs, big applause at the end – the promoter was standing behind the curtain with a small wad of banknotes. In my memory it now appears like a giant wad of cash. More likely it was about £30. She peeled off a wrinkled £10 note and handed it to me. 'Is that okay?' she asked. Okay? Are you joking? Someone was paying me money for performing comedy? I had never even dreamed of this moment, let alone imagined what it would be like. It was one of those weird life moments where everything goes into slow motion and you feel the spotlight on your face and a camera zooming in on you. Remember this moment, I thought to myself. You have achieved something.

Tears had formed in my eyes and I was afraid I was going to hug her and start crying. Try to be cool, I thought to myself. 'Er, yes,' I said, clearing my throat like a teenage boy who is pretending not to be aroused, '£10 is fine.' I suddenly worried that I should have said, 'No. I want more money. I think that was worth at least £12.50.' But I decided this would be pushing it and more likely it would all turn out to be a mistake and they would take my tenner away and give me a fiver instead.

Amazingly, this was not even the end of it all. There were more Hollywood-style rewards in store. 'Do you want a drink as well?' 'Oh, yes, please. Can we really have anything we want?' I was starting to look a bit uncool now. 'Can I have a glass of rosé? Do you think they have rosé?' I do not know why I ordered rosé wine instead of – for God's sake – a Diet Coke or a beer or a gin and tonic (which I thought would be too extravagant to ask for). But it felt like a rosé wine moment and it was. In the event this caught on and all the acts ordered a glass of rosé wine. It was the first time I did the RVT. It was the first time I got paid. It was the first time I got a free drink. I went home and hid the £10 note in my bookcase to make sure I never spent it. It's still there.

Of course, it is not wise to make a career change on the basis of £10 and a free drink. I wasn't going to alter my whole life for a tenner. Or was I? And then there was, of course, one downer that night. There always is. Just after the magical payment and exciting 'free glass of rosé wine' incident, I had a bit of a run-in with one of the other acts. As I stepped out into the dressing room, a woman I had never met before came right up into my face and said, 'That your first time, was it?' 'Er, not exactly. I have done a few gigs before.' (At this point I had done maybe ten gigs.) She looked me up and down, unimpressed. 'Got a lot of friends in, have you?' Oh dear. Was it that I had gone down too well? Or was it that I had been rubbish and only appreciated by my friends? 'Er, yes. I suppose I have got a lot of friends in the crowd ... '. I didn't know what else to say. The woman glared at me and then walked off. This kind of exchange haunted me as I had no idea what it was supposed to mean. *What if I should not be doing this*? That thought is mixed in my mind with the opposite fear: what if I already wasted twenty years not doing this?

Of the 100 gigs in 100 nights, Greenwich gig, has easily been the highlight so far. It was a pub acoustic night with musicians, singers and comedians, attended by an array of drunken, fairly rough but mostly well-meaning and sweet people. There were some extraordinary acts. A ninety-year-old man with no teeth who sang 'Danny Boy'. A woman with the voice of an angel called Evangeline who really should be on *The X Factor*. A raucous double act of middle-aged ladies calling themselves The Office Girls who made lots of jokes about penises. And the host, Dickie Richards, who is the loveliest man in the world, a proper cockney, with a girlfriend who is a nurse and has five children.

This gig is run by a musical comedy trio called We Should Get A Boat. One of them, Steve Bowditch, used to perform in The Greatest Show on Legs in the 1970s with the late comedy legend Malcolm Hardee, Jo Brand's ex. (The Greatest Show is the infamous balloon dance where naked men hop around the stage with only balloons covering their genitals.) It turns out Steve Bowditch is also a mate of Harry Hill. The high-collared one apparently attends this night from time to time; not the night I was there, though, much to my disappointment. I would have happily fought someone for Mr Hill's entertainment. Maybe even the toothless old man. 'Fight! Fight!' Instead I let the toothless man kiss my hand. It was slobbery.

We Should Get a Boat was the house band and they performed an extraordinary number entitled 'Rock God Armsleeves', which featured Steve Bowditch doing a chin thrustingly uncanny impression of Roger Daltrey, as he unfurled, with much great theatrical flourishing, exceptionally long pieces of fabric from his wrists via a home-made Velcro device. Rock God Armsleeves. Why didn't I think of that?

My stuff went down astonishingly well, considering that there was no warm-up, people were not really expecting straight stand-up comedy (a lot of them had just come for the music, and rightly so) and they rather desperately billed me as some sort of feature act when I am nothing of the sort: 'Our headliner tonight is comedian Viv Groskop!' Oh dear. Poor audience. I am not a headliner. I am not a proper comedian. I suppose I ought to get used to people referring to me like this but it just sounds so bogus. I had no idea what I was doing. Dickie whispered to me as I went on, 'Just do as long as you like, love.' I gave him a rabbit-in-headlights look that said, 'I've only got five minutes. But I'll try to stretch it.' One woman came up to me afterwards and said she had been crying with laughter. I swelled with pride. A man said: 'I'm not being misogynist or nothing. But usually women comedians are rubbish. You were good, though. I really liked you.' Heavens. They actually think I am a comedian.

It was the first time I felt wildly in love with the experiment. Simon not so much. 'Day six. Six gigs down,' I texted him on the way home, slightly drunk on a half of shandy and on the train back to Waterloo. His reply: 'Ninety-four to go.'

3: Gigs 15 to 20:

'Oh dear. Are you very depressed?'

Day 14, Gig 15: Piccadilly

Tonight was a waste of a pair of contact lenses. And a total waste of the new joke I tried to do about Derren Brown and Maybelline lipstick. 'In order to appear more attractive to you tonight, I have worn a statement lipstick. The statement is, "Sorry, I've put on a bit of weight, but focus on the lipstick." It's like Derren Brown goes to Maybelline.' As a joke it is kind of not finished and kind of not really working and kind of just awful. Never mind. One important realisation. My advice for any stay-at-home parent who is bored of their life or generally to anyone who is taking their children for granted: go and do one hundred nights of stand-up comedy. You will never love your children more. And you will never want to leave the house again.

Day 15, Gig 16: Brighton

Lovely comics, lovely MC, happy crowd. Not the best performance from me but acceptable and a good night. LOVE Brighton. Love people like Chris Gau, a comic who makes jokes about Jehovah's Witnesses and unicorns. Talked about Nigella recipes with his girlfriend. Why can't all gigs be like this?

Day 16, Gig 17: Caledonian Road

Gorgeous old pub. Relaxed gig. Nice comics. Fun night. Not amazing performance but okay. Middling happiness. Wished I'd ordered Thai food but this is against my principles. Don't understand comics who order food at the venue. How can you eat before going on stage?

Day 17, cancelled gig: Soho

Gig cancelled at 5.30 p.m. Too late to get on anywhere else. Unexpected night at home. Frustrating. Now I am not one gig ahead. Bugger.

Day 18, Gig 18: Islington

Storytelling night. They had a rule about not being allowed to take the microphone out of the stand. I almost always take the microphone out of the stand so this felt very strange, like trying to talk with a straitjacket on. Weird not to be doing stand-up and telling a story instead. Another of the rules of the night is that you are allowed to make people laugh but you're not allowed to do stand-up. It has to be an off-the-cuff story. Passed the test. Compliments afterwards. Happy. Diet Coke expenditure so far: £36.40.

Day 19, Gig 19: Dalston

Bit weird. Long way to travel. Hit on by teenagers and old buffers alike in bar. Enjoyed performance. Weird garden furniture for chairs and weird atmosphere. Overall a weird night. Left as early as I could because I knew it would take me two hours to get home. Still didn't get home until after midnight.

Day 20, Gig 20: Finsbury Park

Big hit at friendly night. Can't complain. Not glamorous gig, next to kebab shop. But friendly people. One of the better ones. Meant to get a kebab after closing time like a proper comedian would. Remembered that I don't like kebabs. Bought a Toffee Crisp instead.

Day 21, Day 22: no gigs

Purposefully took this weekend off because it was my friend Susan's fortieth birthday party and we were all invited to Dorset for the weekend. In theory I could have said no and gigged instead. But in reality I realised that (a) I struggle to get gigs on Saturday nights anyway and (b) what sort of person am I if I cannot take forty-eight hours off this mad project to celebrate my friend's birthday? This did not stop me from looking for gigs in Dorset. But I could not find any.

*

So this is my life now. I leave the house most nights before 6.30 p.m. The children stand on the sofa next to the window, pull back the curtains and wave me goodbye, their skin pressed into the glass as they make idiot faces. Most nights before I go I make a point of asking them what advice they have for me. They always say the same thing. Will, who is seven years old: 'Mummy. Be as funny as possible. Try your hardest.' Vera, aged five: 'Tell some funny jokes. Tell this joke: Knock, knock. Who's there? Mary. Mary who? Merry Christmas.' The next day she always wants to know, 'Did they like my joke?' I reply, 'They loved it.' I never tell it. That would be a bad idea.

If only it were that easy. I always feel bad for lying to the children about not trying out their jokes on the audience, but at the same time I can never quite work up the guts to face a room of people and say, 'Oh, guess what? My children are really cute and they wanted me to tell you some of their jokes … '. I am dying badly enough and frequently enough as it is without having people hate me for pushing some 'yummy mummy' act in their face.

Stand-up is never an easy thing to do. It's not supposed to be. If it were easy, then anyone could get up and tell a load of 'Mary Christmas' jokes into a microphone with a smiley face and we'd all be stand-up comedians. Getting up and doing it once for kicks is one thing. But it turns out that getting up and doing it time and time again, usually the same material, night after night … that is really tough.

I have barely got past the first fortnight and here's the question: do I have the guts to really do it? Not just to get up on stage a few times and try it and get through it. But to actually do it properly. After a week and a bit of doing it every night I am already starting to think that I don't.

The most frightening thing I'm finding out about myself is not that I'm stronger than I thought I was. That's what everyone seems to make out you will discover. 'What doesn't kill you makes you stronger.' 'You must be so brave to do stand-up.' But I am not stronger. I am weaker. I interviewed Dame Judi Dench for work around about Day 10 and it came up that I was doing stand-up. Her eyes nearly popped out of her head: 'By God, girl, you've got some guts.' She said she would never do stand-up, she's not brave enough. Well, I don't feel brave. I feel gutless. I can't seem to rise to some of these occasions. I thought I had the balls but I don't. On the basis of the numbers so far, overall it's not looking great. I'm finding that I'm desperate to cling to what's left of my identity outside stand-up – the fact that I'm a mother, a writer, a grown-up. Anything other than a failing stand-up.

Before all this started, when I had bad gigs I would wonder for days after if I should just give up. The big fundraiser at Leicester Square Theatre (the one where I had no idea what I was doing) came about six months before I started the hundred gigs. I was the least known, newest comic on the bill. The auditorium was packed. Two minutes before I went on the promoter came up to me in the wings and whispered, 'This must be the biggest gig you have ever done.' It was not the right thing to say at that moment. I nearly punched her.

I did okay but not great – by my own estimation, anyway. Evidently, by some other people's estimation it was much worse than that. As I turned away from the microphone on stage, I walked into the red curtains in the wings and straight into the arms of Helen Lederer, comedian and one-time star of the TV series *Absolutely Fabulous*. She held me tightly by the shoulders, looked into my eyes and said, 'Oh dear. Are you very depressed?' I thought it had gone relatively okay. Obviously not.

'It's quite intellectual your stuff, isn't it?' she added. Oh God. Not that one, please. Anything but that one. That is code for: 'No one gets your jokes.' That went straight into my top ten of Unsolicited Feedback From Other Comics Who Should Know Better. Also on that list, these gems: 'You don't exactly make it easy for yourself do you?' 'Your stuff is quite cerebral, isn't it?' 'Your delivery is good, you just need to work on your material.' Thank you for your feedback, people. Thank you for your feedback.

For once I did feel brave after that gig, though, because I just wasn't ready for a venue of that size and I shouldn't have done it and I did it anyway and, to be fair, I did get some laughs. I was beginning to realise the perils of doing gigs before you are really ready for them. You want to take risks and experiment and challenge yourself. But you also risk being so far out of your depth that you will almost certainly bomb and then find it hard to recover or ever feel like performing anywhere ever again. That night I did some completely new material in the middle, which was a mistake – totally new material written on the day and never spoken aloud or tested on anyone. I know now that is an incredibly stupid thing to do. As I fell asleep that night, I could see Helen Lederer's huge eyes looming out of the dark, framed by the stage curtains … 'are you VERY depressed?'

My mood has started to dip slightly between gigs and there's a dread creeping in. It's also coming through on stage, where I sometimes do unpredictable and ill-advised things. At one gig last week I ended up telling the same joke twice in a row without even realising I was doing it until the words were out of my mouth. I am tired and going slightly mad. People think the most difficult thing about doing comedy is writing the material or getting over performance nerves or coping with difficult crowds. It's not. What's tiring is trying to get on with everyone else on the circuit, being nice to promoters and other comics, being courteous about turning up at the right time and leaving at the right time.

All that stuff is completely exhausting, especially when you're starting out and no one knows you. Once people trust you and know that they can count on you, it's easier. You don't have to turn up early and stay right until the end. But until you've proven that to people, you have to be there for the duration. That is tough as often it means leaving home at 6 p.m. to arrive before 7.30 p.m. You usually have to stay until past 11 p.m., which means you're not home until well after midnight or later. That is a big investment for your five minutes of stage time. Add in nerves, stage jitters, the fact that you might have had a bad day, the stress of having to find a babysitter last minute so that you can leave on time, the pressure to have a good gig to make it worthwhile ...

I can't get the nasty gin and tonic girl at Gig 4 out of my mind. She sneered, as I came off stage, 'You've done a comedy course, haven't you? You can tell from your stuff. Everyone who does those courses comes out with the same thing. You're just doing the same thing as everyone else.' The gin and tonic was in a shop-bought can and she was reading the paper at the back of the gig. As far as I could work out, these were the only words she exchanged with anyone for the first half of the night. I didn't stay to see her set.

That kind of poison stays with you for a little while. Feedback can be useful sometimes but it can also crush you – and unnecessarily so. I knew what she said was wrong. I'm not coming out with the same thing as anyone else. Of late I have added a whole section where I am trying to rap about the history of feminism. If anyone else wants to do jokes referencing Mary Wollstonecraft then they are welcome to. I really don't see anyone else doing it. And there's a good reason for that: it's not really working.

I'm now encountering gigs on a regular basis where I feel that people just don't like me. At the one in Piccadilly, where I tried to do the awful Maybelline joke, I could not get past the message I could feel I was sending to the room: 'Hello, I am a rather strange and annoying posh woman.' The Cath Kidston dress probably didn't help. I played to a room of thirteen people who looked at me with a mixture of hatred, sadness and pity. Or rather, they didn't look at me, they looked at the floor. Because when you're embarrassed for someone, it's hard to hold eye contact. When this happens in such a small room with such a small group of people, it's almost impossible not to say something about it just to break the shame of it. But mentioning it – 'Well, this is awkward!' – generally only makes it worse, much worse.

The most disturbing thing about the bad nights? That all the acts think the same: that what they're doing is okay (otherwise why would they be doing it?) but that all the others are crap. And which of us is right? It seems to me that none of us is right. We're all crap. I have not told any other comedians about my theory yet. It may not be very welcome.

On the plus side, I get disproportionately cheered by the random people you meet doing these things. Before that Piccadilly gig, I met an attractive man who was quite funny. He was not a comedian. (Go figure.) I was sitting in the bar, learning my lines for an audition the following week for a comedy workshop I wanted to get into at the Actors Centre in Covent Garden. It was with Tony Allen, the so-called 'godfather of punk comedy'. I had been told this man was 'amazing' and able to unlock everything you need to know about yourself as a performer. I have become obsessed with people like this.

Anyway, this attractive man came in to help one of his mates set up the room for the gig and asked me what I was reading. I said, 'I'm learning a script where I have to play a thirty-eight-year-old French teacher who is having an affair with one of her pupils. Who's going to believe that? I mean, I would need to have sex with an eighteen-year-old boy to get into the part.' He replied, quick as a flash, 'Well, I'm thirty-three but I'm happy to help.' It's the little things that get you through.

4: Gigs 21 to 27:

The consolations of Diet Coke

Day 23, Gig 21: Stockwell

Lost two days of gigging. Now panicked that I won't be able to catch up the numbers. Three gigs in one day planned for tomorrow to reverse things but if anything goes wrong … Decided to have a go at a new five minutes using the Instrument of Truth (Casio VL Tone mini keyboard). It's like a tiny electric organ, the size of two harmonicas. It runs on batteries and you can play it into the microphone. The act I've tried to put together involves me part-playing piano, part-singing. Semi-successful. I like being weird. Shaky new material. Overall poor but enjoyable. But not exactly Bill Bailey.

Day 24, Gig 22: Sheffield

The mother and baby gig again. Like a duck to water now. Enjoyed this even better the second time. Bemused mums and apathetic babies. Helen, who runs this gig, is fantastic. She's an actress and a comedienne and she has no reason to do this other than out of love. She has worked really hard to promote it and make it an exciting event for people and she's getting in over fifty mums a week at lunchtime. That is amazing. This is the stuff that gives you a buzz: meeting other people who are inspiring and funny and making things happen. If I can just cling on to that thought, everything will be fine ...

Day 24, Gig 23: Covent Garden

Surprisingly good night at a classic 'new material' open mic night: only comics in the audience. Enjoyed watching Sara Pascoe (who is on Channel 4's Stand Up for the Week) *show how it's done. Slightly disturbed that even when you get to her level you have to do lame gigs with no real audience. Second of three gigs today: tripling up for the first time. Tired.*

Day 24, Gig 24: Holborn

Third gig of the day. Tough crowd: all foreign students because the MC's day job is teaching English as a foreign language. Messy. They understood nothing. I tried my best but I was weak. Depressing but amusing. Got hysterical on the way home, partly demented with exhaustion, partly overexcited that I am now BACK ON TRACK NUMBERS-WISE. Feel smug.

Day 25, Gig 25: Reading

First competition. A long way to go to die.

Day 26, Gig 26: Stoke Newington

Dungeon. Atmosphere of doom. No audience. Okay, maybe five people. Three hysterically drunk (high?) girls in front row. Did okay as they liked me rapping and pretending to be feminism's answer to Eminem – Feminem. One act did thirty seconds and then threw the mic down and walked out. 'This is a joke. I'm out of here.' Audience horrified. These horrible gigs are hardly their fault. Selfish git.

Day 27, Gig 27: Walthamstow

Bizarrely, 1970s sex guru Shere Hite attended. A play based on her work was showing there the following week so she was checking out the venue. I wanted to go up and talk to her during the interval only to discover that she had walked out during my act. Presumably in disgust. Oh dear. Otherwise quite a fun night.

*

I was always going to have to face a comedy competition. And I was never going to be ready for it. And here it is, the Reading New Act of the Year. Day 25, Gig 25. One of the bigger competitions, although by no means one of the biggest. I have cancelled another gig (the unforgettable Touching Cloth in Liverpool Street) to do this because (a) it's in a big venue and I want the experience of being in a big venue, (b) I want to perform in Reading and it is in Reading and (c) I think it's worth doing as many competitions as you can just to see how you get on – and to exert the maximum stress on yourself because it will force you to learn to cope with pressure more quickly. Like I don't already have enough of that.

Why do I want the experience of 'performing in Reading'? I am making it sound like a residency at Las Vegas instead of a five-minute spot in a nightclub called Highlight. All I mean is that I want to do a gig outside London and I want to do it somewhere like Reading. Not a small place, it needs to be an urban place, but not London. I figure that if I can't make people laugh in Reading, I am going to struggle to make them laugh anywhere. Reading is going to be my litmus test. 'Good evening, Reading!'

I have other gigs booked for outside London: Lincoln, Truro,

Tonbridge. (All the greats, man. All the greats!) I need to know that I can manage these gigs. These dates are not exactly *Live at the Apollo* but they are a very different prospect to what I've faced so far. They mean getting up in front of a real audience with real people in it, as opposed to the unreal audience of fellow open mic comics and comics' friends, who make up a hefty percentage of the audience at most of the gigs I've done so far.

I also have another, more personal reason for doing as many competitions as possible: the children. So far this experiment is a breeze for them. Because it's all in the evening, it doesn't affect them hugely: I'm just going out around bedtime more than I usually would. This is a relief. I had worried that it would be difficult for them. They are obsessed, however, with the idea of me 'winning'. If I could win a competition and, preferably, a large trophy, larger than the one I already have, then it would make all of this worthwhile for them. Children are very basic. They reveal the truth about how we all really feel about these things. Children love competitions and winners. They love the drama and the heartache of winning and losing. For them, the only true measure of the hundred gigs will be whether I am 'the winner' or not. Reading offers this possibility.

'Mummy, you have to go through to the next round,' says Vera, 'you have to.' She demonstrates the technique of impressing the judges by singing an improvised song titled 'I Loved You but Then I Took You to the Bottom of the Ocean.' Her performance includes the important bit we always see on *Britain's Got Talent* or *The X Factor* in the audition rounds, where someone back stage has to press the 'play' button for the music. Vera uses a button on the dishwasher to illustrate this. I feel bad for mixing the children up in my ambitions. It seems pretty unlikely that I will 'go through to the next round' and they are going to be gutted.

The day of the competition dawns and suddenly all this seems a terrible idea. First, I have to get to Reading in time for the start at 7.30 p.m. and I have no idea how I am going to co-ordinate babysitting. I wanted to do gigs outside London to get in front of different audiences and prove myself. But physically getting there is going to prove to be the biggest test. Leaving home before 6.30 p.m. is still a problem. I don't like having someone else put Jack to bed for me other than Simon, obviously, and he is not going to be able to get home before 6.30 p.m. on this particular night.

Jack is not used to what I'm doing yet. At twelve months old he is not drinking milk. Without a bedtime drink (because the breastfeeding has stopped and he refuses to recognise the existence of beakers, bottles or any drinking vessels apart from breasts), it's not easy to get him to go down to sleep. Yoghurt is the answer to this in the short term. But in the long term I would like him at least to acknowledge the existence of non-human milk. When I leave the house I feel like I'm leaving him to starve.

I try talking to Jack about this. 'I have to leave early today because I have to go to Reading.' He looks at me blankly. It's alright for him. He has never heard of Reading. 'I am going in the car. Brrrmm. Brrmmm.' He cheers up at the mention of the car. 'Katie [the babysitter] is coming to look after you.' He cheers up at the mention of Katie. She is young, blonde and very pretty. The sort of babysitter face a friend of mine would describe as 'only fair on the children considering they spend most of their time looking at the face of their raddled, old mother'. He is happy. Katie will give him yoghurt. It's not the same as a breast but it will have to do. (Indeed if only we could replace breasts with yoghurt in all situations. Perhaps a compromise option for the 'No More Page 3' campaign. Free Petits Filous for all readers. Smiles all round.)

Somehow I have a bad feeling about this competition. Listening to Magic FM all the way there in the car doesn't help but I can't seem to find the right radio station to listen to on the way to gigs. Capital FM is too excited and tinny. BBC Radio 4 gets you into completely the wrong headspace. Heart FM is too sentimental and I am usually in tears by the time I get there. The drive takes me ages and I get lost in the centre of Reading several times. It is like the one-way system from hell. I end up having to park in a horrible multi-storey car park which I know is going to be spooky to return to late at night. And I will have no choice but to stay until the end of the competition so that I can find out who has won, at which point I can plaster a massive smile of congratulations on my face for the winner when it turns out not to be me. Oh, how I am looking forward to that moment.

Once I get out of the multi-storey, I'm surrounded by department stores and binge-drinking venues. It's early but some of the binge drinkers are already queuing outside the clubs wearing miniskirts, tight T-shirts and fluorescent stilettoes. I suddenly feel very old. What am I doing out at night on my own at this time? Thinking I can get up on stage in some night club and make people laugh? Make kids in their late teens laugh? I'm suddenly gripped by a horror. I miss my own kids. I want to be at home putting my baby to bed, not withholding my breasts from him by taking them to comedy competitions.

I have tried to get there early but now I'm panicking because I'm late. It had not occurred to me that one of the biggest challenges of doing the hundred gigs would be figuring out where they are and getting to them on time. This is why stand-up is a strange job. No one comes to you, you have to go to them, sometimes in far-flung places. You don't frequently work in the same place twice. It's like having to go to a different office every day and often the office is located in an industrial zone no one has ever heard of or been to and you start to wonder whether you just made the whole thing up and it really doesn't exist.

I walk up and down one street for about twenty minutes asking people for the Highlight Club. I can't understand why one of the biggest clubs in Reading does not advertise itself a bit more obviously; but I guess if you really wanted to go there and you lived there, you would know where it was. However, no one does. 'Highlight? Never heard of it, love. There's another club that way … '. Eventually I find it. It's barely marked and up a staircase next to what looks like a car showroom; I feel I'm walking into a cinema. How can this be the right place?

But it is. I get up there and discover a cavernous nightclub inside. It's like a Tardis. You would never imagine that it's there. Just inside, between the stage and the bar, is a gaggle of comedians looking nervous. A couple of faces I recognise, including a bubbly, friendly girl called Sarah who has a section in her set about taking a sickie from the office and staying at home and masturbating. I am happy to see her. First, because she is friendly, and second, because I know the audience usually enjoys her act. Nothing raises my spirits more than the sight of a comic who pretty much knows what they're doing. Although obviously I don't want them to be too amazing because I will bomb horribly if I have to go on after them.

Buoyed up by Sarah's beaming face, I sign in and let the organisers know I'm there and head into the toilets to put on as much make-up as possible. As if this will somehow help. When I come back out one of the comics, a gay guy who hosts Mr Leather competitions (and, later, I discover to my delight, also Mr Rubber), looks at me and says, 'Well, since we're dressing up … ' and pulls out his leather accessories. I am amused that he thinks that me wearing a bit of glittery eyeshadow is the equivalent of dressing up like a massive gimp. I go to the bar and order a pint of Diet Coke. This cheers me up further; it is the Dutch courage of the delusional. At the very least I will drink lots of Diet Coke tonight. The barman looks at me pityingly. 'You one of the comedians?' 'Yes,' I smile. 'Do I look like one? I hope so,' I say with a manic Joe Pasquale grin on my face. 'Good luck,' he says, shaking his head.

There's a sweet, overexcitable MC who is about eighteen. He is young, cute and, despite his age, looks like he has been doing this for years. It crosses my mind that I feel about 147. I censor this thought and try to feed off the manic energy of the compère. He is endearingly try-hard. To make things more interesting there's no one in the audience. Maybe fifteen people. Which wouldn't be too bad but this is a huge, cavernous venue that seats about three hundred. It's like performing in an aircraft hangar. I have no idea how my stuff is going to go across or how I'm going to get any intimacy in this room. What I do have is a feeling of irrational optimism.

The evening kicks off. The judges are sitting at the back, shuffling their papers nervously. They seem to like the MC and so does the audience. But no matter how much everyone laughs – and they don't laugh much – fifteen people do not create much noise in an aircraft hangar. The space might as well be empty. I think about the car and the multi-storey car park and the long drive home and the fact that I have no real idea of the route out of Reading or when or how I will get anything to eat. I try not to think about the baby because I will start crying. At least my breasts have stopped twitching. I focus on the smile of Sarah, the nice, friendly comic, and the youthful white teeth of the compère and I concentrate on willing a sprinkling of magic into the room.

The first few acts do pretty badly. No one really finds any of us funny. The bank of judges sitting at the back of the room has a sort of throbbing nuclear presence. Like *The X Factor*, only worse. After the initial titters, they are now barely laughing. I don't blame them. The energy is slowly draining from the room. Some people have ordered food and are contentedly gnawing on fried chicken legs. Great. If the size of the room and the size of the audience weren't already enough to contend with, now you're fighting against the fact that people are more focused on their battered poultry than they are on the acts.

I can feel myself getting frustrated as the gap between potential and reality widens. I suddenly realise that I am reacting in a hypersensitive way because I am starving – which is hardly the fault of the competition organisers. But I daren't eat anything now because I feel like I'll just be sick and, besides, I have decided long ago that it's wrong to order food at venues where you're going to perform. A bit like eating a jacket potato in the middle of a work meeting. I can see a group sitting in the front eating scampi in a basket, warm pints next to it, looking up at the stage open-mouthed and munching. I try to focus on the good in them. They have come for a night of comedy and fried snacks with their friends. They just want someone to make them laugh. Maybe I am that person.

I skulk round the back of the room to sneak into the perfomers' entrance by the stage. At least this is quite glamorous, I tell myself, as I balance on a guitar amp for a seat. Often you have to come at the stage via the front, getting up out of the audience like some kind of raffle winner. I can't really hear what the guy ahead of me (Mr Leather Man) is talking about but he's getting some titters. There's hope yet. He comes off grinning. 'That went really well,' he beams. Wow. Is that how it felt to him? Really well? I'm amazed. But maybe I couldn't hear the noise from the room and it was louder than I thought. I am still digesting his reaction when I can hear my name being called.

I haven't thought about how I will come on so I just look down and try to avoid tripping over lots of cables inexpertly taped to the floor.

It feels like miles from the back-stage area to the front of the stage and it takes me for ever to get to the microphone. Up here it feels even more like an aircraft hangar. I have no idea whether to perform to the people just in front of me, to my right, or should I focus on the smattering of people to my left? It feels the same on both sides, like I'm delivering my lines into the Grand Canyon, which stretches miles into the distance. Maybe I should play to the back, where the judges are? No matter. I can feel every line I deliver drop like a stone. I try to put more character into it. Still nothing. Now I feel like I'm really faking it.

Perhaps one or two of my jokes hit the judges at the back – a couple of low laughs came out, or maybe I'm imagining it. But there is nothing else in the room apart from a hum of pity and boredom. It's the longest five minutes of my life. Well, if only it were the longest five minutes of my life. I'm pretty used to having very long five minutes now. I come off, relieved and dazed, and head to the bar for more Diet Coke. (Ah. The consolations of Diet Coke. It's always there for you. It has no calories. It has no detrimental alcoholic effect. It's a friend in dark times. I find myself thinking this and realise, 'I've only been doing this for three weeks and already I have become deeply sad and deranged and obsessed with the comforting properties of Diet Coke.')

I resolve to have a 'good time' with the rest of the comics and go back to see if anyone else wants a drink. They don't and I become disproportionately offended by this. (And I once again have to remind myself that I am offended because I am over-reacting because I am hungry. Not because they are all evil.) There is a certain etiquette around offering drinks I haven't quite figured out yet. In the main people buy their own drinks – one at a time – rather than get locked into buying rounds they can't afford for comics they don't know and probably will never see again. I don't blame them. They don't want me to buy them a drink so that they won't have to buy me a drink. Fair enough.

The rest of the night drags on with no one really achieving any kind of good audience feel. I have no idea how the judges are going to make their selection. We might as well have done this in an audition room at 9 in the morning. There would have been more atmosphere. Eventually it's announced – an excellent one-liner comic, Sunil Patel, wins, with a character act runner-up, Julie 'Psycho' Jones. They both deserve it. (Sunil Patel goes into the finals. So I can say I was in a really tough heat. I later see Julie 'Psycho' Jones – a stage name – do a striptease to the theme tune from the TV series *Casualty*. I cannot compete with this.)

Just as I am packing up to go and realising that I did not finish my Diet Coke, I see one of the judges, Julia Chamberlain, coming towards me. She books acts for a lot of clubs and is something of a legend in comedy circles because she's part of the team that runs the new act competition 'So You Think You're Funny?', which has anointed people like Peter Kay, Dylan Moran and Rhona Cameron in the first year of their comedy careers. For a moment I think she is going to say one of two things: (a) 'You were amazing. Do you have something suitable to wear for Michael McIntyre's Roadshow tomorrow?' or (b) 'You are terrible and I am embarrassed for you. You must give up now before you make even more of a fool of yourself. You are too old to be doing this.' She does not say either of these things. Instead she looks at me kindly and says, 'Good writing. You need to play higher status.' And then she walks away.

Play higher status? She means I should not be afraid to be posh. Or that's what I think she means anyway. In *Fawlty Towers* terms, I have been playing a sort of Manuel idiot version of myself when in reality I am more like Sybil Fawlty. I can correct that. It feels more natural anyway. I've been afraid to be condescending. But someone in authority has now told me to be condescending. This is good. I feel a massive rush of adrenaline. There is hope. There is a place for advice. She saw something in me. There is a simple solution to why this isn't working! I just need to play higher status. I need to be rude and patronising! Is that it? Is that the key to all this?

Status is one of the first things you learn if you take a comedy workshop or study improvisation. It's the basic rule of comedy: everyone on stage has a place in the hierarchy. At a very basic level it's like that 1960s black and white sketch from *The Frost Report* with John Cleese (tall, aristocratic), Ronnie Barker (medium sized, middle class) and Ronnie Corbett (short, working class). Barker: 'I look up to him [Cleese] because he is upper class. But I look down on him [Corbett] because he is lower class.' Corbett: 'I know my place.' Playing high status doesn't mean that you literally are high status. It can mean that you are the fool: Penelope Keith played high-status 'idiot' characters like Margo in *The Good Life* and Audrey fforbes-Hamilton in *To the Manor Born*. You cannot imagine her playing a version of Manuel.

I feel like this might be a breakthrough. I also feel very confused, though, as I am not convinced that anyone wants to feel the force of my full patronising, condescending Margo self. I don't tell anyone else what Julia Chamberlain has told me. I am very excited – but also worried that I am instantly reading too much into her words. I immediately know that I am now going to spend the next three weeks analysing every single word and inflection of her feedback, the first I have had from a proper comedy judge at a proper comedy competition. I have to remind myself that if she really thought I was any good, she would have put me through – while giving me the advice at the same time. But, still, it's something. And I am desperate to cling onto something.

I stumble out of the club, aware that I need to go back to the car before it gets any later. It's already about 11 p.m. and the streets are full of drunk kids – until I turn the corner into the street where the multi-storey is and suddenly there's no one around. 'Great,' I think, 'I come to this stupid competition, I get nowhere, I spend £10 on Diet Coke, I humiliate myself in an aircraft hangar playing stupid low status unintentionally and then I get mugged on the way back to my car. That's if I can even find my car.' At this point I would be glad of a mugger appearing so that I could enlist them to help me find my car.

I manage to work out which entrance to go into and climb the four flights of stairs up to the deserted car deck. It's horrible and desolate and I feel utterly lost. This fights with the feeling of failure and immense hunger. But the only thing that could make tonight worse is if I had some kind of hideous pasty on the way home. I resolve not to stop at a service station to eat. I will drive as fast as I can all the way home and eat bananas and biscuits when I get in. 'This is your life now,' I think to myself.

I get lost on the way home and have to pull in several times to use Google Maps on my phone to get my bearings. Eventually I get back and it's 12.30 a.m. Everyone has gone to bed and there's no one to share my humiliation with. Because it's late at night and I'm tired and hungry and a bit humiliated, I can feel myself going into a tailspin of self-recrimination. I know that what I'm doing looks weird from the outside. The other week I was telling a university classmate I hadn't seen for ages about stand-up. He listened to my tales of this weird new life, rapt and fascinated. When I had finished he turned to me and beamed: 'Oh, Viv. I think it's so sweet that you're having a midlife crisis.'

I bit my lip and looked at the floor to stop myself hitting him. This isn't a midlife crisis. It's my life. Or maybe his words were hurting so much because they were true. Is it a midlife crisis? Sitting at the computer in my sitting room in the dark, too tired to think and too wired to sleep, I could feel that it probably was true but there was no way I wanted to face up to it. And it was too late now because I had made the midlife crisis my life. There was no going back.

The more this experiment was carried on, the more I was beginning to see what I was doing through other people's eyes. Surely it was more than a bit strange, taking yourself away from your family and your actual work to do something that has no guaranteed future and is relentlessly unforgiving and difficult? I needed to have a better reason other than the fact that sometimes I loved it. Especially as a lot of the time I was finding that I did not love it. I wanted to find a way to love it by getting better at it.

The neglect of the children and of Simon was also starting to get wearing for them and for me. I knew it would; but I didn't know how conflicted I would feel about it. I thought I'd just be able to say to myself, 'Oh, well, it's only three months. I'll make it up to them.' But when you're in it, it's not that easy. I have no idea what I would think of anyone else doing this. I would probably think they were incredibly stupid. And mad. I was going to have to do a John Bishop. Without actually doing a John Bishop.

John Bishop is the incredibly successful Liverpudlian comedian who had been separated from his wife for over a year when he first started stand-up, leaving her to raise their children on her own. The first she knew of what he was doing was when she went to a comedy club for a night out with some friends. She looked up at the stage and on walked her estranged husband. After that they got back together and eventually she encouraged him to go into comedy full-time. Then it took him nine years and three Edinburgh shows before he got any recognition. (And now loads of comedians hate him because he is mega-successful. Almost as much as they hate Michael McIntyre.)

If you look at the biography of anyone who has achieved anything in comedy or in anything related to entertainment, it's usually at huge personal cost. You train pretty much on your own with no one to back you up and no idea whether you are going in the right direction or learning the right things. You earn nothing for ages and then even less for more ages. You have no guarantee that any of it will ever come to anything.

On the other hand, though, I could really see that this was what I needed to do – that the children would, in the long term, be worse off if I didn't do this. Because I had committed to this path a little bit – which was already affecting them – and it was only going to drive me mad if I didn't commit to it completely. I didn't want to become one of those mothers who blames things on her family: 'Well, I couldn't do anything because I was looking after the children ... '; 'I suppose I could have gone into comedy, but I didn't really have time because of the children ... '. I didn't want to wake up at forty-five saying, 'You know, I could have been a comedian.' I didn't want to pour my ambitions into the children because I hadn't managed to realise them myself.

The reality of the problem of money and time was also weighing heavily. When you have children, you do not have the luxury of time in order to experiment with new things, network with random people or try your luck in some new career field. If you do something, it has to be a means to an end. It has to lead to something. You can't just mess around, hoping something will come of it. You have to be focused. Still, I allowed myself to feel inspired by little things. Enjoying meeting new people in comedy who seemed talented and interesting. Experiencing tiny gains in my performance and realising exactly how much I loved it when it went well. Being fascinated by all the ins and outs of why it went badly. This was the stuff that kept me going. I just needed to go high status. Yeah. High status.

I eat about six biscuits and a banana and drink a pint of milk. I am like a student having a hundred-day essay crisis. It's pathetic. Shuddering at the memory of the Reading multi-storey car park, I go on Facebook and check who has been gigging where and what gigs are available in the next few days. I am getting a picture of what my life is becoming like and it's horrific. I realise this when I am disproportionately cheered up by reading a Facebook post from another comic: 'Bombed tonight. What's the point?'

Still, though, Julia Chamberlain's words are ringing in my ears. She didn't say anything to anyone else. She thinks that, with a bit of tweaking, I could do something. She didn't have to come up and talk to me. She didn't have to say anything. I didn't ask for feedback. And she knows what she is talking about. This is meaningful. I need to listen to what she says, even if at the moment I have pretty much no idea of putting it into action. I am also frightened. What if what she says means something? A voice sounds in my head: 'You are capable of this.'

I will have to get up in the morning to do the school run because tomorrow is a day when Simon has to go into work early. I watch the video back of my performance and I can see it's a disaster. I'm a gesticulating dot on the horizon in an aircraft hangar, hovering almost ghoulishly above small groups of people trying to eat scampi as quietly as possible. My performance is hokey and I look like a total fake. I can see what the judge meant. It's like Sybil Fawlty trying to pretend she's nice and you know that she's not. You can see that I'm not making any connection with the audience. It's just a very strange, middle-aged, wannabe actress type gurning and talking to herself in a large public space. Whose idea was this? Mine. All mine. I can't blame anyone else. What have I got myself into? A nasty mess. There's a saying about this. Don't know who said it. Maybe I made it up. Or I just read it on Facebook. But it's true. 'You don't do comedy. Comedy does you.'

5: Gig 28:

A night so bad you would rather be a performer
than be in the audience

Day 28, Gig 28: Broadstairs

No. More. Shared. Car. Journeys. Ever. Again. In. My. Entire. Life.

*

Okay. That's it. I have realised what the biggest problem is. It's not money, it's not the children, it's not comedy. The biggest problem is the other comics. Getting up in front of the audience? Tough sometimes, but not difficult. Surviving the other people on the circuit? Sometimes they're inspiring, hilarious, heart-warming. Other times they're impossible.

It is 6.55 p.m. on a cold, damp Saturday night and I have just looked at the time on my phone for the 487th time in the last hour. I am in the back of a white Mini Metro with two other comedians. A fourth comedian is sitting in the passenger seat. A fifth is driving. The back seat is cramped and I am convinced that the rear of the car is so weighed down that it's dragging along the road. The windows are open because nearly everyone is smoking and I keep expecting sparks to fly up from the back of the car, where the axle is virtually bumping along the tarmac.

I am not smoking. I have not smoked a cigarette since I gave up fifteen years ago because I had started smoking forty a day and I was spending more time smoking than not smoking. If I could smoke one or even five cigarettes a day, I would still smoke.

But I cannot. I have to smoke at least forty. So I do not smoke. Which is a shame in comedy terms as you make lots of friends smoking outside gigs. And inside cars.

Instead I feel sick. Partly from the movement of the car and the cigarettes, but also from anxiety. And partly because my support tights are cutting off my circulation. We set out from Finsbury Park, north London, towards Broadstairs, Kent, at 4 p.m – or at least we were supposed to leave at 4 p.m. Most of the comics turned up late so we set off at about 4.45 p.m. It is now close to 7 p.m. and we have not managed to get out of the City of London. We are crawling through Smithfields. If we had taken the train we would have been there two hours ago. Before we have even left London we have had one stop somewhere near Old Street for one of the comics to go to the toilet. Seriously.

I've met a couple of these comics before and, although I don't really know them at all, I have no reason to think that I might dislike them. But that could just be because I haven't shared a car with them to Broadstairs yet. Reading was lonely and difficult because I was on my own. This is going to be lonely and difficult because my fellow travellers are making me insane. They are all, individually, unobjectionable. En masse, however, they are a band of braying, crazed hyenas, all competing over who can tell the most impressive story about the time they 'smashed' it (i.e. had a good gig) and who can boast of the most recent 'paid gig'. (It turns out that 'paid' means 'paid £5', which to my mind barely counts as payment let alone something worth boasting about. But what do I know?)

Their stories are lengthy, angry, bitter, embellished and, weirdly, have no jokes in them. The aim of the stories is not to make people laugh: it's to show their status. These comics travel outside London. They get paid gigs. They know people. They are going places. Which is more than can be said of us at 6.59 p.m.

65

and still in a traffic jam really not that far from Finsbury Park where we first started. We are due at a destination seventy miles away in approximately thirty-one minutes. Welcome to the shared car gig of which I had heard so much.

The shared car gig is a rite of passage for all comics. For many, it is their life. I can't exactly imagine Jo Brand, Jimmy Carr and Sarah Millican sharing a car up to Sheffield, but when you're amateur or semi-pro and you want to gig outside London, this is what you do. There is a whole layer of comics on the amateur scene who swear by gigging outside London. The chance of being paid is higher, the audiences can be bigger and our material is more likely to go down well in front of an audience that is not jaded by being able to see comedy every night, as people can in London. That's the positive theory anyway.

The negative theory is that if you get paid, you get paid about £10 or £20. Or even £5. Or even nothing. Any cash is supposed to cover your petrol. I would say that in those amounts it really doesn't. The size of the audience is wildly unpredictable and wholly dependent on whether the promoter has managed to promote the night properly. And whether the audience appreciates you ... well, that will depend on whether you're any good or not. So just the same as inside London, but with a long journey there and back attached. And even more out of pocket than usual.

The reality for comics who want to gig outside London is that they are going to lose money doing it. Not everyone is honest with themselves about this, just as they're not honest about losing money through doing comedy full stop. There is supposed to be a certain cachet to doing gigs outside London. If you take one on (and talk about it), there's the assumption that you must be doing well for yourself. When it comes down to the maths, though, it's very unlikely many of my fellow amateurs are coming out of any

66

of this in the black. (Me included; after twenty-seven gigs, the Diet Coke bar tab now stands at £50.60.)

I'm not really complaining about the promoters here. Most promoters of amateur and semi-pro gigs do it for love rather than money and I have never seen evidence of anyone making huge profits at the expense of comedians. Some promoters are saints. No, the most delusional ones are the comics. They don't seem to accept that they're doing this at a huge cost to themselves. They will perform any mental trick to make themselves think that it's all worth it. And the sad thing is that I'm becoming one of them. I can feel myself wanting to compete for the biggest laughs and the £5 note. There's a double-think mentality about this: you kid yourself you're making more money than you are so that you can stay in the game and keep going. You do that because it's the only way you can keep going.

This isn't entirely mad. I remember an interview with the (very brilliant) Scottish comic Susan Calman, now hugely successful and a regular on BBC Radio 4, who gave up a career in law to scratch a living on the comedy circuit, where she admitted that she lied to herself for the first year about how much she was making. When she added up her earnings at the end of the year, she had completely inflated them in her head in order to give herself permission to keep going. Similarly, she'd downplayed her loss of earnings from giving up law. If it's the difference between keeping going and stopping, sometimes you're better off deluding yourself.

As we sit in non-moving traffic with me seemingly the only person remotely concerned that there is no way we are going to arrive at this gig before 9 p.m., let alone by 7.30 p.m., they all start bitching about this. The driver has a theory that 'Every gig is a gig but a paid gig is a proper gig, so even if it's only paid £5 you should still take it even if it's in Aberystwyth.'

I do not subscribe to this theory but I have not been going long enough on the circuit to argue – or to say that I worry that this theory might be contributing to his difficult life circumstances. (He has already told us about the considerable financial stress he had acquiring this car, which I strongly suspect is two vehicles glued together and spray-painted.)

The other hot topic on the Car Journey from Hell is the huge argument on the amateur circuit about 'pay-to-play' gigs, where everyone who turns up at the gig – including those who perform – pays to get into the venue. At many open mic gigs you have to 'pay to play'. Or you are not allowed to perform unless you bring at least one friend, which is a sort of human equivalent of 'pay to play' where, instead of paying in money, you're paying in the physical presence of another known person.

Whichever way you look at it, it all converts to money because once you get into the building you will, hopefully, buy drinks. Comedians get annoyed about all this and there is a lot of debate about 'respecting the craft' and 'giving us a space to be creative'. Usually this is code for 'giving us a space to make wank jokes which no paying member of the public would put up with'.

The reality is, with amateur comedy someone is going to lose money somewhere because you cannot realistically charge for it – unless there is an untapped market out there for really bad masturbation jokes. But somehow I think the purveyors and the punters would have found each other by now if that were such a gold mine.

One north London comedy promoter recently put up the ticket price of his amateur night from £5 to £7.50. There was a scandal over this, with other comics arguing that he was ripping them off and that their nights – which were free – were far better value. His argument is that this is what it costs him to run the night. And that he has another night on Saturdays when he books pro comics, giving him a profile and a reputation which means that even on his amateur nights you might get lucky and find yourself being entertained by Harry Hill doing new material.

It all comes down to the argument about whether you do things for love or money. Or maybe you do it for love but hope it will turn into money. Personally I find it endearing that anyone is willing to put on comedy anywhere for very little reward. And in view of how draconian the 'pay to play' and 'bring a friend' rules can be, I consider that comics are lucky that there is not also some kind of law about the sort of drinks you consume; because most of the comics drink (free) water or lime and soda, the cheapest beverage available. No one is making any money from that. I'm just waiting for someone to notice and introduce a £5 minimum drink spend for the comics.

Anyway. The point is, people lie about what stuff costs in comedy, but they lie to themselves the most. I count myself in this. I am constantly lying to myself about how this is not costing as much as it could do, that I've done very well by only buying two Diet Cokes, that if I get paid £20 for a gig (which has happened about, um, twice) it means I'm quids in. In fact the cost of my travel is £8.50 (six-zone Travelcard) – often more if I'm driving – and it's very rare that I spend less than £10 on buying drinks for myself and other people. So I am never quids in. It is all quids out.

This is basically a losers' game; but it's also a game where the only way to even stand a chance of winning is to do whatever it takes to keep going. This is why lots of comics start looking for gigs out of town. It makes you feel as if you're progressing, both geographically and financially. You're not. But it seems as if you are. It makes you feel like you're reaching a new audience. It makes you feel like a proper comic. Because that's what proper comics do: they visit service stations up and down the land, at all hours. They're so lucky!

Indeed back in the Mini Metro, every time we pass a service station we have to stop there, as if it's a badge of honour. The driver is the worst; it's as if he's collecting pasty wrappers to prove something. 'I stopped at a service station. I ate a pasty. Look, this is the pasty. Living the dream.' If we don't stop we will somehow be letting ourselves down. Maybe we'll even jinx ourselves. 'We are comics therefore we stop at service stations.' It is the philosophical moment of willing the comic self into being. 'Comics stop at service stations. If we stop at service stations, that will make us comics.' If only it were true. Sadly the multiple purchase of Ginsters pasties does not a funny set make. I am beginning to understand why many comics are such embittered and angry people. This car journey is turning me into one too.

So the service station confers comic status and so does the car journey itself. Usually the driver is one of the lower-order comics. The headliner or the MC will sit in the front seat. This is what I am given to understand anyway. It is already looking extremely likely that this is the first and last time I will ever travel via a shared car to an amateur comedy gig. Within the next twelve hours I swiftly decide that unless I become Joan Rivers and can have a chauffeured limousine to take me to every gig, I will just take the train. Or drive myself. My sanity is too dear to me to share petrol costs.

No one but me seems to be worrying about the fact that it's now 7.45 p.m., we've only just about left London and we were due to arrive at the gig fifteen minutes ago. We're at least an hour away and in the Mini Metro that could mean more like three hours. (At least I think it's a Mini Metro. It's basically a Reliant Robin with ideas above its pasty-obsessed service station.) Admittedly in London it wasn't just the fault of the car;

70

the traffic was awful. But the car is also awful and now making a terrible straining sound when it hits a certain speed – which, admittedly, it rarely does. I fiddle nervously with my seat belt in the back. 'At least it has seat belts,' I think to myself, imagining the faces of my children if their mother were killed a mile outside a service station on the M25 with a Ginsters pasty wrapper fluttering across her dead face. In many ways they would be so much better off without me.

We make many, many service station stops, either to buy cigarettes, smoke cigarettes or buy drinks or food. I stay in the car the whole time and do not undo my seat belt. I am trying to send a subtle psychological message: 'We are late.' I do need the toilet but there is no way I am going to go when we are this late. I ignore the fact that no one else seems to care and I turn my bladder to steel. This is not easy in view of the fact that I have had three children. At about 8 p.m. I suggest phoning or texting the promoter, who has, after all, booked us and is relying on us to turn up on time. This is seen as slightly alarmist as we could arrive there 'any minute'. I suggest that is unlikely as we are over an hour away – if travelling by an efficient vehicle, which we are not. I text the promoter to say we will be there between 8.30 p.m. and 9 p.m. This is an optimistic estimate.

It's now dark and I feel as if this is the longest car journey of my entire life. That is because it is the longest car journey of my entire life. The conversation in-car is still revolving around paid gigs, including one in particular which is supposed to 'lead to progression' but, when quizzed, turns out yet again to pay £10. There is more talk of 'smashing' it, 'killing', 'slaying the room'. I far prefer talking about times when I've died and hearing about the times when other people have died. It is far more entertaining. And more truthful. And no one wants to hear about the time you did great, they only want to hear about the time when you were just excruciatingly awful. I feel very lonely and wonder if I will ever fit in with this group of people.

The conversation on this journey reminds me of the time I overheard one comic telling a group of friends about a time when he 'smashed' it. 'You should have seen. It was just amazing. There was this one woman and she literally – I mean, literally – wet herself. They had to change the chair at the end.' First, this is a really horrible thing to be telling anyone. Second, really? Are you sure about this? Are you sure there was a woman who literally wet herself? And if this happened – which I strongly doubt it did – then does it really make you look like a great comic if you talk about it? Or could you maybe accept the fact that you had someone in the audience who just happened to be appallingly drunk and/or had very poor bladder control and this had very little to do with your comedy?

There is a lull in the conversation and everyone turns on me. 'How long you been gigging?' Oh dear. I do not fancy explaining my stop-start comedy attempts. 'Oh, not long, I suppose,' I mumble, 'I guess that's why I don't know everyone you're talking about.' Talk moves on to a comic who got a bad review on Chortle, the comedy website. Everyone lives in dread of two things: (a) getting a bad Chortle review, which everyone will read and quote back at you for years, and (b) not ever being important enough to merit a Chortle review, however bad. Chortle is the site everyone reads for news and reviews. It often features spats about paid gigs, pay-to-play and numerous apocryphal, self-aggrandising stories about women wetting themselves on chairs in the front row.

As we get closer to the gig (at least, and most improbably, we have sat nav, although it seems to make very little difference), we get lost three times and end up turning into, respectively, an industrial estate, a supermarket and a garage. At least it's not a service station, so we don't stop. I had decided to do this gig because I thought how lovely it would be to be beside the sea in Broadstairs. I love Broadstairs. It has a beautiful little seafront and 1950s ice cream parlours overlooking the harbour. I keep thinking to myself, 'Soon we will be by the seaside and it will all be worthwhile. Just think of the lights twinkling in the harbour. Maybe fish and chips later!' It turns out, of course, that the pub where we are gigging is a long way from the seafront. Before the night is out I will not even have tasted a chip, let alone seen the sea as it is pitch black and it's virtually the next day by the time we arrive.

As we pull up to the pub, which appears to be in the middle of a housing estate in the middle of nowhere, I have no idea how I am going to do comedy now because my mind is racing with annoyance. My body is giving way from the strain of refusing to go to the toilet for five hours in order to make a point. I climb laboriously out of the Mini Metro (it's a two-door hatchback so you can't get out in a hurry). I am muttering about how I am the only one who hasn't been to the toilet, I've managed to hold it in and I've had three children. Have I mentioned the stress to the pelvic floor caused by three natural births?

In the pub toilet I calm down a bit, fuss with my hair and, in my head, start running through what I'm going to say in my set. When I come out of the door, everyone is in a huddle around the promoter and they look up, guiltily. 'We've put you on first,' says the comic who was sitting squashed up against me in the back seat for the past five hours of what used to be my life and now feels like a tour of Hades. He looks at the floor. I restrain myself from saying, 'WHAT?' I can feel the ground beneath me rumbling and the fires of Krakatoa stirring within.

But I calm myself. 'Oh, that's okay, I like going on first. Best to get it over with,' I say, gritting my teeth and trying not to narrow my eyes, not wanting to seem as if I don't have the guts to go on first. 'Are you sure?' he says, trying to be nonchalant, 'I'm on second half and I'll swap with you if you want.' He doesn't want to go on first. No one ever does. 'No, it's fine,' I say, smiling maniacally, with a histrionic wobble in my voice. I go to the bar. I am going to require several Diet Cokes tonight. With extra slices of lemon.

So. This is how it works. Send the idiot into the toilet and do the running order while she's in there and put her on first. What happened to the grand tradition of drawing lots? What happened to democracy? I try to sell it to myself as a compliment – they must believe I have the guts to open. But in reality I am just the patsy, the schmuck. I am the lamb to the slaughter. Worse, it turns out that, like so many of these gigs, it's a 'competition'. I did not know this. We will be judged by the audience, who will be taking notes and awarding us marks out of ten as they watch. Oh Lord, the humiliation. The winner has a chance at a gig hosted by Rufus Hound – a comic off the telly! – and if you get to that stage you can win £200. So in reality, it's just a 'chance' to do another unpaid gig miles from London where you will have another 'chance' to win something. But most competitions are like that so I don't point this out. The odds of getting the £200 would be higher if I bought a scratch card. I have a sudden desire to be at home with my husband and children watching bad Saturday night television with a hot little Lottery Lucky Dip ticket in my hand and a bowl of popcorn at my feet.

But I am not there, I am here. And I am hot, sweaty and angry. And I need to forget about all of that because we've got a show to put on. If you can call this a show. Which, frankly, you absolutely can't. I look around the space where we are due to perform and it definitely falls into the category of the sorts of places where I feel it would be preferable to go out into the street with a microphone in your hand and deliver your set to a tramp. Nothing against the clientele. They seem very nice, if a little rough around the edges. It's just that you can tell they're not here for the comedy. It has been foisted upon them. They just came out for a quiet Saturday night drink. And now they've got to put up with this bunch of 'look-at-me-look-at-me' amateur stand-up comedians. It is horrific. The only thing worse than being in my shoes would be being in theirs. This is not a good analysis – when the gig is so bad that you would rather be a performer than be in the audience. That is not a good gig.

And I am going to have to open the 'show' (show-free, show-less show) in this climate. There's no chance of me getting anything out of tonight apart from a few mild titters and some light humiliation, if I'm lucky. If you go on first, you never get anywhere in a competition. It's a rule. The opener never wins. First, because the audience has nothing to compare you with and so will mark you harshly. Second, because they will be sober and so will mark you harshly. And, third, because in people's minds the later a comic goes on the bill, the better they must be. The headline spot has the most prestige. So the closer you are to that spot the better you must be. Or so goes the psychological trick. So I already know I am going to look like the least able comic on the bill and I am going to have to live with that.

We're in what is a lovely old pub – a bit shabby, but that adds to its faded charm. It's one of those with a bar in the middle and punters on both sides, sitting round in a horseshoe shape, perched on stools. So there is a whole part of the pub that is behind a wall. In the other part of the pub, where we'll be performing, the punters are all sitting facing the bar. We are to perform to their backs. The spot where we will be is in a booth where normally a table would be. There is no stage, no spotlight, just a ropey-looking microphone. Great. I start to do a tattoo count of the punters but give up when I get past a dozen. They enjoy creativity and artistry, I think to myself, nervously.

The MC (the only one of us who is being paid tonight) does a middling job of warming up the crowd but it is a dead loss. They definitely don't want comedy. They have come here for their Saturday night out and they are not interested in a bunch of kids they have never heard of – and most definitely not off the telly and probably never will be on the telly – coming into their personal space and talking to them, entirely unnecessarily, through a microphone. It doesn't help that we are all amateur and the space is set up to make us look even more amateur. The room is strongly lit and you can see every wrinkle on their frowning faces. A couple of the men flirt reluctantly with the (lady) MC but you can tell their hearts aren't in it.

I get up and throw myself into my set, my heart sinking somewhere deep, deep inside me. A Liza Minnelli chorus girl voice bubbles up, 'Come on, Viv, we've got a show to put on! Raise some hell!' It's tragic. It's not the performance or even the reception of the non-audience – who are not at all bad as a collective and, astonishingly, I get one or two loud laughs for which I am pathetically grateful – it's the whole set-up. Another less showbiz voice is now going off in my head: 'This is your life now. This is your life now.' A movie starts playing in my mind: the service stations, the pasties, the cigarettes, the needing-the-toilet, the being-set-up-as-the-opener.

Even while I'm up there I can see a parallel version of myself leading the life I probably should have been leading tonight. I think of the children sat at home on the sofa snuggled up with their dad, watching *Harry Potter*. 'This is your life now,' the voice whispers from inside. It sounds like Gollum. I try and drink in the energy from a couple of enthusiastic people in the audience who look as if they're too bemused to be entertained, rather than nonplussed, as most of them are, but, again, in five minutes there's only so far I can go. 'This is your life now.' I amuse them as much as I possibly can, hope to remind them of a flash of something vaguely funny that they saw once, hope to tickle them in some way. 'Like some kind of prostitute who is using words instead of her body,' cringes the inner Gollum. But there's a happy side too. It's Sméagol. 'Please love me. Come on, people. You seem nice enough. Give me something.'

By the end I am torn between deep self-loathing and desperation and a feeling of satisfaction and connection with these people. There are moments when I feel it and I know I'm in the right place. 'Oh, you were expecting it to be awful – but it's not so bad, is it?' This is why we love comedy. It reminds us of life. It's about the good in life. Even in a bad set in a weird place where no one wants comedy, you can get something out of it that reminds you why it feels good to be alive and why it feels good to share a joke with other people. Two women near the front look at each other as I tell my last joke. They're not entirely dissatisfied. I could have been so much worse. And now I've stopped talking. I enjoy their relief.

When I come off, I feel as if a poltergeist has been torn out of me. I gave them everything I had in my five minutes. Then I suddenly realise that I've misread the support of the two women at the front. They were looking as if they quite enjoyed it but now they are judging me and deciding what mark to give me out of ten. Please don't let it be zero. Or a minus number. I can see one of the women pursing her lips and marking her score sheet. She is sitting next to a woman who looks like her sister. They are dressed in matching denim outfits. They also have matching husbands with spiky hair and stonewashed jeans. They look like nice, if slightly uncompromising, people and I'm sorry that we've derailed their one evening out at the pub, probably the only time they'll go out this week. 'Five out of ten,' she writes next to my name, which is spelled wrong, not remotely hiding the number so that I can see it from way over the other side of the bar. I am pleasantly surprised. In fact, it feels like being awarded an Oscar. Five out of ten! That is quite good! I order a Diet Coke to celebrate. Hey, this might turn out to be a fun night.

Yeah, right. Meanwhile things have moved on and the next guy is a disaster. It's our driver. She marks him zero out of ten and writes carefully, 'Awful! Bless him.' I have seen him perform before and he can have this effect on people. I wonder if I should tell him about this. Maybe not. Wow. Zero out of ten. I make a mental note to make more eye contact with denim-wearers in the audience at future gigs. Possibly they are my constituency. Five out of ten is good enough for me. That is a constituency I can build on. This is what Joan Rivers is talking about when she says: 'If you can get 1 per cent of the population to like you, you can fill a stadium.' This was always going to be my great strategy. Find an audience for my comedy. Build that audience one person at a time. It's just taking quite a long time to recruit the first person.

As the night wears on – and, boy, does it wear on – I drink a lot of Diet Coke. I am getting a bit sick of it; I might have to switch to lime and soda. I remind myself that I have to find a way to get through the journey home. It is dawning on me that I am not going to get home at around midnight as I had hoped. We will be lucky to leave here by midnight. And God knows what time we will get back into London and how many service stations we will have visited by then. I now pray that I will not be killed in a car crash on the way home as it would be a shame if this were my last gig.

I consider having an alcoholic drink or twelve to numb the rage but that will push the money-spent-on-drink tally onto a whole new level. Plus, I know that I will only end up feeling worse. And, of course, I have another gig in less than twenty-four hours. 'This is your life.' You do this, you torture yourself and you can't even make it any better by getting drunk because you have to start preparing for another gig as soon as you get up tomorrow.

It's still close to the beginning and this is only Gig 28 but already I'm acutely aware of how handicapped I am by my attitude to alcohol. I consider myself a semi-alcoholic because I cannot drink more than one or two drinks without getting completely off my face. This has been proven on numerous occasions over the years. There's the time I was 'allergic' to champagne at the office party and tried to pull my boss's trousers off on the dance floor. There's the time I was found underneath a pile of coats at a friend's engagement party murmuring, 'I just want one more Malibu and Coke.' The time I was sick on my friend on the Tube when we were travelling home after a university reunion.

This is why I drink a lot of Diet Coke. I'm not completely alcoholic; I just have to be very careful around alcohol. So there are occasions when I will drink maybe as much as four or five units, but they are very, very rare. Mostly I will not drink at all or I will have one alcoholic drink. The times when I think I need a drink the most – like tonight – are when it is most dangerous for me to have one because it will end up turning into fifty-seven.

Back in bleached denim hell, the comic who stitched me up and made me go on first is, miraculously, having a good set and everyone has livened up. Improbably, I feel quite proud of him. Inevitably the guy who 'headlines' (i.e. the one who managed to manoeuvre himself into the last position while I was in the toilet) 'wins' the 'competition'. It's not deeply unfair: he got big laughs and he's not completely awful. So it could be worse. Nonetheless, the whole evening feels like a waste of time. There is a tiny, tiny part of me that is clinging onto the denim twins and trying to remind me how I felt up there, even in the most dire and pathetic of circumstances. There was something about it I liked. There was something that made me realise that there might – only might – be something in me that can engage people, even in the most difficult and unlikely of set-ups.

If you can succeed at a gig like that – or at least not die completely – imagine what you can do in front of a decent audience? Somewhere buried deep inside me underneath all the rancour and resentment and not-quite-recovering-from-being-stitched-up-while-in-the-toilet there is a little beam of hope. Above all that, though, is the deep sense that I will never, ever, ever intentionally do a gig like this ever, ever again. Hopefully.

The journey home is as bad as expected, only made worse by the fact that it's 3 a.m. by the time we get back into London, so there are no trains or buses and everyone else in the car lives in north London. I manage to convince the driver to take me to Clapham Junction – which, kudos to him, is inconvenient for him. I get out and wave them goodbye, while still cursing them under my breath for putting me on first. I hand over my £10 in petrol money. It feels like a saving (it is a saving) but also incredibly expensive at the same time, considering everything that has transpired in the past twelve hours. I look around and realise that there are no night buses to Teddington from Clapham Junction and the last train left three hours ago. I cannot call my husband to come and pick me up because even if he would consent to picking me up (which he would not), he cannot leave the children in the house on their own. I still think about it, though.

I try and work out where I can get a night bus from but, realistically, at 3 a.m. there are none. I realise that I am going to have to get a taxi and I don't want to get a minicab because they are traditionally manned by rapists. Of course, they're not really. But there seems to be an attitude that if you do get raped or murdered by a minicab driver, it's your own fault. And I don't want to bear that burden.

The reassuring, tempting orange light of a black cab floats into view, travelling towards me, and I flail desperately towards it. Yes, he will take me home to Teddington. The cost of the cab is more than the cost of a return train fare to Broadstairs, Kent. I do not think about this.

I get home at 4.10 a.m. At least I am alive. Then I remember I have another gig in fifteen hours' time. I check Facebook before I go to bed. The lady MC has messaged me: 'Got home at half 3. It was good fun, though, wasn't it? I am adding it to my "things to tell on *Jonathan Ross*" list.' Hmm. Good luck with that.

6: Gigs 29 to 35:

'I know someone who fancies you'

Day 29, Gig 29: Kingston

Another gig at the place where I was for Gig 1. Really getting into the swing here now. Loving my FREE DRINK payment. A nice gig. I can do this. THIS IS THE LIFE. I love free drink. You cannot know how exciting it is to receive a free drink until you have spent night after night buying your own drinks. Free drink earned through comedy tastes better than any other drink ever invented.

Back on the mic with Mr Soundbytz. Did a 'collabo' with him (his expression not mine) where he beatboxed and I put punchlines on the end of his riffs. Very fun – for us and for the audience. I'm much more experienced now than the first time I came here, Day 1, Gig 1. The change in me is scary. I'm not sure the audience can always see it in my performance but I feel it in how I experience the night. Even when things aren't perfect, I'm managing them so much better and I know how to get the most out of an experience and learn from it.

Day 30, Gig 30: Islington

A good gig. Not amazing. But good enough. Hurrah. If every gig was like this one, I would have no qualms about continuing. Unfortunately they are not.

Day 31, Gig 31: Sheffield

The mums 'n babes crowd is a dream now. I just accept the awkwardness (it's daytime, there are babies in the audience, there are no men) and get on with it. This is the last of these Sheffield gigs because the woman who runs them is heavily pregnant. Sorry not to be coming back. Not sad to avoid seven-hour round trip for one gig.

Day 31, Gig 32: Kentish Town

Ego-crushing near-death in a stinking dungeon with walls painted the colour of blood. Like the Red Room of Pain in Fifty Shades of Grey *but without the satisfying consumer goods-based relationship to match. Just pure masochism. Some comfort, however, that I have edged one gig ahead again. I CAN DO THIS. Where the gigs don't give me strength, the numbers do. Surely by sheer weight of numbers I can beat this thing?*

Day 32, Gig 33: Holborn

Nice crowd, nice place, nice MC, nice comics. Shame I was a bit rubbish. Tired. Uninspired. Uninspiring.

Day 33, cancelled gig: Stoke Newington

Took me almost two hours to get there only to find they were pulling the gig because no one had turned up. Mass panic. Didn't want to miss another night. Don't want to lose my lead in the numbers. I'm one gig ahead and I want to stay one gig ahead in case anything else goes wrong. Makes me feel sick to think that I went up to Sheffield three times to get daytime gigs and now because of stupid disorganisation I am going to fall behind because of this stupid lousy gig.

Day 33, Gig 34: Waterloo

Panic premature. With Stoke Newington gig cancelled, moved on with two comics to another gig where we managed to squeeze onto the bill after the second half. FINALLY an audience member offered to buy me a drink after my set. 'Because I agree with your joke about women comics being awful.' IT WAS A JOKE. Otherwise: fun night. Received alarming message from another (female) comic: 'I know someone who fancies you. Are you single?' Reply: 'I am married with three children.' There are two people she could be talking about and they are both Very Bad News. Now I am scared to go to any gigs in case I bump into the two people this could possibly be. STILL ONE GIG AHEAD.

Day 34, Gig 35: Soho

Gig in pub basement. Stage midway between men's and women's toilets. Directed men's toilet traffic into women's as 'equality protest'. Fun in a place not designed for fun. Proud. (I cannot believe that I am proud of myself for directing toilet traffic. But I am.)

*

Simon has been watching my videos back and has declared that he can see that there is some improvement. I can see that there has been a bit. Even when the gig was difficult because there was no one there or I was tired, my performance is gradually getting more consistent. The entire exercise is possibly – possibly – not in vain. 'The ones where you're not so good, you just seem tired,' he says. The problem is, I can't help but focus on the bad bits.

The thought of the good bits keeps me going. When I am on stage and things are working out for me, I am most myself. In the best gigs I get a feeling I remember from my childhood and I feel a connection with my grandparents. I was very close to them. They both died in the past ten years. I do not mean that I see their ghosts in the room or feel like they're sitting on my shoulder or something weird like that. I just mean, I get the good feeling inside that I only experienced when I was around them as a child. It is a sort of feeling of belonging.

As a child I felt most myself with my grandparents. Growing up, I did not live in the same house as them. But they lived nearby in our Somerset village and pretty much raised my younger sister and me. They were with us most days when my parents were working, right up until I left home at eighteen.

My parents were wary of me. 'Vivienne, please. Stop showing off. No one wants to know.' We loved each other, but did not understand each other. My grandparents, however, were completely different. They indulged my drama queen tendencies. They were encouraging and quick to laugh. In terms of supporting me, if anything they were too far in the other direction. If it had been up to them, I probably would have been sent to the Italia Conti Academy at the age of three (which, of course, I would have loved).

When I am up on stage and making people laugh, I am the person I was when I was with them. It's not so much about receiving the love from the audience – although maybe, yes, it must be partly that – it's about who I am when I am up there. I am just being me. And just being me is enough. Of course, I have that in my family now, with my husband and my children. I have it loads. I'm very lucky. But there will always be a little deficiency in me that needs that bit extra. And being on stage doing stand-up gives me that.

My grandparents were the ones I can remember in the audience at school plays, sitting in the front row beaming and clasping their hands together with delight. I don't remember my parents being present (which is probably unfair as no doubt they were physically there – but it's telling that I don't remember it) and when I do remember them, they just looked extremely embarrassed.

My grandma, Vera, was the person I most looked up to, who most supported me, the one I most wanted to resemble. She was also something of a tease and a raconteuse. She was one of those old-fashioned, working-class-made-good women who was always 'on'. She was the sort of person who lit up a room – and you always heard her coming because she talked loudly and clearly in a wonderful RP accent which she had coached herself into. She was always ready with a laugh. She went to the hairdresser's every week to have her hair set like Sophia Loren's and she always had her face on, finished off with a flourish of pink pearlised lipstick.

Before they moved to live near my parents in retirement, she and my grandfather ran a shop in north London for forty years. They sold the shop when I was five, but by then I had spent a lot of time there. They would put on a bit of a show for anyone who came in, ribbing each other and winking frequently, and I would sit on the counter, helping them to make the customers laugh. Vera was a great saleswoman and the first thing she sold to anyone was herself. She could pass in any company: she'd posh it up among the well-to-do; if you didn't have airs and graces, she'd slip into the Manchester accent of her childhood. But all of this was done naturally and without any artifice. She had learned to talk posh when she trained as a teacher. She taught primary children for a few years before marrying my grandad. After that they ran the grocer's for forty years.

In retirement she became an Avon lady, and woe betide you if you opened your door to her and thought you didn't really want to buy anything today. I didn't realise it until years later but if things had been different in her life, she had all the skills you need as a stand-up: a natural facility with language, rapport with people, an ability to see the joke in anything. She did not have an exciting or glamorous or fun life. But she made everything around her exciting and glamorous and funny.

I loved my grandad just as much, even though he was quieter. He had a sort of mournful countenance, that Stan Laurel face of woe and desperation. He had permanently surprised eyebrows, comical tufts of hair on his head and it took nothing to make him look sheepish or abashed. When I was little and until I was much older, too old for it, I would sit on his lap and suck his ears because it made me laugh to see how embarrassed he looked. He had a squashed nose and slightly cauliflower ears (from boxing for Ford's as a factory worker in the 1940s). He was the perfect character act. But, unlike my grandma, he was not one for the stage. He made the asides. He was the butt of her jokes. He was the sidekick, the set-up man. She took the limelight. He made it all possible for her. These, then, were the two people I spent a lot of time around when I was very young. They were the only people who didn't tell me to stop showing off and who liked showing off themselves.

I think it's disingenuous to suggest that most people don't have fairly deep-rooted reasons for wanting to perform comedy. Not everyone really knows what has put them up there. But there has to be a reason that gets you doing something that most people do not feel a need to do. I once interviewed Dawn French and didn't get the impression she really thinks of herself as a stand-up – she's always been a sketch act and an actor: 'In my experience there is something wrong with everyone who does stand-up. Good luck with your malaise.'

She said this as a joke but there was a curl of the lip, a slight sneer, a twist in it too. She lived with a stand-up – Lenny Henry – for twenty-five years and she must know dozens of stand-ups personally. She laughed as she said it. But she also meant it. And I couldn't agree with her more. I have caught a form of this malaise and I don't expect it to pass anytime soon. I doubt I would have caught it if my childhood had been completely different.

Simon has a theory about why some people do stand-up. (Note 'some'. He acknowledges that a minority of them may be normal.) He thinks that some people are loved inconsistently as children: sometimes they got a lot of love, sometimes they got a little. But they weren't shown love unconditionally or on a regular, predictable basis. He thinks that some people use stand-up as a controlled way to force love in their direction. He may have a point; but I reckon it's more dysfunctional than that. I think there's a masochistic element too, where perversely you're recreating that unpredictability; because no matter how good you get at stand-up and how able you are to control the 'positive flow' of emotion and appreciation in your direction, you always run the risk of losing it and things going wrong.

That's why people are so admiring (often overly admiring) of stand-ups: because what they do is one of the most unpredictable and unscientific things you can do. Apart from acting. But acting is slightly different because (a) you're not being yourself and so you are protected a bit and (b) when it goes wrong you can blame it on loads of other people – the director, the playwright, the other cast members. When things go wrong in stand-up, you can try blaming everything else – the lighting, the microphone, the audience – but, really, you know it was down to you and your material.

I'm not sure anyone would put themselves through that if they weren't flawed in some way. As Lenny Henry once said, 'I think I saw my father laugh three times.' There you go. That is the sort of thing that turns you into somebody who feels that they have to spend their entire life in dark rooms making people laugh – people whom they don't know and can't even see because the lights are so bright.

It's the thing that unites pretty much all stand-ups, whether they like it or not. It is a form of sickness. And it doesn't seem to go away, no matter how successful you become. You'd think that Michael McIntyre would not have very much wrong with him now that he can sell out The O2 and is worth millions. But no. He is still needy. This is what he says: 'I like the stage lights to be bright so I can't see people because I will inevitably only see the ones who aren't laughing. Sometimes I embarrass myself terribly and stop the show and say, "What's wrong with it? You don't seem to be having a fun time." When it's not working it feels awful.'

Jack Whitehall – also hugely successful – says the same thing: 'There are some people you can never make laugh. You can't focus on them. But you do. All you focus on is the one person it isn't working for who is sitting there with their arms crossed. I hate myself doing it because it makes you look so mental. You can have a lovely show and think, "There was this one woman and she really didn't enjoy it. I wonder what I was doing wrong."'

I once heard two young stand-ups I really like and admire discussing this on the Tube after a gig. 'Do you think we do this because we weren't loved enough when we were children?' They both nodded, looked at each other and both said at the same time, 'Therapy?'. Both nodded again and burst out laughing.

Then they went back to talking about another stand-up ('You haven't seen Louis C.K.? You gotta watch him, man') and whether it's acceptable to tell rape jokes.

But I think probably none of us, stand-ups or not, can ever be loved enough when we are children. To be human is to be a bottomless pit of want and need. It's just that some people recover from this and some people don't. If you become a stand-up, you probably haven't, on some level. That's your malaise.

Ironically – or perhaps understandably – in view of the many people who are attracted to perform stand-up who are mentally fragile, there are lots of psychologically unhelpful things around the process. I am often reminded of my friend Ruth's 'You won't let it go to your head, will you?' Because it does go straight to your head. 'They like me. I'm good. I can do this.' You can't help but get a lift from that. It's why people do it. Okay, it's not the only reason people do it but it's a big part.

Is there a twist of self-hatred there too? Of masochism? Yes. You have to protect yourself a bit to make sure you don't expose yourself to too many bad gigs. This experiment is not a good advert for that philosophy. This experiment is an advert for insanity. I interviewed the musical comedian Tim Minchin around about Gig 33 and told him what I was doing. He told me it was really important to choose the gigs you do carefully – to try to do the best ones you can. 'I always say to people, "Don't be ambitious in your goals. Be ambitious in your work ethic." But it sounds like you have a psychotic work ethic.' Oh dear. He may be right. But then he started doing this when he was in his teens. He doesn't have time to make up like I do. And I cannot get on at the best gigs unless I learn to survive at the worst ones.

Psychotic or not, stand-up is a way of messing with your mind. The writer Peter Hitchens, whom I worked with years ago when I was starting out in journalism, says stand-up comedy seems an unhealthily dangerous thing to do psychologically. When I described some of the gigs I was having to get through, he looked alarmed: 'You leave a part of your soul in those places. And you can never get that back.' I tried to disagree with him – 'It's really not that bad ...' – but I think he might be right. Michael McIntyre and Jack Whitehall kind of prove that. It never really goes away. It doesn't really get any better. The stakes just get higher. Sometimes I worry that I'm living out part of my childhood and it's just being replayed, only without regular visits to a sweet shop. (That is not actually true. I usually get chocolate on the way to or from gigs.)

On the other hand, I tend to think my stress and negativity might mean I can actually do this. On Facebook comedians regularly post about the Dunning–Kruger effect, which is 'a cognitive bias in which unskilled individuals suffer from illusory superiority, mistakenly rating their ability much higher than average'. My parents would definitely have categorised me as suffering from this syndrome. Psychologists David Dunning and Justin Kruger were awarded the 'Ig Nobel prize' (Alternative Nobel) for their report: 'Unskilled and Unaware of It: How Difficulties in Recognising One's Own Incompetence Lead to Inflated Self-Assessments'. I would not be the first to suggest that this report is the ideal companion publication for the open mic circuit. Linus Lee, a comic I did my first gig with, told me about it. In his darker moments Simon has hinted that this is why most people become amateur stand-ups: they think they are funnier than they actually are. The more time goes on, the more he seems to include me in this statement. It's getting so I feel like that too.

Sometimes I think I must be quite a good stand-up simply because I think I am a terrible stand-up. This is another recognised philosophical phenomenon. Charles Darwin: 'Ignorance more frequently begets confidence than does knowledge.' I'm not ignorant of how bad I can be so I don't have false confidence. Tick. Bertrand Russell: 'One of the painful things about our time is that those who feel certainty are stupid, and those with any imagination and understanding are filled with doubt and indecision.' I have no certainty. I am filled with doubt and indecision. Tick. Shakespeare: 'The fool doth think he is wise, but the wise man knows himself to be a fool.' I know I am a fool. Tick. But does knowing I'm bad make me good? Try telling that to an audience who are not laughing at your jokes.

7: Gigs 36 and 37:

'Maybe there is somewhere I can go to get drunk?'

Day 35, Gig 36: Kentish Town

Middling gig. Small crowd. Didn't hate me, didn't love me. Only moderately terrible. This description now counts as a good gig.

Day 35, Gig 37: Chalk Farm

Come back Broadstairs, all is forgiven. The singularly worst night of my entire existence. Massive death-on-arse in front of over 100 people. Very close to giving up and deciding that this path is not for me. Truly the worst gig of anyone's life ever. In the history of the universe ever ever ever. With the only exception of anyone who physically ended their life on stage. How I envy those people.

*

Walking down a steep hill towards Chalk Farm Tube Station in north London. About 10.45 p.m. Street empty. Pubs full. My coat is not done up properly around me. I'm shivering, snivelling. I've left in a hurry, running downstairs from the gig, pushing my way through a crowded pub before anyone can see I'm on the verge of tears. I can feel it raining on my chest. Snot is coursing down my face and I can't think straight. The gig is not over and I have left early. I have not stayed to meet the headliner, Scott

Capurro, an outrageous, controversial American comic who says exactly what he thinks and doesn't care what anyone thinks of him. Halfway down the hill I can hear his laughs floating on the wind.

I was excited about meeting him tonight. But now I will not meet him. Because I have left. And I have left because I am crippled with shame. The pavement is slicked wet with drizzle and I keep catching myself from slipping over. I am unsteady on my feet and wobbling around. I am weeping fat, hot tears. And walking in an unpredictable line. I look like someone who needs help. If only being drunk were my excuse. I am not drunk. I am stone-cold sober. Maybe there is somewhere I can go to get drunk?

I am definitely not wrecked from drink: the opposite. Instead I have just spent £20 on buying other people drinks. I have not had a proper drink myself because I knew it would make my mood worse. Ten minutes before I left I bought a pint for another comedian, Tom Wrigglesworth, thinking I'd stay and chat to him, maybe watch the headliner with him. Knowing he had about ten years' more experience than me, I asked him if he had any advice. He had just watched my set. He was silent for a while, then replied, 'Maybe just be funny?'

He meant it not unkindly and half-joking. But he was right and I knew it and it broke me. I knew I'd had a bad set but I was hoping I was being harsh on myself. Turns out I wasn't. It really was as bad as I feared. Maybe worse. I made my excuses and left. Now these words are booming in my head. Yeah, Viv, maybe if you could just be funny? Maybe that would help? Maybe if you could just be funny and tell some jokes that might make people laugh? Instead of them staring up at you in silence and disbelief.

As I stumbled down the street, I remembered something else

he had said: 'Just talk how you talk with your friends in the pub. Just be natural.' That means I was unnatural. I was unbelievable. I was a big fat fake. I was like the idiot talking too loudly in the pub that no one thinks is funny and everyone wants to shut up. I weep more. By this point great big sobs are heaving up from my chest, I'm talking to myself loudly and my mascara is halfway down my face.

Yeah, Viv, maybe if you could have told some jokes that were FUNNY? That would be good advice. Just be funny. Why can't you just be funny? And natural. Like you're talking to your friends. Surely it's not that difficult? More laughter carries on the breeze. That's Scott, screaming some joke about Satan and gays. People think he is hilarious. He brings noise and life and warmth into a room, not silence and death and ice-cold bewilderment. I shudder again. Twenty minutes ago I was standing where he is now to the sound of nothing. Or the sound of contempt, which sounds very close to nothing.

I try to buck myself up. I try to see the funny side of another stage death. Maybe I can pretend my act is a new kind of silent comedy. I choke back another sob and laugh to myself. How stupid am I? I wasn't ready for that gig. It was too big, too much. Too Saturday night-ish. It was the first packed Saturday night I had played. It was a disaster. How could I have let myself down like this? Maybe I just can't do comedy.

I feel the glare of car headlights rush by, windscreen wipers squeaking in the rain. I walk straight through a group of drinkers headed up the hill who look at me and giggle. I look a mess, a bag lady, a woman who has just been dumped on a bad date. And that's pretty much what I am. I'm a woman who has been dumped by a comedy promoter, several other comics and an audience of over a hundred people who have just found me not remotely funny.

Perhaps the most painful thing is that this gig was supposed to be the biggest deal of my life as a stand-up so far. And I ballsed it up, big time. It's not a pro gig, I'm not getting paid, but it's an opening slot on a pro bill, performing alongside comics who are established, well known on the circuit, about to break onto television. It's not a bill of huge household names, but in the comedy world it's an excellent one: Ellie Taylor, a beautiful, sassy young comic from the ITV comedy talent contest *Show Me The Funny*, curmudgeonly Yorkshireman Tom 'Just be funny' Wrigglesworth and the always entertainingly offensive Scott Capurro. When I was first asked to appear on this bill, I could not have been more excited. Now it is to become permanently burned on my brain as the Just Be Funny Gig or the Gig Featuring the Most Horrific Words You Will Ever Hear as an Introduction Before Going on a Comedy Stage. 'The next act is a journalist.' Yes, that is how I was introduced.

No one can do well after that, can they? I have nothing in my act that references being a journalist. Why would you? There is nothing funny about being a journalist, unless you are a journalist who is trying – and failing – to become a stand-up comedian. Maybe that is quite funny. Certainly tonight it seems like a big joke. But as a comedy act it's not funny.

Not that I can blame everything on the introduction. I could have turned it around; I should have turned it around. I should have ad libbed something funny about being a journalist. After all, the evening had not started badly. When you play this particular gig on a Saturday night (yes! a Saturday night gig!) then you usually play two gigs, one in Kentish Town and one in Chalk Farm. The Kentish Town one is in the upstairs room of a pub. It's often well attended but on this night it wasn't; there were maybe fifteen, twenty people. I had gone on first but hadn't done terribly in view of the numbers – a few titters, a few laughs, nothing humiliating. It wasn't the greatest omen for the second part of the evening, but it wasn't a disaster either. A few more acts performed and then I jumped in a cab with Ellie from the telly, to get over to the Chalk Farm pub.

On the way there she quizzed me about my family. 'Doesn't your husband mind you doing this? How many children do you have and what do they think? How old is your baby?' Easy answers: 'My husband doesn't like it much. But he puts up with it. My children are Will – he's eight – and Vera – she's five. They don't mind. The baby, Jack, has just turned one.' Ellie: 'Wow.'

People often ask me these things on the circuit. It is not a big deal to be a woman with children if you are a proper, well-known stand-up comedian like Jo Brand or Jenny Eclair or Lucy Porter. They obviously have an income and a life-plan and a public profile. But it is seen as quite a strange thing to do if you are playing the amateur comedy circuit about twenty years later than you should be, for very little money and a very slim chance of progression. I explained that I was doing a 'blitz' of gigs. My husband didn't mind as long as it didn't last for ever. My children thought it was fun. Although, as a general life rule, they would all rather I stayed at home than went out anywhere. At all. Ever.

That evening I had felt my adrenaline rising as the taxi lurched over the speed bumps of the back streets of north London. This was pretty much the biggest gig I had done so far. I had played to these numbers before but only by volunteering to help out at charity events or because I'd been invited to things predominantly as a writer. This was the first time a comedy promoter had booked me properly as a comic because he had seen me and liked me.

The invite had come two months before when I went to perform at the Thursday night try-out for the Saturday. If you do well, you get offered a weekend slot. Among amateur comics it's a legendary night famed for its eccentric promoter. Promoters are by definition strange – understandably, because it's a strange job. There isn't really much money in it, certainly in the early stages, and you have to be ridiculously tenacious to get anywhere. So it attracts some interesting types. One of my favourite promoter moments was when a flurry of comics went on Facebook to complain about one guy who had disappeared after promising a load of gigs. He reappeared about two weeks later with the following explanation: 'Sorry I haven't been around. I should not drink absinthe.'

Anyway, a few days after I had first performed at this promoter's Thursday night amateur hour, the phone call came. I was thrilled. Now, two months on, I am walking away from the same gig in tears. With hindsight, despite everything I've been through in the past two months, I wasn't ready for a gig that big. Tom Wrigglesworth said that I looked nervous. And he was right. An audience can smell that and, once they have, there is not very much you can do about it. It's too late. They are not going to warm to you.

I began the set with a sinking feeling in my stomach and it didn't go away for the next five minutes. At the worst moments there were audible noises of pity and sympathy coming from the audience. I yearned for a massive, offensive heckle which would at least liven up proceedings. It did not come. I stumbled through my material. A voice in my head urged me on: 'If it starts to go wrong, just keep going. Don't apologise and narrate your failure. That's self-indulgent and even more uncomfortable for the audience.'

It took every ounce of willpower in my body not to shout

out loud, 'Help, people! I am dying up here. You seem like nice people. Do something! Stage an intervention!' Of course, it was not necessary to voice this thought, as every pore of my body was screaming it for all to see. And they did not want to do something. They were waiting for me to do something. To make them laugh. After all, that's what I was there for. Or perhaps not.

I had never been more intensely relieved to finish my set. Although it did occur to me that I would rather stay up there on stage, quietly dying in the spotlight but alone and unconfronted – anything but having to face the comments of anyone who spoke to (or, rather, avoided) me afterwards. The promoter gave me a slightly pitying pat on the shoulder, adjusted his dog-tooth trilby awkwardly and made some hilariously gauche apology to the audience along the lines of, 'Give her a chance. She's a very new act.' He then held his hands up in surrender and shrugged as if to say, 'Don't blame me.' Then he added, as if to justify the fact that he had booked me, 'Er … she is actually very funny.' 'No, she so isn't,' I muttered under my breath, voicing the thoughts of the entire audience. I felt intensely guilty just looking at him. He had given me a chance and I had messed it up. I doubted he would give me another one in a hurry. Or maybe ever.

I did realise that he was surprised at how badly I'd done. After all, he'd seen me do well and that's why he booked me. It was his job to try to save face and make out that every-thing was okay. I suppose you can always pretend that your comedy is incredibly surreal and highbrow and it's not that you weren't funny and you sucked, it's that it's so advanced and clever that people just didn't get it. I would never have the balls to do this, but I have noticed that sometimes it's necessary for a promoter to do it on your behalf because otherwise they look stupid for booking someone as rubbish as you.

I tried to melt into the back of the crowd as the next act, Ellie, went up. But once you've been on and you were that awful and you're still in the room ... it's like you exude a Ready brek nuclear glow. You are the toxic waste of the night. People noticeably shuffled away from me. Ellie, meanwhile, did very well from her very first joke. I would like to say that they were just laughing at her because they were relieved that she was not me. But they were laughing because she is a skilled comic and has good material. It would have helped my ego if she had had a poor reception because then I could have blamed the crowd. But seeing as my ego was already comprehensively destroyed, it made little difference that she pretty much took the roof off.

When she came off stage she was swamped with well-wishers wanting to know when her next gig was and men offering to buy her drinks and asking for her phone number. I, meanwhile, had a fifty-mile radioactive exclusion zone around me. After attempting to regain some kind of composure by buying drinks for everyone possible (because definitely nobody was going to buy me one, they might catch something – like horrific, suck-all-the-air-out-of-the-room failure), I suddenly realised that I was going to lose it and start crying if I didn't leave.

It had taken all of my composure and willpower and self-respect to hold myself together enough to get to the bar and buy drinks. Now it was all used up and I was collapsing internally. I pasted on a pathetic, unconvincing clown's smile to say goodbye, only to register that no one was noticing or caring that I was leaving. When toxic waste exits the building, nobody cheers. They're just relieved.

It turned out that the Walk of Shame to the Tube was the most cheerful part of the experience. I cried all the way home, arrived in tears and cried myself to sleep. When I woke up in the morning I was still crying.

8: Gigs 38 to 42:

'That was like feminism. Shit.'

Day 36, no gig

Couldn't get a gig anywhere tonight. Frustrating. Made the most of being at home. Watched Harry Potter *with the children. Realised that comedy should be like hanging out with Hagrid. Instead it can feel like the Dementors have got you.*

Day 37, Gig 38: Soho

Oh, the horror. The Toothpaste Gig Where Bella Emberg Cursed Me. Another sodding competition. Why do I bother?

Day 38, Gig 39: Covent Garden

Bit of a strange mood. Did new material. Audience laughing a lot but only at my ineptitude. I don't mind and I will take any laugh but I cannot build an act out of being so bad I'm good. Or can I?

Day 39, Gig 40: Clapham

Really went for it with the feminist jokes tonight. I have been working on them for a while now and they are starting to work. 'How many feminists does it take to change a lightbulb? None. Don't change the lightbulb. Because in the dark no one can judge a woman by her appearance.' Next comic after me: 'That was like feminism. Shit.' Perhaps not my target audience. But I antagonised him. So, result.

Day 40, Gig 41: Kentish Town

Return to scene of the try-out night connected to the horrific Just Be Funny gig. Promoter said nothing about my stage death. But he did put me down on the Facebook listing as 'Viv Groskop: Good Fun', which is code for 'Not a Very Good Stand-Up.' I'm not the first and I won't be the last. Still, makes you want to pluck out your own liver and eat it. Survived.

Day 41, Gig 42: Highbury

The lovely gig next to the kebab shop. Performed with the Instrument of Truth (mini keyboard), improvised, was very silly. Enjoyable for all, including me. You can't build an act out of that kind of silliness (or can you?) but it's what I need to start showing more on stage. Completely sick of Diet Coke and getting home late.

Day 42, Gig cancelled: Clapham

A rare Saturday night booking (one of the hardest nights for amateur comics to gig because it's the night people are prepared to see 'names' off the telly). Cancelled because the pub 'doesn't want to do comedy any more'. Back to zero progress with the numbers.

*

Another competition. Gig 38. This one started off beautifully. After the horror of the Just Be Funny night, I had had forty-eight hours off comedy and had recovered my composure.

Before I went on I decided I was blessed. Because, just as I was about to go up on stage, I saw a poster that was about forty years old advertising Bella Emberg's appearance at the same theatre. I thought solemnly, 'I am following in Bella's footsteps. She will protect me.' Bella Emberg played Blunderwoman in *Russ Abbot's Madhouse* in the 1970s. It was one of my favourite programmes as a child. She is very funny, both intentionally and unintentionally.

My thoughts drifted away to how my success would mirror Bella's and I too would perform with the equivalent of such greats as one-time *Madhouse* guests Les Dennis and Dustin Gee (RIP). So I wasn't paying much attention to the act before me. Until I realised that he was cutting himself on stage. And not everyone in the audience could see that he had started bleeding. He had a joke about shaving an apricot, which he was illustrating by shaving an actual apricot, using a razor. The joke was dying horribly and he was succeeding only in shaving off his own skin.

As he came off stage, blood was pouring out of his hand, which he was attempting to stem using toilet roll. His head was jerking and his fingers were shaking. As I headed for the stage, not wanting to delay because you get that awkward moment when the introductory applause has stopped ages before you get to the microphone and you have to start in silence, I panicked for him and made a solicitous 'Are you okay?' face. He replied with a shruggy 'Not really, but I'll get over it' expression. All the blood had in fact drained from his face (not surprising in view of the amount streaming out of his hand) and he looked pale and about thirteen. In reality he was about nineteen, I'd estimate, which was just as bad.

As I stepped towards the microphone, I realised it was worse, much worse. As well as doing weird things with a razor, he had also being doing weird things with toothpaste. It was all over the floor, all over the microphone lead, all over the stand. I hadn't really registered most of his act because I was thinking about my set and about how I would be the next Bella Emberg. That's what you do before you go on. You're trying hard to remember your stuff and stay focused on the first thing you're going to say. You're living completely in your own little world. They could put Joan Rivers on before me and I'd miss her entire set. The act before you could be shaving an apricot and squeezing toothpaste everywhere and you wouldn't even notice.

As I stood there trying to gather my thoughts and sweep away all the audience's memories of Apricot Blood Razor Man, I realised I could hardly breathe as my nostrils were full of the smell of fresh minty toothpaste. I was wearing a black top and the microphone lead, covered in sticky toothpaste, was flapping against me, leaving white marks. You only have a split second to decide whether you're going to reference the previous act or not. It's usually a good idea to create a division between the last person and yourself because once they've gone, generally the audience don't remember who they last saw and they want you to create a new reality. There's no point in trying to piggyback on someone else's act, however good they were. And if they were awful, it just makes you look a bitch to mention it.

What to say? What to do? It was almost impossible to overcome my natural instinct, which was to yell, 'Why have you been doing stupid things with toothpaste, you very silly boy?' I realise now this is what I should have said. Instead, the lights in my eyes, looking out into the echoing darkness, I decided the audience would have forgotten about the toothpaste man and probably could not see the mess on the microphone and the floor anyway. I had a strict five minutes and I needed to get my set going. I didn't have time to waste on doing pointless ad libs about toothpaste, even if I looked as if someone had drizzled white gunk all down me.

Everything I have just described happened in about five seconds, but when you are up there it feels like five hours. Your mind is racing and you are trying to process so many things at once while trying to look totally relaxed and happy, and as if you're in the company of your greatest friends ever. And a bit drunk. But never actually drunk. With hindsight I should have ditched my entire set and talked about the toothpaste. Because my set bombed.

I watched the footage back the next day. A flustered, distracted Penelope Keith-type with immaculately blow-dried hair attempting to tell feminist jokes while looking as though someone has ejaculated down the front of her. It was funny. But not for the right reasons. I didn't get through to the next round.

It's the video that pushes Simon over the edge. He has now been looking after the house and keeping everything together for over a month. I come back from yet another 'disastrous' gig, telling tales of blood, gore and minty horror. Simon watches it and decides that I didn't do too badly and it only went wrong because the audience was just mean and didn't get any of my jokes. I refuse to blame them. It's my fault if they don't get the jokes. I should have done better.

I make the mistake of telling him what another comic told me last night: 'I've never seen you not do well.' This guy has seen me at a lot of gigs. I find what he said bizarre. He has seen me at gigs which I have experienced as total, undeniable death. Maybe he just means that no matter what happens I keep going and I don't fall to pieces. Not outwardly anyway. And I don't narrate the failure of my set. I've now trained myself out of that, because there is nothing worse than an incompetent stand-up saying,

'Oh dear, this isn't going well, is it?' You just have to suck it up and keep going.

Simon is now convinced that I have no self-awareness about what happens when I am on stage. 'It's gig after gig with no respite. One after another. It's making you lose all sense of proportion.' I suspect he may be right. I am very harsh on myself and not really happy unless I have had a strong, unmistakably positive audience reaction. The more I'm learning, the more I'm realising that some of what I'm doing is okay and can be built on. All the same I do tend to rant and rave and be a bit of a drama queen about the bad gigs. Poor Simon is being driven mad by the obsession of it all. Who can blame him?

That night I wake up and find Simon sitting on the end of bed. I know what he's thinking about. 'Do you want me to stop now and just give it all up?' I ask, trying not to raise my voice. I'm whispering because the children are asleep next door. 'Because that is going to be a relief for you in the short term. But in the long term it's going to cause a lot of bad blood between us. I wouldn't have started doing this if it weren't really important to me. You know that.' It sounds like I am hissing now. 'I really appreciate everything that you're doing. I really need your support. I'm really grateful for everything you do for the children and around the house. You know that.' He sighs and says: 'I cannot remember the last time you put a wash on.' 'I'll try and remember to put more washes on. Is that all?' He says, sadly: 'I just don't get why you're doing this. It's like you want to get away from us. It's like some kind of madness. I mean, what's the point to it? Why are you really doing it? It's a joke. Except it's not funny. It's ruining everything. It's just this directionless comedy binge.' This hurts. But I know that he may be right and I can't actually contradict him.

Before things become too tense, he says, jokingly: 'I would

leave you. But I don't think you'd notice.' The joke hides a truth. I take a deep breath. 'Don't be so ridiculous. Of course I'd notice if you left me. Because my life would be ruined.' 'Really?' 'Yes. There's no way I would choose something as stupid as stand-up comedy over you. And you know that. So don't ask me to choose because you will always win. Look, I don't want to go on with this stupid experiment if it's making you desperately unhappy. But if you can hold out just a few weeks more … It's not going to get more difficult. It's only going to get easier from here. This is the worst part, getting to the midway point.' I'm trying to convince myself as much as I'm trying to convince him.

He says, 'The thing is, you're never here. I never see you. The children never see you.' I do feel bad about the children because of course I would be a better mother to them if I wasn't going out every night. But it's partly because of them that I'm doing it. I don't want them to grow up with a parent who didn't have the guts to do what they really wanted to do with their life. I don't want them to grow up with a mother who is defeated and cowed and couldn't be bothered to see things through just because they got a bit tough.

I want them to see that you have to work hard to get better at things. I want them to see that it doesn't matter if you fail initially. What matters is that you keep on improving. I want them to see that it doesn't matter how old you are or what stage of life you're at, you can do what you want to do with your life. It's never too late to have a go at something. And it's never too late to return to the things you always meant to do. I want to show them that having a family is no barrier to doing other stuff with your life.

But at the moment I just feel like I'm showing the opposite of all that. Follow your selfish dreams and your family life will suffer. Go out every night and your husband will want to leave you. Try to become a stand-up comedian and the universe will laugh in your stupid, nearly-forty-year-old face.

'Come on. That's not fair. The children do see me. I pick them up from school. I am with Jack two days a week. Don't make this about the children. I'm sorry I'm not here in the evenings, okay? Maybe I can move around a couple of gigs next week and double up and get an evening off? How about if I did that? Maybe I can come in to see you at work one lunchtime next week. How would that be?'

I am getting frightened that he is going to make me stop doing the gigs. Part of me would love to stop. But I am too stubborn to stop. And I am sort of addicted. I want to prove that I can do it. The problem is, my blind, passionate compulsion is not enough any more: we need a better reason for me doing this. We need some more signs that there's a point to it. 'Do you really think it's directionless?' 'No. Yes. No. I don't know. It's just that sometimes I think you don't know why you're doing it. And I don't think you do either.'

9: Gigs 43 to 47:

Not entirely what I would call daylight behaviour

Day 43, Gig 43: Balham

Daytime mother and baby gig hosted by Lucy Porter. Well-attended, happy gig and a chance to pull ahead by one more gig ... very, very happy. Friend: 'It was like watching early Dame Edna. Which, considering that I know you, was a bit weird.' Now worried that I come across as (a) derivative and (b) like an elderly Australian man in drag.

Day 43, Gig 44: Borough

Comic-filled, audience-free borderline miserable night pepped up by some good ad libs from lots of the comics and general atmosphere of anarchy. A couple of nice comics I like, including an older guy who has had all sorts of health difficulties in his life and does acerbic Tory-hating material. He's good and it's enjoyable to see someone trying to do political material. No one really does it at the moment. Seeing people like that makes it worthwhile.

Day 44, Gig 45: Bloomsbury

Horrific, waste-of-time gig. But quite enjoyed it. Nice-ish crowd. (When I say 'crowd', I usually mean ten people plus the comics. Obviously.) Met a couple of sweet comics. Felt like performing in someone's living room while they waited to hold up their Strictly Come Dancing *marks. Three out of ten. But not painful.*

Day 45, Gig 46: Borough

Bit of a strange mood. Tired. Feeling weird. Acted a bit strange on stage. Insisted on standing on a box for some reason. Nearly brained myself on the ceiling doing this. Getting very bored by my material. It's a huge challenge to keep performing your material night after night, especially in front of other new comics who have already seen it dozens of times.

Day 46, Gig 47: A Place Joy Forgot

Silly man. Horrible. Horrible. Horrible.

*

I should have known something bad was going to happen this night because there was kind of a bad smell in the air. That in itself is not much of a giveaway because overall open mic comedy venues can have a weird smell to them. They literally stink in so many ways. Of hastily applied Lynx deodorant that doesn't really mask the smell of a long day in a much-despised office job. Of a hangover that hasn't really gone anywhere. Of old food, new food and spilled drinks. Of comedians' body odour, often my own.

Generally they never, ever smell of women's perfume and I cannot remember ever complimenting another woman on her perfume at a gig, which is something I would often do in other situations. Possibly most women very sensibly do not bother wasting perfume on such occasions. More likely, the smell of any perfume they are wearing is masked by the overwhelming, competing smells of the venue.

Over the past forty-plus gigs I have almost worn out a bottle of Prada Candy, mostly to mask the smell of my own sweat. I can't even bear to smell it now. And yet I spritz it on night after night, like some kind of talisman. I can't go on without it. It doesn't feel right. And yet I hate the smell of it at the same time.

Because comedy places do not smell like an attractive woman, if you wear any perfume at all people always remark on it, often as if you have worn it especially for them. 'You smell gorgeous,' a promoter once murmured to me, nuzzling his nose into my hair as I shrank away, squirming. I didn't have the heart to tell him that what he was inhaling was not fragrance, beauty or, as he hoped, Essence of Available Woman, but actually hairspray. I usually take my rollers out on the way to a gig, having hidden them under a coat with a hood so that people on public transport do not think I am deranged. I pull the rollers out of my hair just outside the venue and then spray everywhere with industrial quantities of Elnett.

Who are the smelliest people on the open mic circuit? I would honestly nominate myself for being one of them and if no one else backs me up then I would seriously worry about their sense of smell. I have been paranoid for ages that people must have noticed how often I wear my Statement Cardigan and it's really starting to smell like it. Joke: 'In order to make an impression tonight I have worn a statement cardigan. The statement is: "Sorry, I've put on a bit of weight, but focus on the cardigan."' This is what the Derren Brown/Maybelline joke has morphed into. Obviously when I am wearing the cardigan, I'm mostly on stage – or waiting to go on stage – and so I sweat a lot. You are always going to sweat more in stand-up than in almost any other occupation because you are using up nervous energy, you're excited and full of adrenaline and, most of all, it can be really hot up there.

For a while I stopped wearing the cardigan because (a) I thought it was too smelly and I wanted to stop wearing it before someone else asked me to and (b) I was starting to think that the joke was getting a bit tired as well and I wanted to stop doing it before someone else begged me to. But then a horrible thing happened: I realised that I really missed the joke and I missed the cardigan. I had become reliant on it. I had become a terrible hack comedian, dependent on my sparkly cardigan for cheap laughs. So tonight I am wearing the cardigan. Of course I am. It's easier than writing and, worse, learning new material. And I am sweating profusely. I smell and the venue smells. Plus, there is a weird smell of fear.

By this point I had not experienced very many gigs where I feared for my physical safety and still carried that feeling as I was walking home afterwards. Those gigs are the worst. You can't let go of that fear. Sometimes it's not for any particular reason. You just pick up on something in the crowd. A punter who's difficult. A bar manager who's a bit aggressive. A promoter who's not happy. Another act who is in a bad mood with you. But this stuff really doesn't happen that often, and it's mostly just in your imagination because you're tired or hungry or having a bad night.

Then tonight it happened for real. Big time. I had seen one of the club promoters bullying a comedian in the bar earlier. A tall, talented, good-looking young comic with his head bowed like a schoolboy, being berated by a short, menacing promoter, wagging his finger at him. The body language was nasty to watch. I thought it must be a one-off or I was misreading the situation. But something inside me said it did not bode well.

The evening had started oddly. For once I was in a place where the place was packed, people were drinking heavily and swelling in numbers every half-hour. Usually when there's a lot of people and they're all happy and having a good time, the acts are happy and excited too. It's better than playing to a room of ten comics. It's great. It's what you've been waiting for after weeks of rubbish gigs. But tonight was different.

There was an air of something uncomfortable around. Maybe it's because people were drinking too heavily too early. Maybe it's because I had seen the guy getting ticked off in the bar and it gave me a taste of the bad blood in the air. Maybe it was something else. Anyway, it didn't feel like a good night from the off. Things got worse when this serious-looking, frowning man – the same promoter from the bar – came up to the comedians' table. 'We'll be watching you,' he said, eyeballing us. The idea behind this? It's unspoken but it's this: 'If you're any good, we'll have you back. Maybe for money. So you had better be good.'

I went on stage late. It was already past 10 p.m. by which time the crowd was completely insensible with drink. That can be good. That can be bad. Tonight it was bad. They laughed at a couple of my jokes but struggled to understand most of what I said because they were so drunk. Several groups were mostly just talking among themselves. I didn't feel it had gone well, but I felt like it could have been so much worse. I didn't die any worse than the two acts who had gone on before me. I didn't get booed off the stage and there were a couple of moments where I got everyone in the room to listen to a joke. That was about as good as it was going to get.

As soon as I came off stage, grim-faced but not totally defeated, I slumped into a chair and switched off my video camera thinking, 'I am not going to want to watch that footage back.' One of the comics came over to me, still laughing at the situation. When it was his turn he had managed to get more control. When I was up there it sounded as if the people closest to me in the audience were chatting all through my set and I couldn't hear half of what was being said. I felt like a supply teacher trying – and failing – to get her pupils' attention. As one of the comics had said earlier, 'They're a pretty basic audience.' This is usually code for, 'They will laugh at swearing and fart jokes.' I do not have either.

I had survived, though, bruised but not crushed. Not one of the comics said, 'Well done' or shook my hand in the way that they do when things have gone well. That's okay, I didn't deserve it; but it's still embarrassing. The etiquette after these things is usually that if you come up to speak to someone once they've performed, then it means you enjoyed their performance – unless you want to berate them or make an irritating observation. Audience member after my first gig: 'You remind me of Victoria Wood.' Me: 'Oh. Wow. Thank you so much.' Him, smirking: 'Oh, I don't think she's funny. You just look a bit like her.'

If you're another act or a promoter, it's a given that you have something positive to say if you come up afterwards. If you have something bad to say … well, that is basically a huge act of aggression. If you come and talk to an act and you're a promoter, it usually means the act will start thinking that you want to invite them back to perform again. If you don't like them or you think they're rubbish, you just don't talk to them. You don't even make eye contact with them or acknowledge in any way that they were present that night. That doesn't mean that as an act you can never come back; it just means that no one's going to make it easy for you to do so or make you particularly welcome because you're not good enough yet. Suck it up.

So I was very surprised when the promoter came over to the back of the room and made a beeline for me. I was aware that he had been taking people aside all night for feedback, but I assumed it was only people who he thought showed some kind of promise. I had shown promise as a bad supply teacher. But there is no accounting for taste in comedy so I allowed myself to think, 'Okay. Maybe he sees potential in what I did. Or maybe he likes weird comedy that doesn't really work. Or maybe he's another one who wants to tell me I am like Victoria Wood, not because I made them laugh but because I physically resemble her.'

I really did think this. Not for one second did I think, 'I'm a woman. So maybe he is coming up to talk to me because he fancies his chances.' I never think this. Mostly because I have not been on a date since 1997 and I always assume that everyone knows that I'm married and I must give off a vibe of being massively married. It never occurs to me that anything else could be possible. How stupid of me.

So this guy sits down and immediately puts his hand on my knee. I am so incredulous that he has done this that by the time I have registered it is happening, it has become too late for me to say anything about it without it appearing like an accusation, which will cause trouble. I shift uneasily. He asks me if I saw the comic on earlier. (This is the guy I saw him talking to in the bar.). 'That guy is one of the weakest acts I have seen,' he says. 'He's a weak act, he says. I reply, still flinching under his knee-hold, 'That's a bit harsh, he just did a really good set.' He looks at me dismissively, 'Yeah,' and then, meaningfully, 'but I have really high standards'. I can sense that I am about to get my first taste of what it's like to be talked to by someone who thinks they know their stuff and wants everyone to know it. What am I saying, 'first taste'? There are loads of people in comedy who think they know everything. This guy is just even more convinced of it than normal.

Looking down at his hand, which is still on my knee, I recoil slightly, trying to make out that it must be an accident that it is still there. I don't overreact, though, as I can tell he is the type who will get aggressive if I flatter myself by making out that he's coming on to me. His eyes are bloodshot and tired. There's nothing about him to suggest he's drunk but his manner is not entirely what I would call daylight behaviour. He doesn't smile, only grimaces. 'So how long you been doing stand-up?' I give an answer that indicates that I'm not a complete beginner but neither am I an accomplished act who has thus far failed to get anywhere. This is the impression you are supposed to give. 'I did my first gig in 2009. Then I got pregnant. And I didn't gig for a while.' I pause. 'The pregnancy was unconnected to my first gig.' He doesn't laugh. I'm trying to make a joke. But I'm also trying to point out that he should take his hand off my knee.

'Oh, so you're married.' He checks my hand for a ring. 'Yes. I'm married,' I smile sweetly. He leans in. 'Happily married?' He's checking my eyes for the truth. 'Yes, happily married. Thanks for asking.' At least, I think to myself, now we can have a normal, decent conversation as the lines have been drawn. The hand is removed. Then he says, 'Come outside so we can talk.'

What? This is not a welcome offer but what choice do I have? He is in charge. He runs the place. He has let me on stage. I haven't done well tonight but it's one of the only places that always has a good, big crowd of people in. That's what they call it. I need to be able to come back here if possible. I make a quick calculation: I will go outside with him as long as there are other people around.

I am thirty-eight years old, for God's sake. I have pushed three babies out of my body. Over the course of the past forty-six consecutive nights, I have done forty-seven gigs. I cannot run very fast and sadly I don't think I could give a meaningful punch. But I am more than capable of screaming very loudly and kneeing someone in the balls. What's the worst thing that can happen? I do know, however, that 'outside' means standing in an alleyway. It seems, er, inappropriate.

Maybe he just wants a fag, I think. It is not unreasonable to want a fag and talk to someone at the same time, is it? Another part of me is thinking: 'Just by going outside with him I am agreeing to something and I might not know exactly what I am agreeing to.' I am also curious, though, and hoping he will do something awful so that I can knee him in the balls. I am not wearing high heels and am feeling reasonably agile. Anything is possible. I am sort of already looking forward to it.

On the way outside, the girl at the bar shouts, 'You really made me laugh.' I shout back, 'That's the idea!' That makes her laugh more. I am pleased, partly that someone in this place has been nice enough to say something and partly because I am thinking to myself, 'Good. I have a witness. She has seen me go outside.' I am also vaguely wondering if she will be the last person to see me alive.

Just outside there are two or three older men in crumpled suits smoking. They're punters. They acknowledge me, as if to say, 'Oh yeah, we just saw you on stage.' It's not unfriendly, but no one says what they would say if they were nice or polite, which is, 'I liked your act.' The promoter turns to one of the guys smoking and says, gesturing to me, 'Did you see her act? What did you think of her?' The man looks uncomfortable. 'It's okay,' the promoter goads the man, 'she can take it. She's a comedian.' Oh dear, I think to myself, this is actual bullying. I am quite shocked – and not a little impressed – by how brazen it is. The promoter has no idea how well I can take whatever the man might say to me. He knows nothing about me at all. He has just met me.

The man whose opinion has been solicited says, in a friendly enough way, 'You have some issues, don't you?' He is referring to the fact that I got mock-angry in my act. 'It's all for comic effect,' I smile. He seems like a nice enough man. If you like Marlon Brando in *The Godfather*. 'You're pretty angry. I kind of liked your rant,' he says, approvingly. 'Thanks,' I shrug, 'it's good to get it all out.' He finally concedes, having made me earn it: 'I thought you were quite funny, actually.' I turn to the promoter with a smug expression on my face, as if to say, 'See?', but he has got into an argument with someone on their way into the club and is now going back inside. Relieved, I go back in.

Two minutes later, I can feel his hot breath near my neck once more and he motions for me to come back outside again. The act on stage is now doing a Michael McIntyre impression. 'What do you think of this guy?' 'I haven't seen enough of him to tell,' I say carefully, suddenly aware that this comic may be promoted to Master of the Universe or simply killed on the strength of my random assessment. I feel like I have walked into an episode of *The Sopranos*. 'He's a good impressionist,' I add, cheerfully. I do not want the comic to be hit. He looks satisfied with my evaluation. 'Come back outside.' He nudges me back outside by touching my waist and my buttocks as if to guide me. I leap away as if I am being electrocuted. It strikes me that this could be a good way of getting fit. I have not moved so fast in months.

This guy is now seriously creeping me out. I'm wishing that I could just leave. But it would be unprofessional of me to leave and he knows that. I am, I have to admit, also intrigued to see what rude things this guy will say about my comedy. Of course, this is what he's banking on – that I feel I can't leave. And I kind of can't. He keeps asking me when I am leaving and I say that I really need to leave now because I live in Teddington and it's a long way away. Then he looks meaningfully into my eyes and says, 'Do you believe in God?'

Oh dear, this is not a direction I had expected the conversation to take. Except it suddenly feels inevitable: it is going to be one of those conversations. 'For the purposes of this conversation, no,' I say carefully, thinking about the expression and demeanour Tony Soprano's therapist would adopt.

I need to allow for the possibility that he could be either a Jehovah's Witness or a rabid atheist. Of course, it does not matter whether I believe in God or not. The important thing is that I let him talk and not say anything that offends him. 'I believe we all have a spirit and a soul,' he says, still fixing me with a bloodshot gaze. 'Er, right,' I say, wondering where this is going. He looks solemn: 'And that's what you have to let out in your comedy,' he adds. I don't disagree with him – in fact I think this is an astute observation. But, still, this is a weird conversation.

'You need to show the audience what you're like when you're having sex,' he adds, stepping closer to me. 'You need to show them what sort of orgasms you have. What kind of sex you like.' It's said with menace. But it's also laughable. I can feel my face start to flush and I try to back away from him a little. I am scared and angry but also struggling to keep a straight face because I cannot believe he is saying this. He goes on. 'I'm just trying to help you here. Because what I'm saying is that I think you can continue as a comedian … '. At this point I splutter, as if to say, 'Oh, thank you so much for your permission.' He continues: 'I have told three other acts to give up tonight and I'm not going to tell you that.' He pauses for emphasis. 'But at the moment you don't have any material.'

I say as graciously as possible (which is not very graciously at all as I am now shaking with anger): 'Thank you for your advice.' He can feel my hostility and is not happy. 'I know what I'm talking about here. I know about comedy.'

I look him in the eye as amicably as possible and say, 'Thank you so much. That's very helpful.'

My heart is pounding, my flesh is crawling, I'm struggling not to show that I'm shaking with fear and anger. I am feeling physically harassed by this man even though he hasn't laid a finger on me. (Well, technically, he has, if 'accidental' knee- and bum-brushing count. Which they totally do.) I try not to think about other younger women comedians who would have to put up with the same thing and how he would make them feel. Shouldn't I be doing something to protect them? Should I give him a piece of my mind? Not worth it. He wouldn't understand. Although I have nothing to lose – I don't want to play this place again anyway. How could I ever come back here now? Unless I perfect a hilarious orgasm routine, obviously.

I rush back inside, my cheeks burning with shame because I am too gutless to tell him that he's a bully and a creep. As I push through the doors, there's a whoosh of sound and it's the turn of one of the comics who nearly wet himself with amusement when I was doing badly up there. He is getting massive applause. Fair enough. He deserves it. I am just flooded with relief that I can now leave. I pick up my bag and my coat – which I don't even put on because I am in such a hurry to go – and run out of the door. 'You be okay getting home?' the promoter calls after me. Oh, yes, thanks. I'll be okay anywhere away from you. I have never walked away from anywhere faster. Maybe I should get harassed more often. I would get fit.

10: Gigs 48 and 49:

'Good evening, Atlanta!'

Day 47, cancelled gig: Atlanta

Flight to America. Never been happier to be leaving the country. Had the option of going to a gig straight from the airport but (a) I had been awake for about eighteen hours and (b) I would have arrived late and was worried that my comedy wouldn't have been good enough for a late-night crowd. Texted the promoter to say sorry my flight was late, I'm not going to make it and went to bed. Sensible decision. But agonising because I hate to cancel a gig myself.

Day 48, Gig 48: Atlanta

'GOOD EVENING, ATLANTA!' Day after an eight-hour flight. Spent the entire eight hours thinking about how I 'don't have an act' and how I should give up. Back on the horse. Gig at improv night at Relapse Theatre. Audience reasonably receptive. Not my best gig but not my worst and very happy to do improv with lovely Americans, especially because the audience just laughed at my accent so I only had to open my mouth to get love. No orgasm required.

Day 49, Gig 49: Atlanta

AMERICA. I LOVE YOU. YOU ARE MY PEOPLE. *weeping*

*

As luck would have it, the next day I was leaving the UK. This was beyond fortunate. I desperately needed a change of scene. I desperately needed an American audience. American audiences are legendarily easy. You don't even have to say anything funny. You don't have to pretend to have an orgasm on stage. You don't have to do anything. If you have an English accent, you just have to open your mouth.

Before I left I had a long chat with Simon about what to do. I was foaming at the mouth about what had happened. 'I just wish I could do something. I wish I could call the police. Maybe I should call the police.' This was a ridiculous idea. Simon: 'What would you report?' Me: 'That he is a total creep.' Simon: 'That is not a criminal offence. Unfortunately. Just write it all down and you will feel better. Write it all down exactly how it happened.' Me: 'I wish I had punched him.' Simon: 'It's good that you didn't punch him.' He points out that I've been lucky not to meet more people like this creep. And he's right. I do not know what I would do without Simon. We debate for some time what Jo Brand or Joan Rivers would have done. This guy was old-school and presumably they have both encountered loads of people like this over the years. 'I think they would have both got their revenge by taking the roof off,' I say, 'I was not able to do that due to my ineptitude.' Simon nods. 'Jo Brand would also have lamped him,' he adds.

I had to get over all this and move on, though, because only several hours after I came back from the Orgasm Man's gig I had to get a flight to Atlanta, USA. It was by accident that I was going to be ending up abroad in the middle of this whole experiment. In theory I could have warded off this work trip, but in my delusional, all-conquering state I had decided that I could do a gig anywhere, anytime and I would find a way to make it work.

At one point I had visions of doing a gig in the departures lounge or standing up on my seat on the plane. But sadly (or, probably, happily, as it would have been so painful for me and so tedious for the other passengers) it didn't come to that. Which was a shame in a way. I had imagined it like the years of busking that Eddie Izzard did all over Europe – virtually talking to yourself and shouting at people while they ignore you. That's how you get really good at comedy. By doing that fifty million times, I guess, which is what Izzard did.

Anyway, the reason I was going to be in the US around the Gig 45 mark was linked to my disastrous comedy in the first place, so it was almost appropriate. And a sort of a punishment. It was connected to my friend Sam and the night that she came to the Sewage Incident. That was the night I realised that one of the most painful things about doing amateur stand-up is that you have to practise something you are not very good at in front of other people.

People think stand-up comedy is nerve-wracking because you have to perform in front of people who might not laugh at your jokes. As I've said before, that's not what makes it difficult. (Although, admittedly, that is quite hard.) No, what's difficult is the bloody circumstances in which you have to practise. It's not like being a concert violinist, where you practise your instrument at home and with a teacher for twenty years and then when you're really, really good you unfurl your talent to the unsuspecting world at a glamorous gala evening at Carnegie Hall.

No. Comedy is like water-skiing: you have to learn to do it in public otherwise you won't learn to do it at all. Unlike water-skiing, however, comedy is dependent on an audience. There is no comedy without an audience. The audience decides the comedy, not you. Just finding them can be very difficult. And once you've found them they may not necessarily like your comedy. It's like doing a water-skiing lesson in front of people who are not impressed by water sports. 'It doesn't look like you're doing it right. And I don't like water-skiing anyway. Nul points.'

The night of the Sewage Gig was one of those nights when the audience decided that they did not want to watch bad water-skiing. As we left the pub after that interminably awful evening, I asked, 'What can I do to pay you back for this?' Sam looked at me as if she wanted to kill me and said, 'I am going to Atlanta in October for work. For the Oprah Winfrey conference. You better come with me.' It was not an offer or a suggestion. She's a good friend and I did not take much persuading.

Within four weeks I had secured a travel commission with a magazine to do a story on Oprah Winfrey's visit to the home of Coca-Cola, where thousands of her devotees were gathering to worship in her presence. I wouldn't have gone if Sam hadn't given me the idea but it wasn't exactly a hardship. I had always wanted to report on an Oprah event. Plus, this would also give me the excuse of trying to get stage time within the hundred nights outside the UK. 'Good evening, Atlanta!' It also meant that some good would come of the Sewage Incident and that pleased me.

So this is how I ended up doing Gigs 48 and 49 in Atlanta. When the time came for me to go, it turned out not to be the greatest idea because Simon was already annoyed about me being out so much, and having to go to America for four days was hardly going to help with that. The logistics of it were pretty tricky too. I knew what I was doing in terms of booking gigs in the UK, especially around London. I had no idea how it worked in the US.

A few weeks before Atlanta, I started to look for places I could perform while I was out there. I would seriously be messing my numbers up if I didn't gig for the entire four nights I was going to be away. Without Sam knowing that I was doing the hundred gigs (because I feared she would try to stop me, and rightly so), I mentioned to her that I wanted to do some comedy while we were in America. She said, 'I'm never coming to one of your gigs ever again.' After what she had paid £5 to go through at the Sewage Gig, this was fair enough.

I contacted dozens of comedy clubs in the Atlanta area, not knowing whether I would have any chance of getting an open (i.e. unpaid, amateur) spot with them. Most of them very sensibly didn't respond. A couple wrote back asking me to send a video of my comedy. I sent my video and never heard back from them. This made me paranoid about my video. Never mind. Finally I found a place called Relapse Theatre, which seemed to have a strong Facebook presence (always a good sign; it means they're proactive) and had several shows going on over the weekend I would be in Atlanta. I wrote to them explaining about the hundred gigs. I sent my video. They wrote back, 'We'd love to have you perform as much as you can.' Wow. As much as I can? How many gigs did that mean? I think they must have not watched the video.

And so this is how I found myself sitting opposite a sandwich shop on the outskirts of Atlanta in the middle of nowhere at about 6 p.m., wondering if I had the right place or if anyone had even remembered that I was coming. I had flown in late the night before. I was jet-lagged and confused and hungry and still annoyed about how far it is from the plane to the terminal building in Atlanta. You have to walk about fifty million miles, travel on various buses and trains, pick up your luggage, recheck your luggage for security reasons, then walk fifty million more miles and travel on more trains until you get to the end when you can finally collect your luggage – for the second time – and leave. This takes hours.

I was also worried that I had the wrong place because Relapse Theatre is truly in the middle of a highway. This is obviously not a problem in the US because everyone drives everywhere – I had taken a taxi from my hotel – but to me it seemed odd. Why would you have a theatre in the middle of a highway? Also, it didn't look like a theatre, it looked like a church. In fact it was a converted church next to an actual church. I sat outside on a broken chair and tried to read the David Guterson novel I was supposed to be reviewing for work. *Ed King* is quite a laboured and difficult novel about a man who is like Oedipus and you know from the beginning that he is going to end up having sex with his mother. I figured most people would read it just for the sex bit. (It was eventually on page 240.)

I sat on a broken chair outside the entrance and pretended to read my so far sex-free Oedipal book. I kept checking my phone to see if the Relapse people were trying to call me. I kept getting up and knocking on the windows and doors to see if anyone would let me in. It was like no one had ever been there in a hundred years. From time to time I would check the lock on the door to see if I was just being stupid and there were loads of really friendly comedians waiting inside to welcome me in with warm smiles and tales of showbiz camaraderie. This did not happen. There was no noise from inside the building.

Every few minutes a car drove past slowly and I immersed myself purposefully in my non-sex sex book. After a few minutes big, wet, hot tears started to fall onto the pages of the incredibly difficult book. What was I thinking of, coming here? Surely there were better things for me to do in Atlanta than sit outside a disused church trying not to look like a hooker in a very smelly sequinned cardigan and a tonne of jet-lag-disguising make-up?

I thought about what Simon would be doing with the children right now. They would probably be making popcorn and then watching *Pirates of the Caribbean: At World's End* for the fifty-seventh time while Simon fell asleep on the sofa. They would get to the bit where Calypso has to say 'Davy Jones' locker' in virtually every scene and makes it sound as if she is saying an entire paragraph rather than just three words. And they would say, 'Oh, this is the bit Mummy really likes.' They would all fall asleep before they got to the end of the film – apart from Will, who would watch to the end and then start the film again without anyone noticing. Am I really needed in that little family picture? Is it essential that I'm always there? No, it's not essential. Of course, it's not. But when there is doubt in your mind and the reason you've walked out of that picture suddenly seems pathetic and ill-founded ... you just feel terrible for not being in it any more.

It suddenly hit me. All the stuff I'd been holding back from feeling. All the things I didn't want to admit to myself. All the truth. Realistically, I didn't know how much longer Simon was going to put up with the Directionless Comedy Binge. If I carried on like this, it might finish us off completely. And, worst of all, I couldn't defend myself any more. I had been told by a promoter than I had no material and I had no chance of progression unless I start faking sex on stage. I did not feel ready to do this. I did not think I would ever be ready. Should I just give up?

Hot flushes of self-pity and guilt forced their way up my throat and I was half-choking and spluttering with tiredness and defeat. It was so much easier when I thought this was all a good idea and that I could manage it and it might turn into something. I used to think that fairly often in the beginning and it had kept me buoyed up. I'd have a good gig or meet someone interesting or learn something new and I'd feel good about it all. Now that is not happening so much. I've hit a wall. I'm not learning, I'm not developing. Maybe I'm even going backwards. I'm less convinced than ever that it would turn into something. And I don't even know what I would want it to turn into. I 'don't have an act', remember?

It wouldn't matter if I was replacing everything I'm smashing up with something good. But I'm not. I've got to some of the decent gigs and bombed at them. I feel like the only good performances I've had have been flukes. I have no idea whether any of my stuff is funny or not. In any case I'm way too old to be doing all of this. And I have too many responsibilities.

Most of the time it didn't prick my conscience about the children at all; Simon was looking after them and I knew they were fine. But I did feel awful about the effect on our relationship. I knew that we would not split up over this. But what I was doing was straining things to breaking point. Sitting on the side of the road 4,216 miles from home opposite a ramshackle sandwich shop, breathing in the dust from the vehicles of passing potential axe murderers, outside a non-existent comedy venue awaiting what must surely be a non-existent gig ... it all suddenly seemed pointless and insane.

All these feelings mixed up with the genuine fear I had at that point. What if I'm in the wrong place and I'm supposed to be somewhere else? What if I am in the right place but the gig doesn't start for hours? What if the gig is at a much higher standard than I can cope with? After about forty-five minutes, by which point I had decided that the theatre had closed and all the emails I had exchanged had been a hoax and I finally couldn't bear to pretend to read my book any longer, I pushed a door to the side, the only door I hadn't tried. It opened and I stumbled in.

It was like something out of *Alice in Wonderland*. What

looked like a disused church from the outside was a bustling theatre space with several stages, lots of rehearsal rooms, posters for improv shows everywhere and strategic pieces of furniture upholstered in red fabric. Two heavily made-up girls in their late teens bustled past me arm in arm like showgirls in the wings of a Broadway theatre. I had found the right place after all. In a split second, all the doubts and fears I had had while sitting outside crying into my book just vanished. Where had the showgirls been while I was crying into my Oedipal novel? Who knows, who cares. I had found them now. My inner Liza Minnelli burst into life, the shame and horror of the past two months forgotten.

'Excuse me,' I said to another girl dashing past, 'I'm looking for Shellie. I'm doing stand-up.' 'Oh, I'm Shellie,' she said, 'welcome.' I have never been so relieved in my life. 'You can definitely get five minutes on our show tonight.' 'Oh, that's great!' I beamed. She smiled back, 'But it doesn't start until 11.30 p.m.' 'Oh, right.' Crashing disappointment. It was not even 7 p.m. and I had already killed forty-five minutes; I didn't know if I could kill another four and a half hours. The cab fare back to my hotel was about fifteen dollars. The doubts hit me again. Four thousand miles. A five-hour wait. The burden of all the guilt and self-reproach and anxiety. For five minutes on stage?

At least, though, I was in the right place and they had a space for me on the bill. I went across the road to the sandwich shop – 'Subs So Fast You'll Freak' – where I ordered a ham and cheese roll from a boy who looked like a giant, skinny, pockmarked rat. I planned to eat the sandwich very, very slowly. I did not want the sandwich to be made so fast that I would freak. I wanted them to take their time and help me kill at least some portion of the next few hours. I had now been up for about eighteen hours. I was not sure what state I would be in by the time I had to go on stage.

I did not feel particularly inspired at this point; in fact I felt terrified, as it was very difficult for me to figure out what sort of place Relapse was and what sort of performance they would expect from me. There seemed to be a lot of burlesque dancers around. And a lot of improv. All the shows seemed to start past midnight. I just couldn't get my head around this. In London most people want everything to finish by 10.30 p.m. or 11 p.m. latest, so that they can have one more drink and then catch the train home.

I went back inside the church-theatre/non-theatre/burlesque space and headed downstairs to the bar, hoping to meet some other comedians or improvisers who would be able to reveal the key to success at this place. I found a group of young girls dressed for a 1980s theme party, drinking the bar's special: cake vodka. They were talking about the 1980s in the same way I might talk about the Roman Empire, as if it were some hilarious, remote, historical period. A couple of them were improvisers and were chatty. 'Oh, you're from England? Your voice is hilarious. Can you say "water"?' I said 'water' for them. I said 'tomato' for them. Ha ha ha. I got the impression that this might be quite a good gig if I could just speak slowly and keep a straight face.

The next few hours passed slowly but not horrifically. I must have got through about five Diet Cokes by the time I went on. I did an opening five to ten minutes, a bit of ad libbing, some of my feminist jokes. I was near dead with tiredness but the weird combination of the buzz of adrenaline and the hysteria of jet lag were keeping me going. They liked me well enough, but they weren't really there for stand-up, they were there for improv. They were more bemused than amused. I was filled with warmth, though. Despite being tired, confused and crotchety, I got a huge sense of joy from being there. With absolutely no idea of who I was or whether I was any good as a comedian, these people had trusted me and let me onto their stage and share their audience. There is something very special about that.

The group very kindly let me guest on their improv show, which was much better fun than doing the shoehorned stand-up set. Their director is a wonderful man with a fabulously lopsided face called Wes Kennemore. Like a lot of people on the improv scene, both in the UK and the US, he is a big kid: enthusiastic, kooky, endlessly positive. I ended up in a scene where we had to pretend, as a group, to be an alien who is explaining something. I got big laughs for my accent. I can't pretend it was for anything else.

The scene I loved the most was one Wes had invented himself as a game: it's where people play a scene and then the director shouts 'Go chicken!' and the players have to act on, pretending to be chickens, making 'bwark bwark' noises but genuinely playing the scene. It sounds awful and very much like a reason why improv should just be buried and never be performed ever again; but it's very pleasingly silly and after half a dozen Diet Cokes and six and a half hours of waiting and thinking about the many weeks of abject failure and what on earth I was doing here and how much it had cost me to get here, I found it very funny indeed. This is probably more a reflection on me and my state of mind than it is on the prospects for chicken impersonations as a high-class entertainment act.

Once it was all over I had the whole business of figuring out how I was going to get back to my hotel from the middle of nowhere at about 2 a.m. Plus, I had to be up at 6 a.m. to attend – and be in a fit state to report on – the Oprah Winfrey conference. How do I end up mixed up in these things? I managed to figure out how to call a taxi and, after about an hour, it arrived. I got back to the hotel and looked in the mirror: a zombie. But a happy zombie.

After three hours' sleep I was back out and on the red carpet waiting for Oprah. I waited another three hours but she did not come. It was like waiting to go on a comedy improv show but without a rat-faced man serving me a ham and cheese sandwich. The reason I had got up so early and had so little sleep was because I had a message from Oprah's people saying that if we arrived early enough then there might be a chance of getting an interview with her. No matter how little sleep you have had or how demented you are because you are trying to do a hundred gigs in a hundred nights, that is not an opportunity you turn down.

Except, of course, there never actually was a chance that Oprah would be there that morning. I got within a metre of her personal physician (oh yes) Dr Oz and her best friend Gayle. I tried to touch Gayle but couldn't quite reach. Oprah didn't turn up until much later that day and she didn't give anyone any interviews. When Oprah did show up, I was standing about five metres away from her and there was no chance of getting any closer. I cried because she was inspiring and fascinating and weird (she took her shoes off at one point and during the finale of her speech she walked off stage in her stockinged feet). But mostly I cried because I had got up at 5.30 a.m. to meet a person who was never going to turn up anyway. I was doing a lot of crying on this trip.

It was the strangest day during a period when I had known nothing but strange days and strange nights for too long a time. Workshops with Oprah's gurus. A strange, sponsored lunch where your choices were weirdly restricted and you were allowed strictly one packet of crisps and one kind of vegetarian sandwich. And a brownie. At least I had Sam for company, constantly murmuring about how American the whole affair was. Sam was attempting – and failing – to prevent me from getting very caught up in the whole thing.

When Oprah came on stage to address everyone in the afternoon, people virtually started fainting. She gave the most extraordinary, almost trance-like speech, like an old-fashioned preacher: 'I come from The Source. And I will return to The Source.' She spoke for an hour about women achieving power and doing what they want to do with their lives. I was completely transfixed but, if anything, there was a part of me thinking, 'None of this applies to me. It is only for mad Americans.'

But maybe on some very profound level I knew it was seeping into me. I felt as if no one in that room was living what she was talking about in a more intense way than I was. Do what you were meant to do, says Oprah. Find the thing you were put on earth for and do it. Isn't that what I'm doing? 'Fulfilling my unique true purpose?' Or was I really put here on earth to make life easier for Simon and the children and not drive them mad by going off and doing random five-minute gigs opposite sandwich shops manned by rat-faced men?

At least I had a better way to kill the evening this time round. Being in Atlanta with Sam had made me realise how lonely I had got and how much I missed my friends. Stand-up is a solitary business. There are always people around but you spend a lot of time on your own. After the conference Sam and I went out for dinner to Pittypat's Porch, a *Gone with the Wind* theme restaurant. It was my idea of heaven. Sam took quite a lot of persuading to go there. They served us catfish, fried green tomatoes and gigantic pieces of bread. We ate a lot and laughed a lot. I was beginning to feel happier again and realising that whatever happened – whether I continued with gigging or not – all would be well with the world. It was also one of those nights when you think, 'If I can just laugh like this with a friend, why do I need to do stand-up? Why does anyone do stand-up?'

I was due to head back to Relapse for another late-night gig, this time the 1 a.m. Secret Show, which is a proper stand-up show. Understandably, Sam refused to come with me; she was tired and jet-lagged and she'd seen my act before. By this point I was thinking, 'Just let me get this over and get it out of the way and get on with the rest of this.' But another part of me was thinking, 'I just need to get this gig out of the way then I will be close to fifty and maybe I can give up at fifty.' I had it in the back of my mind that I was heading towards my last gig. Or I could be if I wanted to.

Even though I had not had much of a night's rest, I had at least slept on the idea that things were becoming unmanageable. The children were getting restless. Simon was struggling to cope. The promoter had told me that I didn't have an act. I was realising that maybe I'm not cut out to do this. It was starting to feel very all or nothing to me. I couldn't stand the thought of going back to two or three gigs a week. I just didn't know how I'd keep the momentum going. I knew that I either needed to get to the end of the hundred gigs in a hundred nights or give up now and just not bother any more. Certainly no one else would notice apart from me. It would be no loss to the world. I just wanted to get through this one more gig and then I could have a night off as I flew home and worked out what to do.

The second night at Relapse I felt more at home but also somehow less welcome. Shellie, my main contact, was not involved with this show and she couldn't stay to watch. I kept worrying that they wouldn't let me on, all the effort would be for nothing and I would be another gig behind in my numbers. As it was, I was falling two gigs behind with Atlanta anyway because I was travelling overnight for two nights just to get there and back. Plus, it's always nerve-wracking turning up to perform in places where you feel you could be edged off the bill by another amateur comic who knows the MC better. I wasn't convinced that someone wouldn't get a real kick out of chucking me off the bill just because I had come all the way from England.

The more I thought about it, the more I realised that there would be nothing wrong with just doing fifty gigs. God knows, Simon would approve of this idea. Part of me would not entertain it. 'You quitter. You said you would do a hundred. What does it prove if you only do fifty? What example are you setting to the children if you plan to do a hundred and then give up when you get to fifty because some idiot guy has irritated you?' But another part of me was already taking over. 'This is too much. I can't do it. It's taken over my life too much already. The idiot guy is right: I don't have the material. I'm not cut out for this. This isn't for me. Shall I quit tonight?' I wanted the decision to be out of my control. I wanted not to be the one in charge of making things happen any more. I wanted, for once, the audience to decide for me.

The outcome was not what I was expecting. For good or bad, they decided I had no choice but to continue. I got a massive laugh after about three seconds of being up there. It was a cheap shot – the cheapest shot there is – but, hey, you get your breaks where you can. The MC looked like a paedophile and I simply said this. It was true so it got laughs. It's hack, unoriginal and I'm not proud of it. But I don't care. It worked.

As I went into my routine, I could feel one or two small patches of the room who were not 'getting' it but all around there were people who did really like it and who were laughing so hard I was worried for them. It struck me that it's more culturally acceptable in the US to laugh uncontrollably and very, very loudly. It was obvious from the beginning that this was going to be one of the best responses I had ever got from any audience.

In particular there were a couple of comics near the back with stupidly loud laughs who made so much noise that I thought they would make themselves physically unwell. They seemed to like the way I spoke, the rhythm of the jokes and the structure of the jokes because they were really hanging on every set-up and punchline. I had rewritten a couple of my jokes to make them American (putting David Blaine in a joke instead of Derren Brown, replacing a mention of Accessorize with the US budget shop Target) and they really went for those jokes in a big way. The feminist jokes were, weirdly, the biggest crowd-pleaser. ('There was an Englishman, an Irishman and a Sco— WHERE ARE THE WOMEN?') I think they thought it was weird and therefore bold and for once they went for it. It was a miracle.

It came very close to being one of those gigs where you feel you're floating just slightly above the stage because people 'get' you and it means you can reach out to them. I could feel a slight arrogance, almost disbelief, rising in me: 'Oh for God's sake, you'll just laugh at anything now.' I was also thinking, 'It's late. They're very drunk. Don't let it go to your head.' But later, when I came off stage, I watched other comics die. So they had liked me, they didn't just laugh at anything. I had done something right. Best of all, I felt like they had laughed at me but they had also – surely? – laughed at the material. So maybe I did have some material after all. Shove that up yourself, idiot Orgasm Man! (Or maybe not because you would probably like that.)

I felt like bottling their laughs and playing them back to him. 'See, there are people who find me funny. I am not totally unfunny.' I have to admit that they probably would have enjoyed an orgasm impression. Because, of course, the buttoned-up Britishness was 99.9 per cent of the reason why they were laughing at me. Maybe even 100 per cent. As I came off the compère said to the audience, 'Oh. My. God. It's like Hyacinth Bucket was in the room.' A reference which very few people got. 'Do none of you watch *Keeping Up Appearances*? You should.' He chuckled to himself. 'I love the way she says "Pee-do-phile". It's so proper!' Sometimes you don't know why people are laughing at you and you don't care. Just let them laugh.

Things moved on and I was forgotten. But I was still in the moment. I hung around the back of the room for the rest of the gig, a little voice in my head saying, 'You can do this. You can do this.' A couple of the other comics came to find me and they had the look in their eyes that says, 'We liked you. You're funny.' That look cannot be faked. It doesn't come often. I don't want to believe it because I'm scared to believe that I can do it. I'm dreading what I'll have to accept if I acknowledge that I can do this. It means I have to go on.

There's a nagging whinge in my head saying, 'They're Americans. They will laugh at anything. They are just laughing at your accent. You're still not funny. You don't have material. You can't just perform in America and live off your accent. You are going home tomorrow.' And I know all this is true. But I also know that I had a good gig. 'You're funny,' one of the local comics high-fives me. A woman from the audience comes to shake my hand, 'Like your feminist stuff, sister.' Another comic, suspiciously, 'How long you been goin'?' Stop it. Asked the right way, that's the most flattering question.

Here's the question, now, though: do I go out on a high and give up now with a positive gig to remember as my last? Or do I use it as fuel to push me on, knowing that I will have loads of other bad gigs ahead of me? I'm going to have to decide in the next twenty-four hours because if I go past fifty-one gigs I won't be able to bear it if I can't get to a hundred. One of the girls offers me a lift back to the hotel. Before we leave Hyacinth Bucket just needs to do something at the bar. 'Can I get a very small taste of cake vodka, please?' It smelled sweet, sugary, like something baking in the oven … like cake. But it also kind of smelled like a breakthrough. I took a deep sniff. Didn't drink any of it. I didn't know what I was celebrating – the end or the beginning? Or really whether I was celebrating at all. Either way, it smelled good.

11: Gigs 50 to 52:

'You want to talk about "the shit"?'

Day 50, no gig, flying

There was no way I could have got a gig today as the way the flight times worked out I was getting back into London in the middle of the night. Annoying.

Day 51, cancelled gig: Soho

Oh great. The high of Atlanta totally ruined. How the hell am I going to get another gig tonight?

Day 51, Gig 50: Islington

Replacement gig. Perfectly acceptable performance despite being tired. Highlights: first, Tom Webb (one of my favourite MCs/ comics). Lovely man, very funny, always lights up the room. Inspiring. Second, meeting the new clown comic Dr Brown, of whom I have heard so much. He watched me do my stuff and declared: 'There are some elements of clown in what you do.' He is riotously, joyously, uproariously hilarious and amazing. He is everything all of us want to be. Atlanta high recaptured. Renewed optimism that on Gig 50 – the halfway point – there is a sign of hope.

Day 52, Gig 51: Highbury

Hysterical. As in funny hysterical. Waste of an evening performance-wise. Entertaining evening humanity-wise. Unintentionally laughable MC from hell. Lots of comics gathered in a huddle on a collapsed couch at the back of the room, pissing themselves laughing at him. Cruel, hypocritical and so satisfying.

Day 53, Gig 52: Hampton

Sceptical football club crowd. Jack sick down my front as I was leaving the house, already late. Large, tattooed bald man in front row: 'You smell of baby sick.' I hugged him as punishment. Fun. Close to home, glad of an early night.

*

To keep the momentum going, I have decided to sign up for three days at clown school. Having met Dr Brown at Gig 50 and marvelled at his act, he has sweet-talked me into coming to his performance boot camp. I love everything about his performance and really want a piece of what he's got. It was not a tough sell for him. After Atlanta I had the buzz I needed to keep going. I wanted to sustain the high. And I needed to do something, anything, to boost my performing: if there are some 'elements of clown' in what I do, then I want more.

I am clinging on desperately to the feeling of hope. Work is piling up, the children are grouchy, Simon is (understandably) feeling overlooked and I am exhausted from the breakthroughs and the setbacks and the self-loathing and the adrenaline and the wonder and the joy and the not-knowing-whether-I-really-can-do-it-or-whether-I'm-delusional. Clown school – Clowning with Dr Brown-ing at the Soho Theatre – is, I hope, the answer to feeling permanently good. Since getting back from the US, I have been clinging on frantically to the signs of funniness that emerged among the drinkers of cake vodka. But the last few gigs have been too hit-and-miss for comfort. Just when I think I'm getting to the stage where I'm reliably good, I have an off night. I'm not in control of what I'm doing. I can't predict whether I'm going to do well or bomb. I'm still at risk of losing my nerve.

The children are stupidly excited about the clowning and wish they could come with me. I wish they could too. I am missing them so much now. It has got to the point where I have considered developing an act where I use Jack as a live ventriloquist's doll just so that I can take him to gigs. I have even looked up suit-and-bow-tie outfits for one-year-olds on eBay to see if I could dress him up. It's too cruel, I decide. More crucially, I can't do ventriloquism and he can actually say garbled things himself so I don't think I'd be able to control him and the act would not make any sense. This, not infant neglect, is my main reason for abandoning the idea. Shame.

It's not always easy for the children to understand what I'm doing on stage night after night. When they think of comedy they think of Christmas cracker jokes or kids' TV programmes. They can't quite picture what it must be like inside the places where I perform, even though they have watched some of the video footage. Clown school, though? That's easy to understand. Will: 'Can you bring the clown home? Can we come and see the clown? Will he give you a red nose?' From what little I do know about Dr Brown, it is not about dressing up in big floppy shoes and having a flower that squirts water and driving a tiny car that goes 'Honk, honk'. Comics who call themselves 'clowns' do not want to work in the circus. They just want to perfect physical comedy. I try to explain this. Will looks disappointed and confused, 'Oh, okay.' He had got out his Comic Relief red nose for me to use and is now disappointed when I explain that I will probably not be allowed to use it as a prop. I take it anyway so as not to offend him and promise to take him to the clown's show at some point.

Red nose or not, my main fear of the clowning, which is coming up in a few days' time, is that I might be required to take all my clothes off. Dr Brown is renowned for getting nude in his shows, although he doesn't do this at his children's shows (obviously) and he didn't do this, thankfully, when I saw him in Islington. So he does do some clothed comedy. I am nonetheless concerned that he will reveal that the secret to great comedy is nudity. The worst thing is that I am so desperate to hang on to how I felt in Atlanta that I will investigate pretty much any comedic theory in an attempt to keep improving.

If I'm honest, when I think about it I am surprisingly up for taking my clothes off – because I don't want Dr Brown to think I'm a wimp, and I want to do the course properly. This is how English I am. I have no actual desire to get nude and will be completely horrified if I have to; but this is outweighed by my sense of propriety about following the course in the necessary manner. If nudity is required, I will comply. I realise this seems a bit hypocritical. I get offended by someone suggesting I should show people what I'm like when I'm having an orgasm. But the second a cute Californian hippy dude gets all naturist and I'm supposidly ready to strip off, it will certainly be an education for any young people present. And for anyone who has not seen a woman's body after she has had three children.

By this point I suspect that what I have been missing is a guru or someone to look up to. Over the course of the past fifty gigs, I've met dozens of comedians. Many of them were inspirational.

Lots had jokes I would willingly steal. (Joke stealing is not allowed and if you have a joke that is even remotely similar to something someone else is doing, then the best thing to do is to ditch it as soon as possible.) But at these peculiar amateur gigs we do, we're all in our own little world and it's hard to get to know anyone well enough to ask them to help you.

From the moment I meet him, though, I have a strange trust in Dr Brown. I do not really know anything about him apart from one meeting. There is a tiny voice in the back of my mind telling me that he is a total loon and that this course may be absolutely wrong for me. But there is a much larger voice telling me that this is what I have been waiting for. There is just something about him. Maybe it's his mystical beard or his look-at-me-deep-in-the-eyes gaze. He certainly ticks the guru box.

I had heard about him long before I met him. Several comics whose opinion I trust had mentioned him. 'Have you seen Dr Brown? The Californian dude who gets naked?' 'No, I have not. I think if I had I would remember that.' 'You've got to see him. He's amazing.' Everyone who has seen him perform falls under his spell. The people who had mentioned him to me in the weeks running up to my meeting him were all people I liked the most on the circuit. They were all people who laughed at the same moments in gigs as I did, who were prone to laughing at the circumstances of the gig as much as at the comedy and who did not take life – or stand-up comedy – too seriously. Most of all, they were people who were naturally funny.

It's funny – or not, really – how many comics are not that funny naturally. Or whatever quality they have naturally is very different to the sort they use on stage. It's worrying how many people get into stand-up comedy because they think that doing it will make them witty and charismatic. In some very rare cases, this actually happens: someone who is not at all watchable off stage manages to harness something or find a way of speaking that is really funny on stage.

But mostly this does not happen. People who are painfully unfunny in real life can come across as weird and arrogant when they do stand-up. It doesn't stop a lot of them doing it for a very long time, though, and it is exceedingly painful to watch. I have observed them with great attention because I feared for a very long time that I was one of them (i.e. an unfunny person who should not be doing stand-up). I still worry about it. The clown needs to cure me of this.

What he promises sounds very right and very scary at the same time. From the course website: 'As actors and human beings we are always trying to be good. Trying to do and get things right. And when we feel bad for either being bad or doing bad, we want to escape that bad feeling. The clown is different from most of us, in that he/she is happy to be bad. He/she is happy not to get things right.' Am I the clown? Can I be the clown? Am I capable of being different from most of us and happy not to get things right? It gets better/worse depending on your viewpoint. 'This workshop will push us into this place of "badness" (a place we will nominate "the shit") and encourage us to stay in it and not escape it – as our natural tendency will try and make us do. Instead, we will search for a pleasure and a joy in "the shit". Because in "the shit" is where we find a real vulnerability, humility and humour – our clown.'

'The shit' makes me laugh out loud. I need to experience 'the shit'? As if I haven't already been experiencing 'the shit' for the past forty-something nights? You want to talk about 'the shit'? I will show you what 'the shit' looks like. 'The shit' is written all over my husband's face and tattooed on my forehead. My poor children are living and breathing 'the shit'. I need to be

145

encouraged to stay in 'the shit' and not try to escape? I laugh for about five minutes.

There is a danger this course might not be good for me. I am already becoming suspiciously overenamoured of Dr Brown. Despite the recent highs, I realise that I'm not quite myself and am possibly not making great judgements at the moment. I am so tired and confused lately that I have got into a really bad habit of not getting up until the very last moment when the children and Simon are already having their breakfast and I'm like some kind of weird overgrown teenager who is sleeping off a hangover upstairs. (I never have a hangover, though. Unless you could get a hangover from drinking too much Diet Coke.)

Things are not improving at home. On a typical morning Simon is up before me and bashing the children's breakfast bowls down hard in the manner of a person who is trying to signal 'I have to do EVERYTHING'. The last few days I have pretty much given up explaining to him what I am doing most of the time because I feel like he's just bored with it and all he wants to know is when it's going to end. Perhaps six months ago Simon might have been surprised that I have signed up for a clown course. Now he just looks at me with a jaded expression on his face. 'You'll probably really enjoy it,' he says, sighing, 'or at least I hope you get what you want out of it.' Oh dear. That's a metaphor for this whole process. It's all about me getting what I want out of it. The relentless Directionless Comedy Binge. 'I'll try and get a night off this week ... ' I say weakly, knowing that this is not true. 'Yeah, right. Whatever,' he says, hustling the children out of the door to school.

I suddenly remember something else Dr Brown said to me when we met: 'I might break you down a bit. But it will be for your own good.' What does this mean? Is it going to be like some kind of strange torture? Is it going to be cruel and humiliating?

Is it going to make me stay in 'the shit' in a really nasty way? I don't know if I can cope with this. I watch Jack eating his breakfast in his high chair, using two spoons, dribbling half of it out of the side of his mouth and the other half down the side of the chair. That's a real clown. That's someone who's happy in 'the shit'. Why am I walking away from him to spend three days with a load of strangers who want to be pushed into a place of 'badness'?

12: Gigs 53 to 57:

The tears of an Actual Clown

Day 54, Gig 53: Kentish Town

Soul-destroying death in the Red Room of Pain. Mostly comics, disillusioned audience members, stench of failure. Ashamed. Like Atlanta never happened.

Day 55, Gig 54: Richmond

Competition. Lots of friends came to support. Okay gig. Became preoccupied by weird, unfunny magic act. Went through to next round. But so did weird unfunny magic act. So I am not reading anything into it. Friends complained bitterly about plethora of masturbation jokes (not in my set, obviously) but laughed heartily at them at the time. Me: 'If you don't think they're funny then why did you laugh so much?' Frustrating. Drank large glass of rosé wine and felt dizzy.

Day 56, cancelled gig: Surrey

Another rare Saturday night gig cancelled. And I had two booked in with them the following month. So that's three bookings down. Gutted. No more comedy nights at this venue because 'it's a very rough crowd and last weekend a fight broke out'. Lucky escape?

Day 57, cancelled gig: Whitechapel

I reluctantly forced myself to cancel because I had food poisoning. Couldn't even enjoy having a night off. Too sick. What if this goes on? I can't afford to be ill for more than twenty-four hours. Panic. Now I'm three gigs behind.

Day 58, Gig 55: Lincoln

First proper paid MC gig in student union. Cheered by poster of the Chuckle Brothers in dressing room. Unpredictable, walk-in walk-out crowd. Weird venue – basically, the corner of a canteen. Stayed in Holiday Inn. Only moderately appalling.

Day 59, cancelled gig: Soho

That's okay. I don't mind a gig being cancelled – I WILL JUST PANIC THAT I AM NEVER GOING TO MAKE IT TO 100 GIGS AND THIS WHOLE THING HAS BEEN A COMPLETE WASTE OF TIME. THAT'S ALL. DON'T MIND ME.

Day 60, Gig 56: Bethnal Green

Swanky literary-type event. Not my crowd, not my night. Poor connection, wrong material, semi-disastrous. Audience member afterwards, sceptically: 'So you say you're a comedian … ?' Too depressed even to eat free organic goat's cheese artisan pizza which, with the exception of a handful of free drinks and £10 for MC-ing in Lincoln, constitutes the only 'payment' I have been offered in weeks.

Day 61, Gig 57: Tonbridge

The One Where I Loved Everyone.

*

The day of the clown course dawns. On the way into the Soho Theatre, which is where the course is being held, I keep thinking about 'the shit' and trying to understand what Dr Brown is trying to say. I am happy that I am not late. Although I'm sure that if you were late for clown class you would not get into that much trouble. I worry what everyone else on the course is like and what they will think of me. But, of course, when I get there I realise that they all look too stressed about their own position in the world. If you could read everybody's mind it would say this: 'I don't really know what "the shit" is. But please don't put me in it.'

Throughout this whole experiment I have not figured out what to wear on stage that makes me feel comfortable and like I'm being myself. Clown boot camp has to be the biggest wardrobe challenge yet. What do you wear for getting lost in 'the shit' if you are not allowed to wear floppy shoes and a multi-coloured Afro wig? I have decided on something quite clownish: a black top with a drawstring under the bust that gives me a weird 'wench' quality, a baggy black short jersey skirt that allows me to move and purple tights. I have an idea I will be going around in my stockinged feet most of the time and I know I will feel comfortable like that. Or at least as comfortable as can be expected.

There's an atmosphere of the first day at school. Everyone seems younger than me, a lot of them look fresh out of drama school. There are about fifteen of us. There's a burlesque dancer, a street performer, an artist. There's a couple of comics I've heard of – we have mutual friends. But there's no one I know. I am sorry in a way because I could have done with some moral support. But in another way I am pleased, because I am bearing the nakedness in mind. And the bit about 'breaking you down'. I am not entirely sure that I will be prepared to get naked in front of anyone, but I am more prepared to get naked in front of people I don't know.

Dr Brown gets straight down into it. This is not going to be like other classes. Some of it is going to be weird. He is not like a teacher. He describes himself as a 'performer/clown/idiot'. He kind of looks like a happy idiot savant. He is tall, lanky, with a bushy, wiry beard and a matching fuzzy shock of hair, almost like a cartoon athletic bear man. He has a sleepy smile and the eyes of a child. I sound like Kate Bush now, which is appropriate as Dr Brown is very much a Kate Bush sort of person. He is like Kate Bush's grown-up son. Or someone who has walked out of a Kate Bush song. After living in the forest for many years.

He is totally serious about the idiot bit. It is the most important thing to him. If you can't be an idiot for people, you can't be a clown and you can't make them laugh. His technique is all about finding that place of idiocy within yourself and encouraging it in others to help them perform. When he sees it in you, he punches you on the shoulder and shouts, 'That's it, man. That's it right there. Right there you're beautiful.' And he gazes at you with his crazy Californian hippy eyes. He is intense and genuine and the effect is powerful. When he looks at you, it feels as if the world stops.

This happens to me before it happens to anyone else and it happens in the first five minutes. We play a game in a circle which is a bit like wink murder and I keep messing up. I keep looking at everyone and thinking how young and sweet they are and how I am much older than they and should be more sensible and more intelligent and more able to understand the rules of the game and play it correctly, and the more I think that, the more I mess up. I'm out three times in a row on the first go. I have to sit on the floor like a dunce.

The third time I mess up Dr Brown looks at me, disbelieving, checking my eyes to see if I'm faking it and messing up on purpose. I'm not. I'm properly embarrassed, mortified. I can't even get this stupid game right. But Dr Brown is happy. 'That's it right there, man,' he says, pointing to me, as I look up at him, shamefaced, 'that's it right there.'

I try to feel what he means. It's the moment you have sometimes when you're a kid and you mess up, but you know it doesn't matter that you've messed up and in fact perhaps it's even okay that you messed up because it helped other people to feel good because at least they're not you. It's that moment of relief and amusement when, having fallen over, you realise that the only thing that has been injured is your pride. He is trying to get us to feel that banana skin thing and be okay with it. That is all he means by 'the shit'.

It's the fear of falling over flat on your face that keeps most people away from stand-up and performance more than anything else. That's why people hate doing presentations at work. It's not so much that they're scared of speaking; the speaking is okay. It's that they're scared of being humiliated, of making a fool of themselves. I sometimes think people are more worried about people laughing at them – for something they can't control, like tripping up, or having their dress tucked into their pants – than they are at the prospect of people not laughing at them, which is, of course, the worst nightmare in comedy. What people really want is to control others and control their laughter. And on stage you have to give that up and stop controlling everyone and let them enjoy whatever they want to enjoy.

According to this theory, once you enter into the world of

the clown you have to allow yourself to be humiliated and allow people to laugh at you. This is much easier for some people than others. Even seasoned comics, actors and performers who are in the clown world find it really difficult. Some of us want to control the humiliation. And that is not going to be any fun for the audience. The audience does not want you to be in control; they are in control of you. This is the hugely difficult thing for you as a performer: you can't force yourself to trip over and keep it real. You can't make a banana skin appear out of nowhere. But you have somehow to carry the spirit of that in everything you do, so that the audience gets its kick from your defencelessness, from you being in 'the shit'.

What happens over the next three days is hard to describe. Part of the reason it all works so well, disarms you as a performer and forces you out of your comfort zone, is that it's a surprise to you when you experience it. If you knew about it all in advance, it wouldn't work as well. Dr Brown uses performance exercises and techniques designed to bring you closer to the audience. He trained at the École Philippe Gaulier in Paris for two years. Everyone who is serious about physical comedy goes there. Sacha Baron Cohen (Borat) is one of his ex-students: 'Philippe Gaulier is the greatest living teacher of clown and modern theatre. He is also the funniest man I have ever met.'

Gaulier's techniques are brutal and exposing. You have to get up on stage and pretend to be an animal and make the appropriate noises. You have to make interesting shapes with a chair. You have to join with a group of people to make a 'group alien', where you all move in unison in the manner of the alien. Most people would not want to do this in a million years but this is normal, run-of-the-mill stuff to most actors and performers. For stand-ups, it's less so. Lots of stand-ups hate improv. They want to be in control. I am the opposite: I want to learn more about letting go. I have got used to doing this sort of thing through doing lots of improv over the last couple of years and I am not remotely bothered by any of these things. I am relatively happy in 'the shit'. I am much happier in it than out of it, to be honest.

People respond surprisingly to being dumped in 'the shit'. The burlesque dancer fears nothing, happily pretending to be a snake in the spotlight or just standing up on stage staring at us for minutes on end. She is a gorgeous, wild-haired Italian girl in her late teens. The comic who has worked the most with Dr Brown, a shy, sweet Australian, will do anything on stage to appear ridiculous. And it's effortless. At one point he imitates a sheep perfectly, emitting the most tragic, heartbreaking bleat while keeping a look on his face that says, 'I can't believe I'm doing this. I'm so sorry.' It's very funny.

The one thing that really scares me is a physical exercise where you have to stand in a circle and four people surround you. You then close your eyes and allow your whole body weight to fall stone dead to the floor. The idea is that the people surrounding you will catch you long before you hit the deck. I struggle to trust my group, which is not necessarily wrong of me as they do nearly drop me at one point. (Although I guess Dr Brown would argue that they nearly dropped me because they sensed my lack of trust. Or something.)

With the best will in the world, even if they are there to catch me, it's going to be a challenge. I feel extremely overweight, which is definitely stopping me from trusting everyone around me. Would you want to be one of the ones on the outside trying to catch Bella Emberg? This is the position I have put people in. I feel sorry for them and worried for myself that they are going to break me. Or themselves.

There is another odd thing we have to do – massage each other. 'To get the city out of our system. The city is a cruel place,' says

Dr Brown solemnly, in his hippy voice. Again, this doesn't really bother me. But whenever I mention it to anyone else afterwards, this is the aspect of the workshop that horrifies them the most. It's just a way of breaking down people's boundaries and making everyone feel like part of the group. 'Shrug off the city, man!' The massage also makes it sound like it is some kind of secret sex society – which, I promise, it isn't. (Although some of the group were quite attractive, I must admit.)

The Gaulier clown techniques are brutal: they put you up on the stage on your own with no props, no lines, no exercise, nothing. And, without any preparation or ideas in advance, you must do something – but ideally not speak. Once you've been massaged and thrown like a dead weight between four people, you are not that scared because you know that everyone else in the group will go through the same thing. I immediately have to fight the urge to perform my set or 'do' something that I've done on stage before. But that is not the idea. You are not supposed to perform. You are just supposed to 'be'. And see what happens.

As everyone takes their turn up in the spotlight (and it's a big stage and pretty lonely), I find that I love being in the audience as much as I love performing: I like supporting the other people. When people are up there with nothing apart from themselves, they need everything the audience can give them. This is what Dr Brown means about being in 'the shit'. It really is a kind of nakedness. It's not literal – happily, or rather, sadly, I never do get to take my clothes off and educate people about the state of the real-life post-baby body. Instead, the stripping-off we have to face is much, much worse. This is emotional nakedness. It's the most exposing thing you can do with your clothes on. One man goes up and cries for about ten minutes. He is rewarded with the highest praise from Dr Brown: 'You're beautiful, man. That was generous.'

When it's my time I have to fight very hard not to think of something to do in advance. If you do, it shows immediately and everyone can tell you've cheated. I also have to try very hard not to speak – not just because I am used to doing stand-up and speaking as much as possible and as quickly as possible, but also because, I realise, when I'm performing I hide behind words as much as I can. It's not as bad being up there with nothing as I thought. In fact I quite like it.

'Look, she loves us,' says Dr Brown in his hippy voice. 'It's nice that she loves us. We love her too.' He shouts: 'She's funny, man. We like her.' Part of what he teaches is about being comfortable on stage and loving the audience (no matter how horrible or indifferent they are) and being comfortable with them loving you back. I am not doing anything funny but that in itself is funny for some reason. I think my face just looks stupid and that is entertaining to people.

Unfortunately I can't progress beyond this point. They get bored of laughing at my stupid face. 'It's good. We like her. She's funny, right? But now you need to do something,' Dr Brown says to me, not hiding his exasperation. 'Do something. Anything. Do something with your boobs. Whatever, man.' Oh. Is this turning weird? Is this the naked bit? I squeeze my boobs. But this is not funny, it's desperate. 'Ay, yay, yay,' Dr Brown whines disapprovingly, his plastic golf club of judgement hovering over the dustbin lid he wields when anyone is on stage. Three strikes and you're out. If he says, 'Ay, yay, yay,' two more times then my turn is over. I gulp. It's like the man said: I don't have any material. I was okay up there. But, basically, I didn't have anything to give.

This goes on for three days. There's not much chance to get to know the other people from the course because we spend so much time in class, there's very little time even to eat. So it feels strange. I'm doing all these intimate things with these people and I feel very close to them. But in fact I don't know them at all. If you put this many people in a group together doing these things for long enough in a confined space, they would all end up having sex with each other.

That is not a random thought. Dr Brown has theories about sex and performance. Dr Brown's theory is that it's important to give away something of yourself at a comedy show – and if it's at night and it's an adult show, on some level the audience will expect something sexual. Without it necessarily being sexual. It's complicated. I am beginning to realise that unfortunately Orgasm Man was not such an idiot after all. All he meant was that people want to see you at your most intimate and unguarded, which is the same thing as Dr Brown is saying. For most people that's a sexual moment. Dr Brown says you have to be on stage the way you are 'when you are post-coital'. (Asleep? Why would anyone want to watch me sleep?) But I get what he means. It's about having all your defences down.

The trouble with having your defences down is that you can get yourself into trouble. On the third day my massage partner ends up being a guy in the class who is, I think, a real clown. As in, someone who makes a living from being an Actual Clown. Or at least some kind of clown-like performer. (I am sure there are very strict distinctions about these things in the clown world but I have not figured out what they are yet.) I'm happy to be his massage partner because he seems sweet and I sense that he doesn't trust everyone in the class, but I think that he trusts me.

Halfway through the massage (the massage is fully clothed, by the way, I should have said that before), he starts crying. I don't know what to do. It is not small, discreet crying. It is full-on shoulder-heaving blubbing with snot and big, wet tears plopping down his cheeks and onto his clothes.

I feel cruel just leaving him to cry but I hesitate to stop the massage and I don't want to ask Dr Brown what to do because that will just draw attention to my partner, which might embarrass him. I decide to hold my hands out to the Actual Clown and see what he does. If he ignores me, I will just continue with the massage and pretend that I have not noticed that he is weeping hysterically. He reaches back to me and I hug him and he keeps on crying. I am still not sure I have done the right thing but it seems to have calmed him down and now the class is about to start.

When I get home at the end of the day, I have forgotten that all this happened. But there is a message waiting for me on Facebook. It is from the Actual Clown. He is upset because during the massage I did not allow him to go deeper into his pain. Instead I tried to 'mother' him and it prevented him from accessing his inner feelings. He wants to tell me this for future reference, in case I am ever in a situation like this again. He writes: 'I wish you had not overwhelmed me with hugging.'

I feel guilty and shocked – and bemused. I have offended an Actual Clown. This has to be bad karma. What will happen to me now? I have visions of tripping over my feet as I walk down the street. Or being squirted in the eye next time I smell a flower. Or waking up with an actual red nose that will never go away. I was just trying to do what I thought was right; but I have to admit that it was probably my instinct to mother him. When someone is in pieces in front of you, what else can you do? I'm not sure I will be able to learn the lesson for the future reference he is referring to. I am also struggling to see that this situation will be replicated again ever in my life.

I reply that I'm very sorry and that if I had known that was how he felt, I would not have acted as I did. Does this mean I am a bad clown? I'm also wondering whether something of my own life came into that moment. I'm not much of a mother at home right now so maybe I was trying to mother everyone else. I'm not being a good mother to the people who really need me to be their mother. I'm being an annoying mother to Actual Clowns who wish I would go away so that they can access their pain. In any case, now I really am in 'the shit'. So for that I must be thankful. But his complaint is a little dispiriting.

It would seriously bother me if I were going through all this and it did not improve my performance. The only real test of Clowning with Dr Brown-ing is whether it makes me funnier. I don't get to test that after the first day with him because a gig is cancelled on me. I had been waiting to do – finally! – Touching Cloth. Somehow I never seemed to email the people organising this gig at the right time or get my dates right and I had messed up again. I wonder if I messed this up subconsciously because I sensed that I needed a night at home.

After all the fuss before and after Atlanta, Simon had not really calmed down much and was still jittery and wanting me to consider pulling the entire experiment. Also, it was getting to the point where it wasn't just eating away at the two of us as a couple, it was literally eating away at me physically. I was falling apart. It felt like I had a permanent cold. I looked a total mess.

In the two weeks running up to the clown course, which was taking up the entire day as well as gigging taking up all my evenings, I had been to Atlanta and away from Simon and the children for four nights. I had then been away in Lincoln for another night, MC-ing the terrible student gig. I myself had cancelled a gig for the first time because I had food poisoning for twenty-four hours. And I had done eleven gigs in fourteen days. I was completely exhausted. Of those eleven gigs during that fortnight, only three or four of them had been any good. Two had been absolutely awful and had left me in tears.

So the first night after Dr Brown, it was good to have a night off. I always find that however bad things get, if you have time to sit down and talk, suddenly it all improves and that was how that evening worked. It helped that Simon could see I was energised and transformed by the process of being in 'the shit'. I think he also got some perverse satisfaction at the thought of me being in 'the shit' as well. 'In "the shit"? So now you know how I feel.' He smiled tightly with a grim sense of satisfaction.

But that night was just one night's respite and I had over forty gigs to get through in less than six weeks if I was going to make the numbers work in this sodding experiment that I had set my heart on. Much as I recognised how important it was to have a night off and get things back on track with Simon, I also really hated skipping a night because I was getting behind on numbers. And the last thing I wanted to do was to end up having to do doubles or triples (two or three gigs in one night) once I got into the last ten of the hundred days. That would be really stressful and high risk. Now it was going inexorably in that direction: one cancellation or another bout of illness and the whole thing would be made pointless at a stroke.

After the second day's clown workshop, though, I was back on track. I had a gig I had booked ages ago in Tonbridge in Kent. Having an out-of-town gig is always exciting and annoying at the same time because it could be really good, with a great crowd and an interesting venue (Brighton), or it could be a nightmare scenario in a place where no one really wants comedy (Broadstairs). In the case of Tonbridge, it turned out to be a bit of both. It was in a nice enough pub, not that far from the train station. And Tonbridge is not a hassle to get to from London, it's barely half an hour away. Plus, I set out with my new clown's attitude: I can do this. I love 'the shit'.

As it turned out, as far as gigs go, it wasn't the best. The pub was all kitted out for Hallowe'en. The room was split into two sections. The top part was supposed to be for comedy. The lower part, where the bar was, was intended for anyone not interested in comedy. And yet, in the bar, where they couldn't see the performers, there was a tannoy system piping the comedy through to them. So as a comic you were in a catch-22. You were supposed to entertain the upper part of the room – who, at least, had chosen comedy. But there was noise pollution coming from the lower part of the room, where they had chosen not to watch comedy. And at the same time there was some kind of vague idea that you would capture the attention of everyone in the pub via the tannoy, even enticing people who were on the other side of a brick wall to come and join you in jovial hilarity. Oh for Christ's sake, why do they do these things to the poor comics? We are nice people (mostly). We do not deserve this.

Usually all this would have pissed me off royally. But somehow a different part of me had taken over, thanks to all the massaging and the animal noises and not quite being thrown onto the floor. I looked around the room, with plastic pumpkins and rubber spiders hanging from the fake Tudor eaves, and thought, 'I just love everyone.' And I genuinely did. This resulted in my spending most of the evening with a local character at the bar who told me all about his life history, including a long-standing vendetta with his brother. In my 'I love everyone' state, I attempted to coax him towards a reconciliation. 'Life is short. Are you sure it's beyond repair?' Oh dear. First I had over-mothered the clown. Now it was the local character's turn. Dr Brown had not necessarily made me a better comic, but he had certainly turned me into an excellent counsellor. Perhaps I could become a vicar. Or Oprah.

I was on fifth before the break and all the comedians who had gone before me had pretty much died. The audience upstairs were not that interested in comedy, or at least not the sort of comedy that was being presented to them. The audience downstairs – who were not an audience and resented the fact that a tannoy booming out comedy was interrupting their conversations – was getting louder and louder. But, still. I was deep into the clown zone and I loved everyone.

I had spent two days in the company of Dr Brown, the world's hippiest man, and when you are with him you just cannot help but adore the world and everything in it. Somehow all your troubles melt away, everything seems wonderful and you genuinely don't care that you are performing in a strange, dilapidated, mock olde worlde alehouse decorated with cotton wool cobwebs. You don't care because in your imagination you are on *Live at the Apollo*. Or singing a silly song for your baby, who is at home wishing you were breastfeeding him. Or dancing on a sunny beach somewhere. Wherever you are, you're in 'the shit' and it's a happy, don't-care kind of place.

When I stood up in front of them and saw their little faces marked with disgust, disappointment, a tinge of hope, the effects of long days at work and too many Hallowe'en special offer drinks, I loved them even more. I launched into my set with the sort of attack I had not experienced in a long time, possibly ever. It wasn't exactly as if I were a different person; it was as if I were a slightly better version of myself. Much better than I had been in a long time.

The audience didn't particularly like my stuff, though, and it wasn't particularly right for them, but I gave it my all and tried to put it over to them as best as I could. A few of them came on board and I could see them looking at their friends encouragingly, 'Actually, this one's not bad. For a woman, anyway.' But sometimes, even if in your heart you're on *Live at the Apollo*, in reality you are in a pub in Tonbridge. And there was only so much I could do. I knew, however, that I had turned around a bad situation that only a week before would have finished me off completely.

And it was all down to the Master Clown. I cried with happiness on the train all the way home, weeping to myself, 'I had a good gig.' It wasn't even that good – I knew it – but it had felt good. That was a big difference. I knew that if I could hang on to that, I could build on it and make all my performances better, especially in front of audiences better suited to my stuff.

The strangest thing was how it felt inside. I knew I had not had a terrific gig where everyone loved me and thought I was brilliant – I knew what that felt like and this was different. When that happens, it's as if you're overtaken by this feeling of warmth in the room and you feel as if you could soar off the edge of the stage and fly. The circumstances of the gig would not really have allowed for anyone to experience that sensation. But I had felt good up there and I had felt completely connected to the audience, almost as if I knew what they were thinking. To be fair, mostly they were thinking, 'How soon until she gets off and I can get another drink?' But I had still felt them. And this counted as a breakthrough. And I hadn't had to get naked to achieve it.

I phone Simon on the way home and I am crying. 'I think I've figured out how to do it,' I gush. 'Really? Did you have a good gig?' 'Not especially. But I kind of felt like I knew what I was doing and I was very happy and I just loved everyone so much. I just really loved them, you know.' More crying. 'That's great, darling,' Simon replies. I can hear the effort in his voice. 'It sounds like you are making progress. That's just great.' 'There is progress. There is definitely progress. It's all because of the clown. I need to do more stuff with the clown.' I'm crying again now because I'm worried that once I'm not with the clown any more I won't have this love thing any more and it will all be doomed.

'Well,' says Simon, wearily, 'at least you've got another day with the clown tomorrow? Maybe you can cement everything you've learned then.' 'Yeah, I guess. Did I already say how much I loved everyone?' 'Yes, Viv. You did. You did.'

13: Gig 58:

'Step up to the mic and say what's on your mind'

Day 62, Gig 58: Finsbury Park

Cheery, heart-warming gig with old friends and nice comics. Irrelevant in comedy scheme of things. Necessary for battered ego. Seriously need to figure out how I am going to catch up on the numbers. Where can I double up?

Day 63, no gig

Just couldn't get a gig tonight. Tried to enjoy being very, very happy at home. Tried not to think about the fact that maybe I can't make this experiment work. Thought about Doris.

*

If only I can crack the numbers again, I'm on the home straight. Most of the time, thanks to Atlanta and thanks to the clown man, I'm feeling it's all worthwhile. Then one mediocre gig hits and I feel I should never have done any of it. This process is like being thrown between two extremes. The more difficult it gets, though, the more I remember about why I wanted to do it all in the first place. And that, at least, helps.

When I was growing up, the person who made me laugh the most was Doris Schwartz, the aspiring actress and stand-up comedian played by Valerie Landsburg in *Fame*. Wild-haired, kooky and ditsy, Landsburg played the role between 1982 and

1984. For those years Doris was the person I most wanted to be. I was obsessed with her. I loved her. She was my idol.

I was nine when the series started. At the time I had already half-fixed myself on the idea of being a writer, but I also loved drama and comedy. I used to lie in front of the television on my stomach, chin in my hands, open-mouthed, lost in love for Doris. She in turn was lost in love for the even wilder-haired Bruno Martelli, the moody keyboard maestro and protégé of Mr Shorofsky, the curmudgeonly piano teacher. My love for Doris was only slightly influenced by a subconscious desire to appeal to the Italianate Bruno and to obtain approval from Mr Shorofsky. (I only found out recently that he was called Mr Shorofsky and not Mr Schwarovsky, such was the way I heard the New York accent as a child.)

To my mind Doris did not have an easy time of it. While all the other girls in the cast wore leotards and had big hair and lots of make-up, Doris wore headbands, dungarees and massive cardigans. Even when she got to sing the lead vocals on 'Hi-Fidelity', bouncing around a music shop as Bruno tried out the latest top-of-the-range electronic keyboard, she still came across as the geek of the piece. She always had the most open, vulnerable face and I can't think of her without crying, swaying in her peach twinset during 'Starmaker', singing 'I keep measuring what I lost … ' with a sad little smile on her face.

Doris was involved in a big-production, saxophone-heavy ensemble number set inside a makeshift open mic comedy club which was part of the New York High School of Performing Arts' 'Talent Night'. It was titled 'Step up to the mic and say what's on your mind'. Doris bravely opened the song, stepping up to the mic in a red polo neck and hideous black and grey cardigan, while the principal looked on in a checked suit and kipper tie with an expression of concerned indulgence that said, 'These kids shouldn't be doing this. But maybe they have a point.' The whole episode was dominated by a woman in a apricot jumpsuit doing jazz hands at every opportunity. But it was Doris's heartfelt contribution that had touched me somewhere deep inside.

The gist of the episode was something to do with the fact that some people need to get in front of a microphone in order to say what they really need to say. And even if you don't want to hear what they have to say, you must let them speak. As a child who felt her many contributions and pronouncements were not always greatly valued, I lodged the importance of this song somewhere at the back of my mind. It contains the immortal lyrics: 'How 'bout you, young lady? Come on, step up to the mic!' and 'Step up to the mic and say what's on your mind … Don't be shy, come on, make some room for the lady.' I obviously felt this song expressed the contents of my soul.

I'm not sure I knew where Doris ended and I began. In my nine-year-old's mind I had the two of us muddled. To confuse things further, there were two Dorises: the one in the TV shows (Valerie Landsburg) and the one in the 1980 Alan Parker film *Fame* (Maureen Teefy), which I did not see until I was much older as it had a 15 certificate because Coco (Irene Cara) takes her top off in it. In the TV show, Doris did not do that much stand-up; she mostly swooned over Bruno and looked smiley during big dance numbers.

When I was little I adored Cupid Stunt on Kenny Everett and would annoy my parents by doing open-legged impressions of her wailing, 'It's all in the best possible taste.' I thought Cupid somehow really was a woman. And I definitely did not understand anything about her name for at least another twenty years. In any case, I was repeatedly told off for copying her and showing off. I was also wide-eyed over Tracey Ullman in *Three of a Kind*, I loved the impressionist Janet Brown and was vaguely aware of Pamela Stephenson and her Janet Street-Porter impression. I loved Josie Lawrence in *Whose Line Is It Anyway?* (Around the time I did my first gig I remember telling a young comedienne I had just met that she reminded me of Josie Lawrence. 'Oh, I'm much better than her,' she replied. I realised we would not be friends.)

I grew up in a tiny village in Somerset and had never met anyone who lived in London or America, let alone anyone who did acting or writing or comedy or improvising or any of the things I was interested in. I always wanted to be front- and centre-stage at school plays. I played Widow Twankey when I was about five, all big lipsticked lips, rouge cheeks and fake Les Dawson bosom. When I was seven, I played a mad scientist in some Dickensian skit and insisted on having proper knickerbockers and an intricate moustache. I learned to play the piano and even when I was sitting on the stool, banging away furiously on the keys, I would lean out from the side of it at school shows so that the audience could see my face. Come on, make some room for the lady.

It occurred to me around the age of eleven, however, just as Doris was being written out of *Fame* (she disappeared after Series 4), that it would be a huge stretch to become an actress or a comedian. Apart from Doris, I had never seen a woman doing stand-up comedy. It did not seem a viable career path for me or for anyone who did not live within walking distance of the New York High School of Performing Arts. I lived within walking distance of the Bruton Conservative Club, where my dad played snooker; if you walked the same distance in the opposite direction you were standing in a field of cows. From an early age I did not envisage that this would be an easy place to get out of. It was best to keep things simple. And to choose stand-up comedy would not have met that requirement.

We were not badly off as a family, but we were not comfortably middle class either. Neither of my parents had gone to university. My grandparents (my dad's parents) had run their corner shop for forty years. My mum's dad was a builder and her mum worked in a factory. My mum was a secretary at the GP's; my dad was a travelling sales rep. We did not know people with jobs in media or who worked in the theatre. I did not take it for granted either that you got to do what you wanted with your life or that other people you knew would help you to get places. My grandma had a friend who worked in the box office at the Prince of Wales Theatre in the West End and she got me a signed photograph of Bucks Fizz just after they won the Eurovision. This was about as showbiz as it got.

For a while, when I was about eight or nine, I did impressions of David Bellamy with a beard of washing-up bubbles, Margaret Thatcher with a wagging finger, heavily lifted from the TV impressionist Janet Brown, and an appallingly Oirish Jimmy 'Come 'ere' Cricket (not that the original was any less appallingly Oirish). I could make people laugh but I knew in my heart these were not good impressions. Oh, how I would have loved to be good at impressions. Intuiting that drama school or the 'Step up to the mic' talent contest was beyond my wildest dreams, I decided to become a writer. That, I reasoned, coming from where I came from, would be bad enough. I started by getting a scholarship to the local posh school.

Once I was there I volunteered for plays but I wasn't chosen for the lead parts because I wasn't one of the pretty girls. I did public speaking and balloon debates and all the things that are supposed to prepare you for Oxbridge, which I eventually got into. At Cambridge I signed up for Footlights, but when the audition was cancelled at the last minute I took it as a sign that they didn't want me and didn't darken their door again. Pathetic.

But I had only so much self-confidence then, and it had taken me all the guts I had to get away from home and into university in the first place. I didn't want to push my luck. Slowly, over the years, the idea of performance was ebbing away and my attention was turning elsewhere.

For a couple of terms at university I was in a sketch group with some college friends and we even muscled in on a slot on a Footlights bill with Stephen Fry at an AIDS benefit at the Cambridge Corn Exchange in 1992. We were called Juicy, Fruity, Fresh and Cheap. I think I was Cheap – or at least Juicy, who ended up being my boyfriend for a year, would have argued that I should have been. Ha ha. We weren't that good, and we didn't stay together after the benefit gig. But we weren't that bad either. And we put on a good show that night – so much so that one fleeting Stephen Fry moment is fixed in my mind as if it were a Royal Variety Performance.

I was eighteen. I was nervous, excited and pumped up with adrenaline, dressed as a St Trinian's schoolgirl complete with freckles drawn on with an eyebrow pencil. I squeezed past Stephen Fry in the wings, pushing far closer into him than was strictly polite. 'I like the costume,' he boomed at me in a wonderful, breathy, actor-ly voice, with a hint of a wink. Later that evening I stole a packet of Marlboros from his dressing room for Juicy. There was one cigarette left in the packet. We shared it. I felt bad for smoking a cigarette really belonging to Stephen Fry – but also I felt good about having something of Stephen Fry's which he wouldn't really miss. Juicy, Fruity, Fresh and Cheap disbanded; I broke up with the boyfriend. I wasn't to know it but the Stephen Fry gig would be the last time I would do anything on stage for twenty years.

By the time I was in my early twenties, I was focused on writing and getting into journalism. I didn't think about performing anymore – although get me anywhere near a karaoke mic and I would hog it for hours on end. That was a sign. For a long time, though, I didn't think about stand-up or comedy much at all. Doris was nowhere. I didn't think about her for years. I suppose I continued to enjoy comedy whenever I saw it but I didn't make any connection between comedy and me. It was a road I hadn't taken and I didn't want to think about it.

It must have been in 2008 that I saw an article in a newspaper about a man who had been made redundant and virtually lost the will to live. He did a stand-up comedy workshop and it completely transformed the way he felt about himself. I was shocked and intrigued. I had never imagined that some people attempt to train to be stand-up comedians rather than just 'become' them by some mysterious means. I cut out the article and kept it. Thirty years before, as a child, I thought you just become what you're meant to be. Now, as an adult, I had already realised that most things don't just happen by accident. Life is made up of a series of decisions, often random decisions. And lots of us don't become what we're meant to be because we're too scared.

14: Gigs 59 to 61:

'Boom. Boom. Boom. Another one bites the dust.'

Day 64, Gig 59: Islington

Semi-bomb, semi-okay. I'm torn between being extra determined that I can make this work and I can turn the numbers around and make it to 100 in 100 nights ... and thinking that I just can't do it and it's all been too ambitious.

Day 64, Gig 60: Soho

Fun night with lovely people. Small audience. They liked the Instrument of Truth (mini keyboard)!

Day 65, Gig 61: Soho

King Gong at the Comedy Store. On stage for 52 seconds before I am gonged off. Fifty. Two. Seconds.

*

Loving everyone and having fun is all very well. Ultimately there is not much point in doing any of this unless you can survive in front of a proper, serious comedy audience. And for that there is really only one place everyone wants to play in London: the Comedy Store.

There are loads of semi-pro gigs people want to play because they're in good venues, have good crowds and offer some hope of progression: Downstairs at the King's Head, the Comedy Cafe, Up The Creek. But if we're talking about an amateur comic's ego, to play the Comedy Store has got to be right up there. It's not easy to get booked at 'the Store'. (I do not call it that. There is no way that I have graduated to the stage where I can call it that and not sound like an idiot. Possibly no one can.) I have serious reservations about playing the Comedy Store. Because the only way to get on there is to do King Gong. Most people want to play the Store. But they don't want to do the Gong.

The Gong is evil and the Gong is cruel. The Gong is the great leveller. The Gong can fell even the most experienced of comics because it's all done on the whim of the audience. If you do the Gong, you might get to say that you did a barnstorming five-minute set at the Comedy Store and get an amazing video that you can put on YouTube and get invited back to perform a paid set. Or you might get gonged off after two seconds.

All stand-up is on the whim of the audience but this is the most extreme version of that dynamic. It's like stand-up crossed with wrestling with a bit of the lions' den at the Colosseum thrown in. But if you win it, you get your video (this is a big deal). And you get a chance to perform there on a regular night with comedians off the telly. This is the main reason people do the Gong. They hope somehow they'll get into that hallowed spot and it will catapult them into the Comedy Store for real. If you lose it? If you get two, three, four seconds up there? You get a serious kick in the teeth from four hundred people.

The night I do the Gong, I'm in a funny mood. I'm bemused by what I've gone through in recent times and am feeling pretty reckless. This is usually a sign that I am either going to do very well on stage or very badly, nothing in between. I have the feeling I don't really care that much how I get on tonight. I don't think that I'm ready to play the Comedy Store for real in any case so it doesn't bother me whether I make it through on the Gong or not. This kind of mentality usually means you have a better gig. But you can't fake it. You have to really not care. And tonight I just don't.

Doing the Gong is a strange experience if you're used to open mic gigs. It's run like a proper comedy club – because it is a proper comedy club. There's a cloakroom and everything. And proper seating. And an actual front row. Most places I have gigged there isn't necessarily a front row because there aren't enough punters to force people to sit there; the second row ends up becoming the first row by default. The numbers alone here are impressive and different from normal. As an open mic comedian, you don't have much experience of having to fight your way past bouncers and get up in front of a crowd of about four hundred.

This is what is great about this gig – a proper big crowd of people who really want to see comedy and who have paid to see it. Okay, so they have also paid to see a gladiatorial fight, because that is what the Gong promises. But what they want most of all is a great night out at the Comedy Store. It is exciting even to be cannon fodder in that set-up.

Not all comics agree. Some professional comics counsel against doing gong shows because they are so arbitrary. I've heard it called 'the death of creativity'. Some think that it's gong shows like this that are killing off comedy. You never learn to work the audience because the second you die, you're off. You can get the impression that your material is bad when in fact the audience is just tired and wants to see someone different from you. You can really get your ego punched in at these shows.

Also, gong shows demand a very specific skill set. They encourage you to hone your comedy in a very precise direction: tight, fast, cruel. In a way, that's a great discipline. And if you have five minutes that can win a gong show, you probably have five minutes of really good material that will work in a comedy club anywhere. On the other hand, this is a sort of accountancy version of comedy: it's about reliability, gags by numbers, 'banker' jokes, guaranteed laughs. It can risk becoming formulaic.

Again, there are pros who worry that all these new young comics are trying to be the next Jimmy Carr and coming out with the same one-liners and grooming themselves for *Mock The Week* on television. They argue that comedy has stopped being experimental and exciting. I'm not sure where I stand on this. There are a lot of bad Jimmy Carr impersonators; but there are also a lot of comics who are masquerading as experimental and who do not have a good five minutes and who are just not funny. The thing is, though, you're not going to get through a gong show unless you have a really good club set. And right now it seems to me that having a really good club set is no bad thing to have.

It's about 7 p.m. and the audience is swelling to around several hundred people. I can feel the nerves of the comics rising. We are not used to these numbers. I am starting to get a buzz. I like it here. I'm scared. But I also don't care any more. The comics all line up to one side, behind the audience, and hassle the man in the sound booth who is deciding the running order. He will not let anyone move from their spot. I end up fifteenth out of about twenty-five. I have no idea whether this is a good position or not. There are more comics coming on the bill the longer things go on so I'm glad not to have got on even later.

The MC is Jarred Christmas, who is very funny. They are going to hire the best MC they can get at a night like this because they cannot rely on the acts, who are unknown quantities. The MC deals with the braying crowd easily, ridiculing their accents and where they're from. The usual stuff. It's the sort of crowd where if you're American you're toast. Australians get love. Gingers get hate. He explains how the night is going to work. He gives big red bits of laminated cardboard – 'red cards' – to three random people in the audience. If you're one of the three people with a card, you get to hold it aloft when you've had enough of the comic on stage. As the first red card goes up, a Voice of God announcer booms, 'One red card!' As the second is raised, 'Two red cards!' Once the third card goes up – 'Three red cards!' – the Gong sounds and then three drumbeats as the music blasts out Freddie Mercury: 'Boom. Boom. Boom. Another one bites the dust.' It's brutal. But it's also funny.

The comics are basically lambs to the slaughter. The first three barely get a few seconds in the spotlight and they're carded off. Most of them are booed off. That is a loud and frightening sound coming from four hundred people. Sometimes the people holding the cards are harsher than the rest of the audience. They hold up the cards more or less straight away. At other times, a couple of the card holders will really hold out while the entire audience attempts to boo off the act.

Most of the comedians just about cope, although I do watch one really hard man come unstuck. I know he's quite a good comic and a pretty tough cookie but this crowd is too much even for him. I'm standing way at the back and I can see him shaking from where I am. They give him just over a minute and then he's carded off. He looks gutted – and surprised. Surely he could feel from the first second that it wasn't going well up there? Sometimes a comic has no idea what things look like from the outside.

One girl barely makes it to thirty seconds and comes off in tears. Again, she's surprised. She can't see that from the second she walked on they wanted her to get off. That's how it goes sometimes. The audience couldn't care less about the performers' reactions. They don't care or notice what happens once the performers are off the stage. They don't especially want to see people's weakness or humiliation. They just want to have their moment of wielding power.

I am bemused by the whole thing but also starting to feel vaguely uncomfortable. I can cope with being booed and failing and not going through – and I really like the idea of the drumbeats followed by 'Another one bites the dust'. But I am suddenly not sure that I can face people booing jokes which I have taken ages to make work and which I know can and do work in most situations now. After hating my material and thinking it's rubbish, I'm suddenly in a position where I want to protect it. I have not gone through four decades of self-doubt, three natural childbirths with no drugs and sixty gigs in everywhere from Sheffield to Atlanta to have these people vote me off just because I am not twenty-three, male and sporting a Kings of Leon T-shirt, skinny jeans and a gelled quiff.

There's an interval before I go on. I go over to the bar to listen to what people are saying. They don't remember much about any of the comics – there are too many of us. They are just talking about how much they love booing people off. That is what they have come for. 'Are you one of the comics? Are you on?' one girl asks me at the bar. She must have seen me standing at the back, looking nervous. 'Yes. In a couple of people.' 'Good luck.' 'Thanks, I think I'll need it.'

When things start up again, two acts in a row get through to five minutes. If you go through, instead of 'Another one bites the dust' you get a piece of music that plays, 'Hallelujah! Hallelujah! Hallelujah!' The last few acts are strong and they deserve it. One of them is a woman – Samantha Hannah. She has an excellent set and is likeable. The next one who goes through is Gatis Kandis. He's a Latvian with a series of bonkers one-liners which mostly revolve around him wilfully misunderstanding English. 'Hello!

Are you well?' he asks. 'Yes, thanks,' replies the audience member. 'No,' giggles Gatis, 'You are not a well. You are a person.' He does it with such innocence and stupidity that you think it's for real and sometimes it's not clear whether the audience is laughing at him or with him.

Someone puts the red card up quite quickly but it doesn't seem to 'catch' with the other two, as it has with a lot of the other comics. Often it's the first red card holder to put their hand up who determines the fate of the comic. I find myself mumbling angrily at the red card people. I think the MC purposely chooses people who are mad or drunk to make it more fun. Gatis manages to get through an entire set with one red card held aloft. He keeps looking around at the sound booth, expecting to be gestured off, but he keeps telling his gags as well and the audience keep laughing, half in disbelief, half in delight. It doesn't matter why they like him in the end because they put him through. He looks completely amazed. He will now go into the joke-off with the other comics who get to five minutes.

So by the time I'm waiting to go up, several people have gone through and the audience has heard the 'Hallelujah!' music pretty much three times in a row. As Gatis goes off, I can feel them baying for blood. They have had enough success. They are bored by good comics now. They have heard this music and they're fed up with it. They want some people they can boo. They want the drumbeats. They want another one to bite the dust. Boom. Boom. Boom.

As my name is called and I bound up onto the stage, I've already made my decision. You can tell it in the bounding – I would not normally bound onto the stage, I would walk slowly and deliberately. But I have a strategy and I'm not going to be my usual self tonight. I have decided that I'm not going to do any of my material in the first minute. I can't face my material being booed off. I don't mind them booing me off just because they don't like the look of me. But I'm not having these people reject jokes that I know work just because they're itching to ditch someone.

This is a bold move and I'm quite proud of it. Of course, it's born of cowardice. I'm not secure enough in my material to feel I can face seeing it destroyed in this space. Either they like me for who I am and let me stay on and then I'll do my material. Or they don't like me and they boo me off and then at least I won't have had my material rejected. But it's also a noble thing to do: go up there with nothing.

In some ways this is a sensible strategy and a very self-protective and responsible one; in other ways it's complete suicide. All you have as a stand-up comic is your material and you are not going to be able to sustain being up there without it for very long. The only thing standing between you and the disdain of the audience is your jokes. Your personality and your charisma might last you for a few seconds, but after that you need some gags. This is the case even if you are famous. As Lenny Henry put it: 'If you're a famous comedian, you've got about a minute to impress on stage. You get a clap at the beginning and "My mum used to like you!" and then there's nothing to do but roll your sleeves up.'

I did not have the benefit of a minute. Or even much of a clap. And I didn't even get to the stage where I was rolling my sleeves up. Turns out I was able to sustain it for fifty-two seconds. This is my official Gong time. As the seconds ticked past, I looked out over the sea of faces and thought: 'They are good people. They are tired and drunk. There's a couple down here at the front who really don't like me at all and one of them is about to put the red card ... ah, yes, there it goes.' But I also felt good up there and that I would like to have been up there again for longer.

It's a weird feeling when you're up on stage in front of that many people when you're supposed to make them laugh but you don't really know what you're doing. I had a feeling of profound calm and profound excitement at the same time. And I very much wanted to be there – without feeling that it would be terrible if I had to leave the stage. I made the mistake of carrying on some banter which the MC had started – something about one of the guys in the audience looking like a squirrel, which he did. What I said was funny enough (I can't even remember what it was now) and some people got it and laughed.

But it wasn't enough. They wanted to know who I was. And they wanted to know what my jokes were and what I was about. When that didn't materialise after about thirty seconds, they wanted rid of me. And fair play to them. Fifty-two seconds. My gags hadn't bombed because I hadn't done them; but I personally had bombed. I had learned an important lesson the hard way. The audience don't really know who you are without your material. You can ad lib and you can chat to them (which is what I did – and not entirely disastrously), but ultimately you're bottling it if you don't do what you went up there to do.

I raced down the steps to get off the stage and up the steep ramp back into the audience to hide behind a pillar. The annoying thing was that just before I went on stage one of the bouncers noticed that I was trying to set up my video camera (I usually leave it on a little tripod while I'm on stage) and attempted to confiscate it. I managed to get it off him somehow – he was going to destroy it but I threatened to start crying and screaming, which I was fully prepared to do – but basically I have no film of my fifty-two seconds which is a big, fat shame. As I cowered behind the pillar, shaking, the bouncer eyed me suspiciously. I could see what he was thinking: not only did I want to undertake illegal filming but I was also not funny. No sympathy: 'Why do these loons bother? Who told them they were funny?'

My heart was racing but I still felt calm inside. I had not beaten the Gong but I had been true to myself and I hadn't sacrificed any of my material. Cowardly or brave? Who knows. At least it meant that my material was not toxic to me and I could still use it. Although maybe it would have been better to put it to the ultimate test in front of this braying mob. I guess I'll never know. Unless I go back.

I now faced the decision as to whether to wait and see out the competition or just cut my losses and go home. It wasn't even really a decision; I found myself pulling on my coat without even thinking about it. As my heartbeat slowed and the adrenaline calmed, the reality of the past few hours hit me. I had left home at 5.30 p.m. to get here on time. It was now close to 10.30 p.m. and they were a long way off the finale. There were another ten acts to get through. I decided to leave so that at least I could get home at a reasonable hour for once. I still didn't get home until after midnight. So that was six hours of my life gone for fifty-two seconds of stage time. It was the least economical evening so far. Their Diet Coke was expensive.

The thought of all this defeated me, slightly. Yet again another evening of huge emotional effort for pretty much zero reward, verging on a negative result. The Gong books up to six months in advance so it is a pain to get a slot. It's only on once a month. I had waited four months to get on. Four months for fifty-two seconds. Fifty-two seconds. One second for each week of the year. A whole room of people hating me and not wanting to see me for even one measly minute. Well done me. So why had I enjoyed it so much? It was beyond logic.

This was what I was already thinking: 'I want another go. How soon can I come back and do this again?' I didn't want to feel this way. I wanted to have hated it, all fifty-two seconds of it. But I didn't hate it. I had been well and truly bitten. When I got home I messaged Dr Brown. 'How can I hold on to being a total idiot?' He replied, 'Don't hold on, you idiot. Just be with us however you are.' Bloody hippy.

15: Gigs 62 to 72:

'This is shit. Get off.'

Day 66, Gig 62: Shoreditch

This was the week Steve Jobs died. And so did my miniature electric piano. (I bought it on eBay. It was made in the 1980s. It can't be expected to work, really.) Experimented with playing piano app on my iPhone instead by holding my phone up to the microphone and playing the piano on it. Disaster. Old man at back: 'This is shit. Get off.'

Day 67, Gig 63: Forest Hill

Riotous mother and baby gig with Lucy Porter where one baby laughed so hard it fell off a chair and hit its head. Disturbing. Also funny.

Day 67, Gig 64: Farringdon

Very sweet, try-hard new night with an overly keen promoter. Bar staff getting extremely excited about 'mixing new cocktails for the comedy night'. About eight people turn up. But they are nice people and it's an okay night. Relieved to leave early to get to another gig. Feel super-determined about making the numbers up now.

Day 67, Gig 65: Warren Street

Arrived late because coming from Farringdon. Low-key gig, not badly attended, in the basement of a wine bar. Messed around with the little keyboard (Increasingly Tempramental Instrument of Truth). I'm not entirely 'with it' at the moment so I came across as slightly mad person. Not necessarily funny mad person either. Just scary.

Day 68, Gig 66: Islington

Weird show in a basement with very little audience. Still seemed to manage to make the best of it and enjoy it. Comic saw me who hadn't seen me for ages. 'You have totally improved. It's like you're a different person.'

Day 69, Gig 67: Greenwich

Lively, heart-warming, cosy night. Love going back to places where I've had a nice gig before. Very funny We Should Get A Boat trio. Simon's Video Verdict: 'Wow. You are actually getting better. This is quite good.'

Day 70, no gig

Couldn't get a gig anywhere on a Saturday night. Absurdly happy to be at home with the children.

Day 71, Gig 68: Borough

Bog-standard, notch-on-the-bedpost gig. Neither awful nor great.

Day 72, Gig 69: Hammersmith

Totally embarrassing. Two friends came to support and there was literally No One There. Typical unpromoted disastrous amateur gig. Shaming. Performance not much better. Silence in the room. HOWEVER. I seem to cope much better now at these events. I don't take them as a personal insult. I just see them as a chance to run through my material. This is progress. Realised on the way home that people seem to enjoy the eccentric, shambolic nature of some of these gigs, especially if they haven't paid. Important lesson.

Day 73, Gig 70: Islington

They. Got. My. Stuff. Finally feel like I can really do this. Massive high.

Day 73, Gig 71: King's Cross

Two gigs in one night. From success to failure. Did exactly the same set, bombed the second time. Why do you do this to me, universe?

Day 74, Gig 72: Vauxhall

Wonderful venue. The Royal Vauxhall Tavern. Four of us are hosting our own comedy night: there's me, Ben Fogg, who has many outfits with him including a stars and stripes adult Babygro, and The Electro Future Beard Club, a surreal duo who have been compared to Vic Reeves and Bob Mortimer. This night has taken a huge amount of organisation and stress and it took every ounce of persuasion for me to get them to accept the compromise name for the night: Comedy Cabinet. They all wanted to call it Wank Tank. Great crowd of 100. Acts mostly successful. I did okay but not great. Headline act bombed so badly he walked off the stage and out of the club. So it's not just me.

Day 75, no gig: Taunton

I was hoping I was going to be able to count this as a gig. But no. In Taunton for the night for work, talking to a group of mothers and midwives, which I had been booked to do months in advance of deciding to do the 100 gigs. I was hoping that instead of discussing 'motherhood and journalism' (which is what they wanted me to talk about), I could just do stand-up. When I arrived, I discovered that the person going on before me was presenting a talk about stillbirth. This included her showing photos of her dead baby. I revised my idea of telling jokes and instead gave a serious talk about the perception of motherhood in the media. It was quite nice to talk in public without the expectation of getting laughs. Maybe I should follow more stillbirth presentations.

Day 76, gig cancelled: Soho

Immense frustration. Too late to get another gig.

*

The emotional dam that is Simon is about to burst again. Having been twitchy but supportive, he has turned permanently cross. Sometimes he has a sense of humour about it all: 'Next time you choose a challenge, can't you do having sex with your husband a hundred times in a hundred nights?'

The experiment has had its inspiring moments, but it has also been so frustrating. For every good gig you have somewhere like Brighton, you have seven bad ones in some hellhole in Kentish

186

Town. The idea that this is what I should have done with my life has kept me going. But lately I've started to think that we weren't 'meant' or 'born' to do anything. We pretend this is the case because it makes it seem as if life makes sense and that there is some kind of plan to the way it turns out, instead of us all just filling time in random occupations until we die. This pretty much sums up my view of life. We make out there's some logic to all this. There isn't. To paraphrase Woody Allen, it's better than the alternative – death. Or maybe there is some weird parallel here anyway. Because I am experiencing death on a pretty regular basis.

Simon is struggling to see why I am sticking with it. He was briefly interested in it all after I did my fifty-two seconds at the Gong; he could identify with how painful it must have been. Now he's bored by the whole thing again and wants me to give up. I want to give up too. But I can't. Not now. In order to get through this, I have retreated into my own little world. On an average morning I make a cup of tea for myself and take it into the living room to go and look at last night's video footage. 'Hello? What about my cup of tea?' Simon shouts after me.

I don't blame him for joking about the 'sex for a hundred nights' thing. There was an American couple who did this as a relationship experiment. Their motto? 'It's all about just doing it!' They got sick of it halfway through and had to use Viagra. What I'm doing is the opposite of their 'Getting Closer Together' programme. It's the hundred-day 'Drive a Wedge Between You' workshop. Or, basically, the fastest route to divorce. It's entirely possible that I set all this up on purpose. Did I subconsciously want to wreck our marriage and find a get-out clause? Meanwhile I need a psychological equivalent of Viagra to get Simon through to the end of the hundred nights. Valium is the only thing I can think of. Or a horse tranquilliser.

If the sex experiment is all about 'just doing it', the only person I'm 'just doing it' for is myself. Or at least that's how it seems from the outside – and to Simon. At the very least he knows that he can trust me and that has not turned into a problem. Which is just as well because if I was out this much doing anything other than stand-up then it would be pretty obvious that I was having an affair. The affair bit would be fairly easy as I am meeting an awful lot of people who would just have sex with anyone or anything (99 per cent of amateur stand-ups do material about being single and desperate).

I have received a message via Facebook from someone else I met at a gig which says this: 'Your husband would kill me but … if you were single and didn't have babies and stuff, I definitely would.' Oh dear me. The problem is, at the moment I am so tired and fed up that I generally wouldn't. I am already cheating on my husband with stand-up comedy, which turns out to be the equivalent of having a third person around who is extremely demanding and annoying. The last thing I need to do is bring a fourth person into this already crowded relationship.

The real issue of trust here is whether he really believes that I am not wasting time and money doing something which I'm not entirely serious about. That would be embarrassing – to put so much on him and the children and not do it 100 per cent and for it not really to work. He knows how much this means to me and what I want to give it and how much I want to make it work. I am trying to put a brave face on it all. When we have a rare meeting at the breakfast table – which is pretty much the only time we're seeing each other at the moment – I beam regularly: 'Not long to go now.' I ostentatiously count the days down and cross them out in my diary. 'We've still got a month of this,' he grumps. 'We'll get through it,' I trill.

Accusations come from him all the time and I can't deny

their accuracy. 'You are a nightmare.' (Guilty.) 'It's all about you.' (Er, yes?) Simon expresses these thoughts mostly in anger or frustration or tiredness, and we do have times when we are together and we catch up properly and get on. And those are the times when I manage to persuade him that it's okay, we are going to get through this. They are also the times when I consider secretly crushing some pills into his tea.

There have been a few dark moments when I've reached the point where in my confusion I fear it's too late for me to choose him over the experiment (which I would do if I had to) and we will just have to split up. Although there's never a time when I think he is actually, properly going to leave me, the practical implications are at their worst now. We never see each other. I'm home very late so if we want to talk about things and catch up then it has to be after midnight. When we do see each other, I'm really tired.

Now he's getting really tired because I'm coming home late every night and waking him up when he's half asleep. He's having to do extra childcare and fill in all the gaps at home: housework, washing, cooking, shopping. Weekends should be a good time to catch up and paper over the cracks, but weekends are when I get work done and weekends are when we argue.

I'm slacking on everything at home and in my day job because I am stressed and exhausted and can only keep my mind on so many things at once. Just booking the gigs and getting the gigs done and organising childcare and keeping work ticking over is bad enough. Things get much worse when I try to make them better. I try to buy 'sorry' presents. I leave Simon a steak in the fridge for him to find when he comes home from work. He buys something else on the way home. He forgets to eat the steak the next night and then it goes off and has to go in the bin. 'Why didn't you tell me there was a steak in the fridge? Why did you put it where I couldn't see it? Why are you creating food waste?' 'I thought I told you. I thought I put it somewhere, um, prominent. Sorry. I do not mean to create food waste.'

I buy him a packet of his favourite biscuits. He has one or two and then within twenty-four hours I have eaten the rest because I am having a stressful day. Food-wise, I am not looking after him or the children and I am not really looking after myself. I have started taking detours to Waterloo on the way home instead of going straight to Vauxhall Station (the quicker route) because they have a Burger King at Waterloo and I can get onion rings there. I tell myself it's okay to have them because I still have not had any kebabs.

I don't want to leave him. I know he is the only thing holding me up. But there are times when I get scared that I might have to leave him just because I am so difficult to live with and it's cruel. Sometimes I think it would be in everyone's interests because I am evidently so bad for him and I am making him so unhappy by having chosen to do this crazed experiment. It seems all he wants is a wife who isn't trying – and failing – to become a stand-up comedian. Is that so much to ask? Looking at him from the outside, it's all I want for him: a decent wife who has time for him and is not a nightmare. I love him enough to want that for him, even though I know that person cannot be me. Not for the next five weeks anyway. He needs someone who will cook him a steak in the evenings and buy special biscuits for him that she will not actually eat herself. I am not that person.

And all this in pursuit of what? Everything is miscommunication and there is not enough time to talk and I'm focusing on just getting through the stupid hundred days. 'Please just stop putting us through this,' he says one morning as he is getting the older two ready for school. 'I don't know if I can take it any more.' And you wonder why people with full-on jobs and people who are obsessed with their work and people who work in the entertainment industry are always getting divorced. 'We have been here before,' I say, 'you were saying the same thing about fifty gigs ago. We are near the end now. I can't give up now.'

This happens the morning after I've come home in tears after a very bad gig. This is the hardest part. Not the logistics – which are bad enough – but the psychological impact. How can you persuade someone that you want to do something and you need to do something and you can't stop yourself from doing something, when it's obviously hurting you and is hard and doesn't always go your way? How do you do that when you're not certain yourself that you should really be doing it anyway?

So many people never attempt what they want to attempt in life because they're not even certain of wanting it enough. If they hit setbacks, they give up. They take failure as a sign that it's not meant to be, not that it's just a necessary knock-back. There's research that shows that people who succeed at anything have something psychologists call 'irrational optimism'. And I suppose the Directionless Comedy Binge has to be irrationally optimistic, otherwise there would be no point in undertaking it. Simon has no irrational optimism about this experiment. He only has realistic pessimism that it is all a Very Bad Idea.

The one thing that keeps me going is the children. I've arranged things carefully so that their lives are not too disrupted. I still have childcare three days a week and those are the days I write, book gigs and organise everything. During this time sufficient money must be earned to pay for the childcare, pay for life generally and pay for this experiment (and the Diet Coke bill). On the other two days of the week I'm looking after Jack and picking up the older two from school. Simon is still doing the school run in the mornings most days.

Bedtimes have been easiest as I can usually put Jack to bed before I go out and often I'll do so at 6 p.m., just so that it can be me who puts him down instead of Simon or a babysitter. There's often a babysitter around for the next hour or so before Simon gets home. I cannot imagine what the babysitters must think of us or, rather, me. Generally as they arrive I am cooking tea for two children and feeding Jack in his high chair, with my hair in rollers as I try to put make-up on. Katie, the babysitter who looks as if she just walked out of a Timotei advert, has been let into the house by Will only to see me running up the stairs in my bra and pants, rollers bobbing up and down, shoving a fish finger sandwich into my mouth.

The food is always the same: Nutella sandwiches, ham sandwiches, pizza, fish fingers or scrambled egg. Sometimes broccoli. I would feel bad about this but they get a decent meal at school at lunchtime and I can't beat myself up about everything. I'll give them organic vegetables when the Directionless Comedy Binge is over. 'Mum, when are you going to make pancakes?' They ask this nearly every day. About once a week I make pancakes and it's like Mary Poppins has come to visit and everything is going to be okay. Except Mary Poppins is semi-naked, wearing heated rollers, trying to apply foundation and mascara at the same time and fiddling with her laptop to try and recharge her video camera.

The domestic mess comes to a head at the weekend. Simon is barely speaking to me and I feel so guilty. After the children go to bed, an almighty row erupts. I start it. 'Why are you so frustrated? Do you still think this is a Directionless Comedy Binge? You do, don't you? It's not directionless. I'm trying to improve. I am improving. I am getting somewhere. It's not going to happen overnight. But I can't do it without your support. I can't do it at all if it means it's going to break us up.

I need to know that you're okay with me doing it.'

There is a long pause while Simon evidently tries to decide how honest he can be with me. And whether he is going to offer me an ultimatum. I can feel something inside me go cold as I realise that he might be about to say that I have to give it all up. Eventually he sighs, 'You are just so caught up in it all, that's all. And it's relentless.' 'But you knew it was going to be like that when I decided to do it and you agreed to me doing it.' 'I guess I didn't realise quite how relentless it would be.'

'It's going to be over in less than a month,' I say, trying to sound cheerful. In fact it's more than a month. And I cannot disguise the fact that I am scheduled to be out every single night for the next seven weeks. 'Barely weeks to go. And then I'll be at home the whole time.' 'No, you won't,' he says, 'you will just do more gigs. I would not be surprised if after doing these hundred gigs you just do another hundred gigs.'

Oh dear. Now he has hit upon something I have already thought about and considered, although I also know it's madness. I realised very close to the start of the experiment that in terms of performance and knowledge and experience and contacts, this is the only way to do anything. The more time has gone on, the more I've realised how true this is. Immerse yourself, practise, fail, improve, fail more, expose yourself to more opportunities, more people, more failure.

This is the cost–reward ratio. Improved performance traded for a worse marriage. The more I gig and the closer together the gigs, the better I get. The more I fail, the more I improve. I can see that this is just the start. How much worse is my marriage going to get until I get good enough to do comedy properly? I don't need to do a hundred gigs. I need to do a thousand gigs. I need to do ten thousand gigs. And that is not even going to get me up to the ten thousand hours' practice that they say you need to get remotely skilled at anything because I only get about five or ten minutes of stage time at a time. This is the worst thing about stand-up. There is no shortcut to getting in front of an audience.

I say all this. Simon turns red in the face. He looks as if he will explode. When I stop talking, he picks up a toilet roll which is sitting next to him on the table, and throws it at my head. It misses. It's more exasperation than anger, like when a child smashes up their favourite toy because they're frustrated the batteries have run out. I am shocked. I have never seen Simon throw anything before. But I am also amused at the fact that he has ended up throwing, of all things, a soft white toilet roll. Or rather, pale-ish grey, not white, because it's a recycled one. I burst out laughing. He storms out of the room and, later, out of the house. We don't speak for another few hours.

'You know I would choose you over this any time,' I say when he comes back, 'I don't want to continue doing this if it is going to break us up. You only have to say the word and I will just stop it. I don't have to go to a hundred days. I don't have to go to a hundred gigs. It's not as if anything is riding on it. Come on, we have had this conversation before.' He looks relieved. 'But that's the thing,' he says, defeated, 'I can't exactly prohibit you from doing it. I know that you feel like you need to do this.'

'I do need to do this,' I admit. I sound like some tragic drug addict, when there is no real defence for me to carry on taking my drugs but I am going to do it anyway. 'I need to get it out of my system and work out if this is what I am supposed to be doing and, awful though all this has turned out to be, I honestly think this is the least painful way of doing it.' As I am desperate and we have really reached a low point, I raise the spectre of the alternative. 'Would you rather I did four or five gigs a week for a year? At least I'm doing it in a really concentrated way so it's only disruptive to us for three months. Three months! It's nothing. We'll be back to normal before you know it.'

'I'm just worried that all of this is eventually going to take you away from us,' he says, sadly. Oh. He thinks I am going to leave him. 'Oh for God's sake,' I say, trying to make a joke of it, 'if I wanted to leave you, I would just leave you. I would not do bloody stand-up comedy instead of just leaving you. Leaving would be a lot less effort and a lot less humiliating and time-consuming.' He laughs. But only a bit.

16: Gigs 73 to 77:

'You had them at the beginning!'

Day 77, no gig

As usual I could not get a Saturday night gig. So instead I went round to friends for dinner with Simon. I am definitely going mad because I felt I would be more comfortable at a gig. Shocking to have a normal life. Strange not to be gigging. Preoccupied by the whole 'homewrecker' thing. (Have realised that is what I am.)

Day 78, Gig 73: Gipsy Hill

Trying to ignore the fact that I have not had a gig in three nights and the numbers are looking extremely dodgy. How am I ever going to catch up? Friendly, happy gig with lively MC and lively old-school one-liner acts. It felt like there were about fifty-seven acts (okay, fourteen) and so it went on late but fairly enjoyable. As these things go.

Day 79, Gig 74: Islington

Ah, the reliable 'nice' gig from the early days. Another useful, fun gig with a warm, receptive audience. Not some huge highlight but lovely enough to keep me from despair.

Day 80, Gig 75: Kentish Town

Aaargh. The Red Room of Pain again. I hate this gig. Am I doomed always to bomb in this hideous room? I had maybe two jokes that landed. Horrific.

Day 81, Gig 76: Brighton

Totally lost my voice. Used antiseptic spray to get it back for ten minutes (count them!). Still bombed. Great rider: biscuits, bananas, KitKats.

Day 82, two gigs cancelled: Islington, Farringdon

Voice totally gone so no choice but to cancel the chance to double up tonight. I could not have done this more against my own will. I would have done anything to get to these gigs as I really needed them to push the numbers back up again. Eighty-two days and six gigs behind. I just don't even know if I can do it now.

Day 83, Gig 77: Richmond

Voice back. Dream gig. Hardly any audience but lively, warm room and people who understood my jokes and just LIKED me. Allowed myself to feel smug for about seven minutes.

*

Whether I can make the numbers work and get to a hundred or not, all this is going to be over soon. It's just hard to know whether I'll be able to say that it has been worth it. I'm not sure I ever meant to put things at home under so much pressure. I guess I tried to ignore how difficult it would be for Simon because thinking about that was inconvenient for me. If I'd really thought about it properly I would never have done any of this.

It's not enough any more for me to say that I did this because I had some burning compulsion to be a stand-up or some long-buried childhood wish. I've put too much on the line for that to be the only thing behind it. What I've done is not some simple midlife change; it's a massive disruption. It's scratching some itch I can't even define. What makes anyone change direction in life like this? Is it arbitrary? Do we work our way towards the things that are meant to be? Is it supposed to be this difficult?

Long before I even dreamed of doing the one hundred gigs and around the time I first found out that you can learn how to do stand-up, I was writing an article about childhood influences. I wasn't supposed to be writing about my own life – I was interviewing other people about the figures who had inspired them – but every time I started an interview on the subject the face of Doris Schwartz would pop into my head. What was she doing there? I could see her in my mind's eye, standing at the microphone, happier on stage than off, gesticulating wildly, lost in her own thoughts, talking nineteen to the dozen. A hot feeling came over me when I thought of her; it felt something like shame and regret. I had not turned out anything like Doris. The part of me that was like Doris was non-existent. What had happened? How could I just have forgotten her?

Around the same time, I was seeing a careers counsellor who was a friend of a friend. I was hoping she was going to help me work out what to do since I'd lost a couple of work contracts. I thought she'd put together some kind of schedule for me or make me rework my CV or something. Instead she asked, 'What's the one thing you want to do which has nothing to do with what you're doing now?' I didn't blink. The image of Doris Schwartz flashed back into my head. The words 'stand-up comedy' popped out of my mouth before I could stop them. And there was Doris looking at me, smiling expectantly. 'But there is no reason for me to do stand-up comedy,' I protested quickly, worried that this woman would force me to do it. Or was it that I wanted to be forced to do it? Why had it come out of my mouth? Oh, for God's sake, Doris, why don't you bugger off? This was the last thing I needed in my life at that moment.

I tried to focus on other things I wanted out of life to try and put this woman off the stand-up comedy. 'I also want to have another child, by the way.' (This was true. And I was trying to work out how I could square the fact that I was feeling miserable in my work and looking for some new, unknown direction with the fact that I wanted some security because I wanted to have a third child.) She wasn't going to let it go.

'Let's just set aside any thoughts of expanding your family for now,' she said. 'Is there a course you can do or somewhere you can go to try out the comedy thing?' 'Yes,' I mumbled, 'I suppose there is. Well, I know there is. I read about it.' 'So what's stopping you? The money? The time?' 'Both. Except it's not impossible. It's on a Saturday so my husband could look after the children.' 'So what you're saying is that nothing's stopping you?' 'I guess not.'

I was angry but also confused. I was torn between elation and dread. I suppose I could have ignored this woman's advice. But she was a friend of a friend. What was the point of consulting her if I didn't pay attention? And anyway, would it really be so terrible if I went on some stupid course? I might enjoy it. It would not mean I had to become a stand-up comedian. I read and reread the workshop information. You learned how to write jokes. You learned how to use a microphone. You met other people who were interested in comedy. Crucially, the small print said that you didn't even have to do a gig. That sold me. I could just do it to learn more about comedy. I would not do a gig. I certainly would not become a stand-up comedian. No, I definitely did not need to become a stand-up comedian. That's for sure! I made Doris into a pinhead in my mind. Get lost, Doris, I do not need you in my life. I'm doing this my way. I know best.

So this is how it came about that a month later I did the comedy workshop with Logan Murray. It was a weird set-up, like an AA meeting in a pub downstairs in Covent Garden. A group of about twenty people sitting awkwardly on chairs in a circle, some of them already stand-ups, some of them best men working on wedding speeches, some people not really sure why they were there. I was excited about what we were doing and very pleased when one exercise I did, a spoof Sylvia Plath tribute poem, got a good reception in class. (Oh, how we laughed.) But I didn't see how this would translate to actual stand-up comedy in front of an audience. Everyone I had told about the course said the same thing: 'If you're doing it with that group of people, don't you all just collude to make each other think you're funny? You won't be able to make anyone else laugh apart from the people in that group.' I tried not to think about this, concentrated on enjoying the fact that Logan Murray was brilliant (which he is) and focused on the fact that I would get as much as possible out of the course without performing.

By week three I was completely evangelical and had signed up to the end-of-course showcase after all, giving myself the excuse that 'If I don't do it, I will be letting the group down.' I still batted poor Doris away in my head and pretended to myself that I was not that interested in stand-up comedy and was just having an early midlife crisis. When Logan said things like, 'Of course, if you want to do stand-up properly then you will have to get past a hundred gigs as quickly as possible', I just laughed and thought, 'That is not relevant to me. I am a journalist.' Unfortunately, somewhere much deeper in my subconscious this fact lodged and then eventually conspired to take over my life.

But anyway. I did my first gig at the Lion's Den in King's Cross, a legendary try-out for first (and sometimes last) gigs, forgetting my words halfway through and fishing a piece of paper out of my pocket. It was compèred by a cute young MC called Tyrone Atkins, who runs gigs across London with new-ish acts. I got my first laugh when he handed me the microphone saying, 'Good luck, love,' and patted me pityingly on the shoulder. 'Hmm. That wasn't patronising or anything,' I replied. Doing it for the first time was mortifying, it was horrific, it was wonderful. Most of all, it was intriguing. There was something about it that I found fascinating. You only got five minutes up there but the connection with the audience when it worked – in the tiny moments when it did work – was incredible. You felt you were breathing at the same time as everyone in the room. I barely slept that night.

During this period I visited a friend in Washington DC when I was working in the US for a few days and she persuaded me to do an open mic gig there. I had no idea whether the Americans would understand me or whether I would be able to do ten minutes' worth of material. (At London open mic the norm is five minutes. In the US it's ten. Which, believe me, is a long time.) But I liked the idea of being able to say, 'Hello Washington DC!' so I did it. I wasn't great. But I was okay. And I was discovering that I was capable of surviving gigs that weren't that great and learning from them.

I kept in touch with other people from my course and vowed to support them on the circuit. I put on a gig for my birthday and made myself into the MC. I went to the Edinburgh Festival – as a punter – for the first time and loved it. I did seven gigs in about six months. That is not a number that is going to set the comedy world on fire. All this time I was still pushing Doris to the back of my mind, as if it were just for fun and meant very little to me. Weirdly, the happier I was doing my little bits and pieces of comedy, the easier I seemed to find my journalism. Suddenly I was inspired again. I had more ideas. I was more confident dealing with people.

Then two things happened. Someone I knew was killed in a freak accident. And I got pregnant with my much-wanted third child. One of the people who had come to see the gig in Washington DC was a guy called Ian, the English boyfriend of a friend of a friend who was working in the US. I had barely met him or spoken to him, but I felt bonded with him because he had come to see the gig to support me, another Brit in town, and he had said something to me afterwards that had made me laugh and cringe at the same time. He rushed up to me as I came off stage, hugged me and said, accurately and with great sympathy, 'You had them at the beginning!' It was a brilliant assessment of my performance, which had started riotously well and descended into embarrassing tumbleweed amid a stream of ill-advised gags about Michelle Obama visiting the Queen's vegetable garden. Although I didn't really know him, I felt very warmly towards him. He was one of the first people to give me feedback on my comedy. He had liked it. Even if only the beginning bit.

Ian was killed a couple of weeks later in a climbing accident. He was an outdoorsy type who was often going off to do rock climbing and abseiling; that was his idea of a fun weekend. He was on a routine climb when one of his ropes snapped. His death was none of my business – I had only met him and his girlfriend once so I could hardly pretend to be bereaved – but something about it preyed on my mind. Possibly because I had liked him so much, just from one meeting. Possibly because whenever anyone young – he was about forty – dies in a freak accident, it's upsetting because it's so unfair and pointless. Or possibly just because at this point hardly anyone had seen me do comedy and he, a stranger, had seen it and been supportive about it. Even though it wasn't very good. A big sign just flashed up in my mind: 'Life. Is. Short.' You can guess who was holding the sign: bloody Doris.

At the time, this in and of itself didn't make much immediate difference to how I viewed life, though. We like to think that big things like this affect us, the sudden waste of the life of someone we didn't really know. We think things like that will help us to wake up and do the things we really ought to be doing with our lives. But of course this does not happen. Usually we think, 'Wow, that's a wake-up call,' and then do nothing. Which for the moment is exactly what I did.

Around the same time, though – probably exactly around the time that I did the comedy showcase, which was my third ever gig – I got pregnant. I was exceedingly happy as I desperately wanted a third child. Things were improving at work by this point and I felt more in control. (Otherwise I would have not have tried to have another baby. I can be reckless but not that reckless.) By the time I went up to Edinburgh to watch other people's shows and support some comics I knew who had got through to competition heats, I was about ten weeks pregnant, enjoying the secrecy of not drinking and feeling impatient about the twelve-week scan when we would be able to tell the children, who were then aged five and three, that they would be having a brother or a sister. Doris and her sign receded a bit.

My first pregnancy scan was delayed to thirteen weeks for various reasons, and the day before I was due to turn twelve weeks I was flying to America again for work. I decided to get a scan done privately because I felt superstitious about going on a flight without having had a scan. The fact that I was thinking about something going wrong should perhaps have already shown me that something was wrong. But I was oblivious because I felt fine and had a blooming bump.

That morning, as I lay on the couch with the ultrasound jelly turning cold on my stomach and the doctor frowning, not wanting to make eye contact and saying nothing as he pushed the probe into my skin, I knew. 'It's not alright, is it?' The doctor said, 'I'm sorry.' The baby had died probably about four weeks previously, before I'd even gone to Edinburgh. It was a 'missed miscarriage', when the pregnancy is over but your body still thinks everything is fine and carries on as if you are still going to have a baby. Even though the pregnancy had ended a month before, I looked twelve weeks gone. I tend to put on a lot of weight when I get pregnant. Turns out I put on a lot of weight even when I'm not pregnant but just think I am.

I know it happens to people every day but I was devastated. The flight to the US was cancelled and I booked into hospital that day for an operation instead. Then life went on as normal. I went to the US a week afterwards because work is work and they do care about these things, but only up to a point. I started thinking about whether I really wanted a third baby after all. And suddenly, despite all the revelations and Simon saying 'this is the most relaxed I've seen you in five years' and the friend's boyfriend who had died unexpectedly, comedy definitely did not seem like the biggest fun to me any more. I had one gig booked in, about a month after the miscarriage. I suppose really I should have cancelled it but there was something in me that forced me to go through with it. I wrote a load of embittered, terrible material about miscarriage, because it was the only thing I was thinking about at the time. ('Bad news: I've had a miscarriage. Good news: I can go back on my diet.' Oh how hilarious.)

In the end, I ditched all those terrible 'jokes' about half an hour before the gig because I felt sorry for the audience and thought it wasn't fair on them to make them listen to that stuff. I at least had that much sense. (Although I now slightly regret not having done that material as it would have been an entertaining car crash and a good lesson for me.) Instead I just did some old jokes from my first gigs and some impressions of my younger sister, Trudy. The impressions were helpful because people found that bit really funny. Sorry, Trudy. But my heart wasn't in it any more. A couple of friends had come to see me. I can remember one of them saying to me in the bar afterwards, when I was relaxed, 'See how funny you're being now!' 'Yeah. I know,' I said back, 'it's all very well being funny when it's too late. I can't be that funny on stage. It comes and goes.' I didn't plan to do any more gigs. I just wanted to have another baby. I didn't want to think about all the other stuff that was wrong with my life. And I definitely did not want to put myself under pressure to make people laugh.

Another six months passed. I did not do any gigs. I did not think about Doris bloody Schwartz. I thought about Ian, the man who had died pointlessly in the climbing accident. I thought about the baby I had lost. And I thought a lot about my grandparents who raised me, who had died in the previous ten years. I tried to get pregnant again. I got pregnant. I worried. I thought maybe I was not meant to have a third child and something bad would happen. I became extremely large. By the time I was about six months pregnant, I was going to comedy improv classes. If I couldn't face going on stage, I could face going to class. Again, allegedly, like the first time round with the workshop, this was 'just for fun' and not because it was what I wanted to do with my life.

During class I started to realise that I was potentially laughable to look at because I was so enormous. I had a prominent, space-hopper bump that was only going to grow bigger. It struck me that it was too good to waste and I would not be that physically funny for a long time or possibly ever again. I wrote a pregnancy rap, performed it with a Ting Tings' 'That's Not My Name' backing track and booked in some gigs. 'They call me bloater, they call me bowling ball, they call me spacehopper, they call me blimp. That's not my name. That's not my name.' It was borderline demented and I very much enjoyed it. 'They call me large for dates, they call me heavyweight, they call me incontinent, that's not inaccurate. That's not my name.'

I began to think of myself as a person who might do stand-up again. I booked in a few more gigs and started writing what I thought of as 'pregnancy patter'. Opening gag: 'This is awkward. I don't know anything about any of you. But you all know I've had sex.' 'Performing in this state [point to bump] is difficult. If you don't laugh, I will cry. If you do laugh, I'll think you're laughing at me. It's a lose-lose situation. Like childbirth. If it goes wrong, I die. If it doesn't go wrong, I have a baby.' These jokes wouldn't last beyond forty weeks but I didn't want to think about what would happen after I had the baby and whether I'd go on with comedy. So I didn't care. I did my bad pregnancy jokes and my Ting Tings song. Mostly people liked it, although one comic did send me a message on Facebook which said, 'Can you play a musical instrument? Because I think that might help.'

Then just as I was about to have my baby – and, hooray, I did have my third baby, although he was three weeks late, which was scary – some odd things started happening. While I was busy thinking, 'I definitely don't want to be a stand-up. I'm a journalist', other people were noticing that I did stand-up and asking me to help out at things. I was basically free of charge, which was popular. I told myself that you don't have to be that funny if you come for free. If they wanted guaranteed funny they would have booked Michael McIntyre.

When the baby, who turned out to be Jack, was a few weeks

old, I was booked to perform at an event sponsored by Nigella Lawson. I ridiculed her brownies. I was booked to host Jo Brand's book tour. I raced her down the aisles of a theatre in Worthing and let her win. (It wasn't much of a race as I was heavily lactating and had just spent half an hour milking myself in the front seat of my car in Waitrose car park. And Jo Brand is, well, Jo Brand.) I was booked to do a charity gig with Sandi Toksvig where I insulted her trademark Showaddywaddy suit and she came back with the biggest laugh of the night: 'She criticised my suit? Bless her Primark soul.'

I let it all happen without thinking too much about it. Then, about six weeks after I had Jack, I was doing a charity gig in Richmond hosted by the TV presenter Gabby Logan where a couple of comics who were supposed to turn up didn't and so I ended up being the 'headliner'. The audience had paid about £50 a ticket. I did my best for them. To my amazement, they did not seem to mind that I was not a proper headliner. If you put yourself in front of people as a comedian, they tend to believe you are one – until your bad material and poor delivery prove otherwise. One night with Jo Brand there was a terrible moment when someone in the audience shouted, 'You're a comedian, Viv, tell us a joke' and I found myself telling an awful, half-remembered children's joke. 'How do you catch a squirrel? Climb to the top of a tree and act like a nut.' This was terrible. But no one minded, not even Jo Brand. And so my delusion was maintained. Encouraged, even.

Doris continued to picket my brain with her sign. 'Life. Is. Short.' I began to feel sorry for Doris. She spent the entire six series of *Fame* trying to get attention and being ignored, especially by Bruno Martelli, who was destined to be with Doris if only he could just see it. Did she really deserve to be ignored by me too? Or was I ready to sit up and listen and do something about the sign she kept waving in my face? It took me about twenty years, two dead grandparents, the death of a person I didn't even really know, one miscarriage and a new baby to realise it. I needed to pay some attention to Doris. The only thing was, now I'd paid her a bit too much.

17: Gigs 78 to 82:

'It's very rarely as bad as you think it is'

Day 84, Gig 78: Truro

Announced as 'headline' act to very drunk, very young crowd who had had a long night of very strange acts. Happy with my stuff but difficult to keep control of a rowdy late-night crowd. Survived. Got some petrol money. Result!

Day 85, Gig 79: Brixton

So-called 'urban' gig (predominantly black audience). Weirdly popular with the gentlemen. This is code for 'accosted by chubby chasers'.

Day 86, Gig 80: King's Cross

Demented, unsuccessful set against a wallpaper backdrop in a room above pub that looks like someone's living room. Humiliating. WHEN WILL THIS HELL BE OVER?

Day 87, Gig 81: King's Cross

'Weirdos' comedy night too weird for most of the audience. Bombed, basically, except for one comic laughing at the back. I'll take it.

Day 87, Gig 82: King's Cross

Two gigs in one night. Gong show. Almost got to five minutes. Better than fifty-two seconds at the Comedy Store. Fun night. Good comics.

*

Throughout this experiment I have been strategically releasing footage for Simon to watch in order to prove to him that it's all worthwhile and that I am getting better. Occasionally I've shown him bad gigs so he can understand the difficulties. The one video I have suppressed is the Just Be Funny gig because it is too humiliating. Now the end is in sight and Simon needs to understand why I've put us through all this, I decide it is time to embrace it.

Once he has watched the video footage he can see that it was an incredibly frustrating experience. He also thinks it wasn't as bad as I was making out before he saw the video. He finally understands what it's like to live through these gigs. Maybe the gig itself is not that bad. But if you're the one standing up there, it can feel like hell.

His body language when he is watching the Just be Funny gig is hilarious. He is visibly wincing and cringing. I can hear the soundtrack as he watches (I cannot bear to watch it myself). There's my voice booming out crystal clear because there are no laughs punctuating anything. Usually if someone gets a joke but they don't like it, you can hear a disgusted exhalation of breath, 'Cuh'. It is the sound of an audience member's disappointment and disbelief. It says: 'I can't believe you just told that joke.' It says: 'That is not really a joke at all.' It says: 'Get off stage now.' There were quite a few of those. He has only watched a few seconds, though, when he pauses the video.

'I thought you said he said you were a journalist and that put you off?' 'He did. Honestly, it was horrendous.' He looks at me, perplexed, scrolls back and listens again. 'You can't hear him say it. Are you sure he said it? Watch it.' Reluctantly I watch it back. He is right. Very near to the end of his introduction, the promoter muttered in passing something that sounded like 'journalist', but the audience was already applauding and didn't really care what he was talking about by that point. I had heard it, of course, and it had screamed out to me like the voice of God on Judgement Day. But no one else had caught it. I had gone into massive panic attack mode and ruined my own set for nothing.

'You experience things very differently to how they actually happen,' Simon says. 'Now I have no idea whether to believe anything you ever say about any of your gigs. It's very rarely as bad as you think it is. Maybe it's never as bad as you think it is. I just don't get why you do this to yourself.' I didn't get it either, but I was not going to admit that to him. 'Well, thank goodness for the video evidence,' I say, brightly, 'if you watch on, you will see that objectively I did die.' 'Yes, I can see that,' he says.

This footage helps, though, because in the recent videos I'm so much better. My own attitude to gigs is also improving. I keep bumping into comics I like. Seeing them makes it all worthwhile. There's Chris, the man with the unicorn joke (I would tell it but it's very long and convoluted). David, an Australian comic with a dry wit who was the first person to tell me about Dr Brown. Gemma, the MC at Comedy Virgins who has a line in wry, caustic asides about life in south London. Tim Shishodia, the 'oddball newcomer' who has been compared to Tony Hancock and is still my most favourite act on the circuit ever – I could watch him all night. Shishodia also shares my violent dislike of acts who arrive at a comedy venue and order food. 'What's wrong with them? Why can't they eat at home? Why would you order a lasagne if you were about to do a gig?'

But it has to be a special night for all the people you love to be there at once. And sometimes there is no one. There are lots of cliques and groups on the amateur stand-up circuit. These groups are informal and unintentional and people don't even really notice that they're in them, but if you arrive at a night run by a clique it can feel pretty lonely. There are a lot of gigs that aren't on everyone's radar because they're not in the right group. By doing so many gigs in such a short space of time, I have managed to sidestep getting caught up in any group and I have been able to get on lots of different bills with lots of different people. But I've also ended up a bit of an odd bod, not really having my own group of people that I belong with.

For once, though, at the Alternative Comedy Memorial Society, I find somewhere where I really, really want to belong. This is a special gig and it feels like the right place for me. It is run by Thom Tuck, nominated for a Best Newcomer award at Edinburgh a few months previously, and John-Luke Roberts, who writes lots of BBC Radio 4's comedy output. I don't know either of them well but I have seen them perform at Karaoke Circus, the musical comedy night that used to be on at the Royal Vauxhall Tavern among other places.

I suppose if you were going to say that there's an indie comedy scene, they would be part of it. 'Indie comedy scene': is that an embarrassing thing to say? Do I sound like a High Court judge talking about The Beatles? Yes. But never mind. It's like the difference between Josie Long and Sarah Millican – hip versus mainstream. On the semi-pro circuit it's the difference between people who dream of playing a stag night at Jongleurs and people who want to play a weird, undiscovered venue where Dr Brown is headlining. I can't say that I feel I fit in either camp at the moment. But no one is asking me to play Jongleurs. And yet I do seem to be able to get on the bill of these more random gigs which are less about straight stand-up and more about experimentation.

I end up going on second and do well. This is an audience where you can do jokes about Betty Friedan and (a) no one minds and (b) some people actually get them. And the MC is doubled up laughing, which is always a good sign. I can't quite explain what turns a gig from a bog-standard stand-up gig into one that celebrates alternative comedy, because there are plenty of comics who move between the two extremes. I have noticed, however, that when there is a feel of alternative comedy, the venue usually smells better. This is because alternative comedians are less likely to wear Lynx aftershave.

I am happier among this crowd but I have no idea whether what I do can be classed as 'alternative' or just, as Simon might put it, 'an alternative to comedy'. I did eventually get into the Actors Centre workshop with the punk comedian Tony Allen, the self-styled 'king of attitude'. He helps you to work out what's unique about you and sell it to the audience. Unfortunately, he could not really tell what was unique about me or whether I could be classed as 'alternative'. What he said to me instead was this: 'For someone who is not exactly slim, you come across as very self-possessed.' This was almost certainly code for: 'I would have thought someone as fat as you would be a lot more insecure.'

The one interesting thing he did say is probably true of all good stand-ups: 'You don't need props. You don't need nuffink. You just need the clothes you're standing up in.' Unfortunately the one piece of clothing I really liked to stand up in was my Statement Cardigan. He would have thought that was rubbish, an unnecessary crutch. But it was pretty much all I had and I was sticking with it.

It had indeed got to the point now where that cardigan could virtually stand up on its own. In fact it could have pretty much done the gig. I couldn't live without it. It was 'hand wash only'. And took ages to dry. Which is why I never washed it (or, more accurately, asked Simon to wash it because at this point he was doing all of the laundry). And so the unfortunate cardigan kept on going on stage, masked by more and more Prada Candy and deodorant, but never quite masking the smell of stale sweat, a stand-up set which has passed its sell-by date and the unmistakable stench of desperation.

After a while I stopped caring about whether I smelled good or not. I was just marking time. I was chalking up the gigs and the hours and the money spent on Diet Coke (now in excess of £250). I had by this point decided that it was kind of pointless making an effort anyway, because even if you smell nice, you're soon engulfed by the smell of everything around you – which, for once, at the Alternative Comedy Memorial Society, was not the smell of failure and self-loathing. Oh, no, that was just around the corner at the next gig that night, Party Piece, a gig in a pub in King's Cross where I had one of my first early, amazing gigs, which I think of as the Clock Gig (because in the video I am standing in front of a massive clock). I always have fond memories of this gig because I love the MC, Tom Webb, and because I did well there and it really set me up in the early days of this experiment, before I became jaded and demented. On that day it all smelled fresh and exciting.

Today, though, it's a different story. Tom is not MC-ing, there's not much of a crowd and I'm tired and overwhelmed and too pumped up from how exciting the previous, non-smelly gig was. I get up and do five minutes but I'm not interesting or engaging and I don't capture the room's attention. This is turning into a pattern. I'll have one really good gig to two or three bad ones. I'm getting the feeling that the truly awful, mega-death ones have sort of stopped now – or at least if they're truly awful I don't ascribe the failure simply to me. I can see more easily how and why things are likely to go wrong. I can walk in the door and know that the light is in the wrong place or the audience is too far back or the MC has a bad vibe. I don't know yet quite how to get over these things but I know that I'm learning. Before I would have just had a bad gig and blamed myself for being rubbish. Now I know when I'm rubbish and when the circumstances make it difficult to be anything other than rubbish. What I need to work on is transcending the circumstances. And not always being rubbish.

This comes together from time to time. This is also the week that I survive my first 'urban' gig. And if that is not transcending circumstances, I don't know what is. I had no idea what an urban gig was; turns out it means 'no white people'. This rule is not literally enforced, nor does anyone speak it out loud. A hip, talented young comic called Junior Booker has invited me to do his 'urban talent night' in Brixton. I'm happy about this because it's a Sunday night and Brixton is not inconvenient to get to and I like Junior Booker's stuff. He is known on the circuit for having a 'very tight five minutes'. Translation: he's really good and the laughs come thick and fast. I've done a lot of gigs with him and he always does well.

The two of us could not be more different, however. He is young, cool, makes jokes about taking ketamine and fathering illegitimate children. I am pushing forty, the only substance I take on a regular basis is evening primrose oil and I have a Mothercare charge card. One time I gave Junior a lift to the station in my car from a gig. When he got into the car, the passenger seat was virtually horizontal because the last time I had been in it, Simon was driving and I had gone to sleep on a long journey. Junior was so embarrassed to be sat in a seven-seater Volkswagen Touran driven by me that he kept the seat exactly where it was, hidden from view to the outside world. If anyone had looked in the window they would have seen a flushed, harassed middle-aged woman in a replica 1940s Cath Kidston tea dress driving an attractive, young black dude in a puffer jacket with a beanie pulled down over his forehead, lying prostrate in the passenger seat. It looked like a drugs heist sponsored by John Lewis.

So I appreciate Junior reaching out to me when we are poles apart. And I am intensely intrigued to know what his 'urban night' will turn out to be. As soon as I walk in the door, all my suspicions are confirmed: there are indeed no white people anywhere. Now I know what it feels like to be an ethnic minority. I try to look cool and unfazed when in reality I am quite frightened. I worry that if I reveal that I am feeling nervous and out of place this will make me seem racist. I have already accepted that my car – which I have parked around the corner – is unlikely to survive the night unscathed. That is not a racist comment, that is a Brixtonist comment. Although to be fair the last time I was here for a gig I got a £65 parking ticket that was entirely my fault (caused by the fact that I am too dismissively middle class to read road signs correctly). It probably would have been cheaper if I had parked legally but the car had been broken into.

There's another comic I know here. I also like him – Mr Blair. He's a big, beefy guy who specialises in accents and punctuates his set with big belly laughs, a sort of Barry White of comedy. I do like a comic with a funny laugh. As the place fills up, I realise that I am the only white act as well as the only white person. I wonder if I am supposed to do my act or whether I am meant to just stand there and let people laugh at me. Turns out to be a bit of both. It's a bar where most of the audience is sitting on sofas and chatting among themselves. There is no real stage and no real spotlight. And yet somehow you are expected to command their attention. It's just me and my (now broken again) miniature keyboard, which I can't really use without a microphone stand and there is no mic stand here.

I stand in front of the assembled sofa-seated crowd of around thirty and feel like Penelope Keith addressing the Women's Institute in *To the Manor Born*. (High status! Good, surely?) I have all the Tinie Tempah and Jessie J material so I bust all that out and the room falls silent. They have not heard a serious, teacher-like white woman wearing a Michelle Obama women's activism T-shirt ('Yes We Can!') trying to rap before. There is silence for a while as they look on, shocked. And then the laughter spreads. They aren't really paying huge amounts of attention, I'm just like a fun YouTube viral video playing in the background. But they don't hate me and it's better than being booed.

I am also popular in other, unanticipated ways. Afterwards I am approached by several men who want to 'get with me' because I have 'got it going on.' This is a veiled appreciation of morbid obesity. It's flattering. In a backhanded compliment kind of way. But I need to get out of there. When I get back to the car there is no parking ticket and no vandalism. It's a miracle. Junior messages me afterwards: 'Great performance, Viv. Everybody loved you.' I think they may have loved me for the wrong reasons. I was a bit fat. I made inappropriate racial references. I was ridiculous at rapping. But you take what you're given. And that will do me nicely.

18: Gigs 83 and 84:

'Just be as weird as possible.
That's why we booked you.'

Day 88, Gig 83: Brighton

Bloody pianist. I blame him for not laughing at me enough.

Day 89, Gig 84: Brighton

Tough gig but some people liked my performance. Several did not.

Day 90, cancelled gig: Gipsy Hill

Slightly hysterical about this gig being cancelled after I had driven an hour and twenty minutes to get to it. Went for a curry with a friend who had turned up to watch instead. Three hours spent thinking, 'I am still normal. I can still go out for dinner.' I miss going out for dinner.

*

If I hear any of the following phrases ever again, I will not be responsible for my actions.

I love internet porn.
Get in.
Strap in.

Boom.

Have you ever noticed that … ?

Is it just me or … ?

If I hear one more reference to bukkake, vibrators, Two Girls, One Cup, bell-ends or fat girlfriends who look like beached whales who need rescuing by Greenpeace, I will shoot myself. (If you do not know what 'bukkake' is, please do not look it up on a computer. It is basically a Japanese practice where men abuse a woman in the most unpleasant manner. It is frequently depicted in pornographic films. Apparently. I only know about it because of stand-up comedy. And I wish I did not know about it at all. I do know that it is also a sort of hot noodle dish and it is best if we think of it in that context.)

That said, one of the recent Brighton gigs, number 83 (the one with the sullen pianist), had buoyed me up because it was one of the good ones. I asked what the tone of the night was and how long I should do. The bespectacled student type running the night said earnestly: 'Just be as weird as possible. That's why we booked you.' That I can do. Fairly quiet audience but I could feel that they didn't hate me, they just didn't want to laugh out loud. This is what I am telling myself. Is this the first sign of delusion? 'They just don't want to laugh out loud.' Indeed. What am I becoming? I once heard a story of a comedienne who watched one of her best friends sit through an hour of her material without once cracking a smile. It nearly killed her to keep going. Afterwards she said to her friend, 'Wow. You really hated it. I could see it on your face.' Her friend replied, 'Oh, no. I loved it. That is my listening face.'

It didn't help that there was a man on the stage sitting at the piano throughout my entire act and it's always distracting for the audience when there is someone on stage whom they are not supposed to be watching but whom they cannot help seeing. I rewarded myself with a rare gin and tonic and fish and chips on the seafront on the way back to my single hotel room where the 'trendy' theme is that everything is knitted, including the lampshade and a knitted seagull sitting on the corner of the lonely single person's bathroom sink. It appeared to leer at me, mocking and pitying. In my gin-induced euphoria, I found it endearing.

I have come to Brighton for three nights to get away from the London circuit and to try to shake off the self-hatred that has set in. I've almost always had really good gigs in Brighton so it seemed like the place to go to make me feel better about myself. Comedy crowds are kinder in Brighton: they are happier people, they are less jaded. It's a numbers game, really: there aren't as many comedy nights as there are in London, so if people have chosen to come out, then in Brighton they're really looking forward to it and they're really up for it. That is the sort of audience you want.

Plus, people in Brighton always seem so much more relaxed. They listen hard, they laugh easily, they go out of their way to be supportive to the acts. It's not that that doesn't happen anywhere else; it can happen a lot, especially at certain nights in London. But it's just not guaranteed the way it is in Brighton.

There's always an exception that proves the rule. I suffered one gig at a wine bar with a theatre space in the back room where I just bombed horribly. This failure was compounded by the fact that one of the acts, a young comic called Ingrid who had done hardly any gigs, had come up to me and said, 'Wow. You've got amazing credits next to your name. You've met Jo Brand! You must be really good.' This is always the kiss of death. Five minutes after she said this, she watched me go on stage and be completely rubbish. Ingrid then went on and was amazing. It's like Jo Brand says, 'Viv is brilliant. But I still quite like Billy Connolly.' I can occassionally be brilliant. But I am not there yet.

This is a big reminder of how humiliating this business is. It's hard to plug away doing your apprenticeship while still bigging yourself up the whole time too. Ideally I would never mention whom I've gigged with, what reviews people have given me and what competitions I've gone through in – because it's all just embarrassing and, really, if you were that amazing, then why are you not already on the telly? In reality you have to play the game. It's important for the promoters, even the ones in charge of small, free, open mic nights which no one comes to. Even they need to think that they're giving stage time to people who are going somewhere. So you have to make it sound like you're going somewhere – even if in reality the only place you are going is straight on stage for another live stage death.

That said, one night in Brighton is fantastic. Not because of my performance, which is mediocre. But because of the atmosphere at the gig and because of being able to spend time with lovely comics back-stage. It's not always that you get a good feeling of camaraderie among inexperienced open mic comics. People are often too nervous to talk much beforehand; they're running through their material, worrying about where they come on the bill and stressing about whether they're going to try and do one new joke (which, if they are me, they will forget to do when they are up on stage anyway).

At this night at Gentlemen Bears, though, at the Marlborough Pub and Theatre in Brighton, I get a real feeling of warmth and excitement. Sometimes you happen across a venue and you just think, 'This is how it should be.' The Marlborough is a lovely old pub in a Brighton back street about five minutes' walk from the pier. The bar is snug and cosy and poky and split in two, like the best old-style Victorian bars should be. Upstairs, improbably, there is a proper old-fashioned theatre which seats about eighty people.

There's a huge room off to one side which the performers can use as a dressing room. The comic presenting the night, Laurie Rowan, is performing as Chapsom Bear, a six-foot-plus furry gentleman grizzly in a smoking jacket. His costume is extraordinary. It's like Stephen Fry in a bear outfit. He is exceptionally tall, stiff-looking and covered in brown bear paint all over his face. He has an elaborate furry ears contraption over his head and a plastic bear nose.

He has managed to look like a bear. It's spectacular and I am thrilled to share a stage with him. The only problem is, the make-up starts melting off him by the time the third act has been on and his skin begins to show through at the bear's hairline. Every time he comes off stage we fan him manically with our hands and blow on him.

This is one of the only nights when it's not until the end that I realise I'm the only woman on. Everyone is so friendly and so supportive that it doesn't register initially. Not that it really bothers me being the only woman; in fact I've pretty much given up noticing it. My age probably bothers me more than being a woman anyway – I feel I stand out because I'm older, I have children, I'm not waiting for my life to start like most of the other comics. I'm waiting for my life to restart. But the woman thing is always noticeable if you want to take note of it. I've learned to ignore it, mostly because it's a bit boring and there is nothing I can do about it. On average, if there's a bill of ten comics, there will be two or three women maximum. Sometimes there might just be one. Get down to a bill of four or five and there will almost certainly only be one.

There's no conspiracy in comedy against women; the circuit just reflects reality. There are fewer women who want to do this than there are men. Or fewer women who can be bothered. There are a million reasons for this, just as there are a million reasons why there are fewer women on FTSE 100 boards, commentating on sport on TV or being head chefs of Michelin-starred restaurants. It is not comedy's problem. It is society's problem. But society doesn't like acknowledging that it differentiates between men and women. So it pushes the problem onto comedy.

I don't notice any difference between men and women doing comedy; the women are just as tenacious as the men and have just the same difficulties. I don't think it's harder to do as a woman – if anything it's made slightly easier for you by the fact that you stand out. I've even been given a space on a bill that was full just because I was a woman. In theory that's unfair. But that night there were about fifteen men performing – and me. Lots of clubs are desperate to get more (good) female comics because audiences really like difference and variety.

But any change is slow and the numbers do get to you after a while. For every woman who wins a new act competition, there's another competition which has no women in its final. Again, though, I don't blame comedy, I blame humanity. I do like a broad, pointless target that way. People do say mad things to you sometimes, in relation to the fact that you're a woman. My favourite: 'I don't like women comedians.' This is qualified with a shrug and a reluctance to expand on what is implied by the comment, which is, basically, 'And you didn't change my mind about them. As far as I am concerned, since seeing you I am even more confirmed in my belief that there is not a woman on this earth who is funny.'

These are the ramblings of the unimaginative, though, and

you can't let it get to you – although it is annoying that whatever you do is seen as having to stand for all women. No one looks at Joe Pasquale and says, 'Oh dear. I don't like male comedians.' I'm not saying they should …

19: Gigs 85 to 87:

'Do you feel that went well?'

Day 91, Gig 85: Soho

Performed on the main stage in Soho Theatre to a terrifying group of children who are learning to perform comedy. They laughed at about one and a half jokes. Brutal. But I enjoyed it. What's wrong with me?

Day 91, Gig 86: Walton

Rough pub, rough comics, rough crowd. I could feel there was more interest in the room about whether it would be appropriate to 'do' me (whether or not I wanted to be 'done') than there was in listening to my set. Loads of drunken heckles, most of which were not even intelligible and mostly seemed to be female audience members shouting, 'My friend's a slag.' 'Shurrup, you're a slag.' And so on, culminating in (directed at me): 'Get off, you slag.' I also overheard this while I was on stage, referring to me: 'Check her out. Would you?' 'Nah.' 'Don't worry, I wouldn't either.'

Day 92, Gig 87: Balham

Another successful mother and baby gig. Lucy Porter MC: 'You are much more confident on stage now.'

*

Ever since I started doing stand-up there have been times when I really get the fear. The usual things come up, the things that go through everyone's mind. What if I'm rubbish? What if I forget all my stuff? What if no one thinks I'm funny? What if I have to go on after someone who has completely died? Or, often worse, what if I have to go on after someone who has completely 'killed the room' and who can't possibly be topped?

If the Directionless Comedy Binge has proved one thing, it's that the only way you get around fear is by preparing. I am not very good at preparing and I am slowly realising that if I could get better at it I would probably do better gigs. I am learning how proper comedians live, the ones who do this for their full-time paid job. They spend their days writing and learning jokes. Memorising the material is one of the hardest things. Then they spend their evenings testing and honing stuff.

I first sat down and wrote jokes when I signed up to various comedy workshops. Some people are just able to do it. Or they're happy to go and try out something they think might be funny at an open mic night without really thinking about how it should be worded. I needed a teacher to tell me to do my homework. That was what led to me getting five minutes of material. I performed that same five minutes for a while, adding and tweaking bits. Then I realised that most of it was awful and completely rewrote it. Then I added and tweaked the new bit.

Most comedians work from a script. How much you deviate from that script is completely individual. Most people don't ad lib as much as it seems; come back tomorrow night and you will see exactly the same ad lib. One of the biggest things you have to get over is how uncomfortable it is to perform the same material night after night, often in front of the same people (because all the other new comics are doing the same gigs as you). I used to find that excruciatingly embarrassing.

Doing so many gigs back to back has helped with that. There has been no time between gigs for me to work on new material so I've had no choice but to do the same thing night after night. I've varied it by using the Instrument of Truth and I've occasionally decided that I'm not going to do any material tonight, I'm just going to ad lib. Sometimes you need to do your five minutes until you are completely sick of it; then you leave it for a while and when you come back to it it feels new and fresh.

This is the other challenge: how do you make something you have prepared and learned by heart sound spontaneous and off-the-cuff? This is the wonderful contradiction in terms of stand-up comedy. In some ways it's the most fake performance imaginable: it's the recreation of natural speech but under controlled conditions. This is why it's so easy to get it wrong. When you're talking to someone in everyday life and making them laugh, you're not speaking from a script – if someone suspected you were, they'd immediately hate you. That's what comics have to overcome. They have to give the illusion of 'I just thought this up.' But the reality is that it's almost impossible to think up things on the spot which are punctuated by laughter every thirty seconds or, ideally, less.

While mastering the material and figuring out how you're going to make it sound natural and unrehearsed is one thing, getting your performance right and connecting with the audience is another. Plus, you've got all the politics of the other comedians and who's been put where on the bill and who's getting paid and who's not getting paid and having to go on after people who are completely amazing and having to go on after people who are absolutely dire. I once interviewed Tim Vine, who is the ultimate one-liner comic and who once held the world record for the most number of jokes told in an hour (499), and he told a story about going on stage after someone who had done fabulously. As they passed in the wings, one going on, one coming off, Tim said to the other comic, 'I hope you've left something for me.' So the fear of getting it wrong never goes away.

Between the pressure to succeed and the pressure not to fail, it's hard to work out which is worse. Sometimes you just get this horrible feeling that there is someone out there in the audience who is desperate for you to do really well and can't bear to see you bomb. You can sort of feel their disappointment even more strongly than you feel your own. This is worse for me if it's a friend or someone connected to my work. It also happens whenever Simon is in the audience. That is why he is not allowed to come. (Also because he hates stand-up comedy. Or, at least, he used not to be that interested in stand-up comedy and now he hates it.)

I have sort of got over this now but it doesn't take much for me to be reminded of it and for me to think, 'Oh God, I can't bear for that person to see me fail.' The awkwardness afterwards is, however, hilarious. You can see them readjusting things in their mind. 'So she's not so funny.' 'So she's not who I thought she was.' 'Does she know it wasn't that good?' 'What do I say, in view of the fact that I did not like it that much?'

Generally, afterwards, if this has happened people say, 'Wow!' or 'Hey!' Then they say, 'So did you enjoy that?' This comment is code for, 'No one else enjoyed it. So I'll put a question to you to see if you realise that.' The 'enjoy' thing is probably the worst thing that people say. Although, 'Wow. Hey! You're really brave!' is a close second. But they will say that even if a gig went not too badly. They will not say, 'Wow. Hey! So did you enjoy that?' at a gig that went even remotely okay. 'Did you enjoy that?' is code for 'You should give up.' Someone even once said to me, 'Do you feel that went well?', which is maybe even worse.

At a gig that is moderate but not that good people who know

and like you off stage will say, 'You were great!' But you see the lie in their eyes. Although at least they're not saying, 'So did you enjoy that?' At a gig that is really good they will say, 'Wow. Hey! You were great!' and you can see in their eyes that they really mean it.

My problem is, I register all this stuff and I find it hard to let go of it. You need to get into a frame of mind where you are playing very high stakes, where you're giving your absolute best and there is no way you're going to let go of this moment and this chance – but where you're also so relaxed and carefree that you just don't care about anything at all. This is completely contradictory. But that is the way many things are in stand-up.

It's the same with material. You need to be so familiar with it that there is no way you could forget anything – no matter how rough you feel on that particular night, how hostile the audience is, how badly you get heckled, no matter who went on before you or how much you can't stand the MC. And yet you need to deliver the material with total spontaneity and lightness, as if you literally just thought it up on the spot and you really couldn't care less what anyone thinks of it. This is the joy and the hell of stand-up. Say what you like about it, it is very rarely boring.

This, of course, is the biggest challenge for many stand-ups and it's the reason not many stay in the game and only a handful make big money out of it. It's very difficult to keep the same material perky night after night. This is why great stand-ups are often great actors too. An actor needs to keep a stage performance fresh and different but also reliable and consistent every night. This is exactly what stand-up needs, except what you're playing must not come across as a character, it must come across as you. Ideally it should be you.

I see very few new stand-ups who are able to do this and so far I am achieving it rarely. The ones whom I admire the most are those who are having a bad day (or a bad life) and who leave all that in the dressing room. (I do not mean this literally. There is no such thing as a dressing room at 99.9 per cent of all gigs I have ever attended. When I say 'dressing room' I mean 'bus on the way there'. Leave your bad mood and bad life there.) They are their best selves when they are in the spotlight and never anything less and it seems real, even though it is not remotely real and they will come off stage and say, 'God, they were gits out there tonight.' And then they will go home back to the mess of their life. Because we all have a mess of a life. Not just stand-up comics. All of us. That's why comedy exists: for us to acknowledge that and recover from it a little bit. If you are a pro then anything can be going on in your life and you can still be 'the comic' on stage. When I did Jo Brand's book tour, there was one night when she was particularly relaxed and funny (although that is not saying much because she is always relaxed and funny). After the gig she had to leave straightaway and it turned out that someone in her family was very seriously ill. She had known that before the gig. She had been completely faking her state of mind and yet it seemed entirely real. That is the difference between a professional and an amateur.

But stand-up is also about a slightly aggressive relationship between the audience and the performer. 'Go on. Impress me.' 'So you think you're funny? I could do better than that.' This is why all everyone really ever wants to know is what it is like to be heckled. This appeals to the good and bad in people. They want to know what it feels like for you and, to some extent, sympathise with you. But also they want to gloat and feel relieved that it wasn't them. And they want to relive the cruelty of the moment. 'What did the heckler say? Why did they say that? What did you come back with?'

There is something very basic in human nature that makes

us love these exchanges. Perhaps it's because confrontation is generally not socially acceptable: you have to have a good reason for having a go at someone. In comedy it is somehow part of the package. The audience is not obliged to sit there and say nothing. You're having your say so why shouldn't they have theirs? One of my favourite hecklers ever was a very drunk man sitting in the front row one night at Up The Creek in Greenwich. He was called Bernardo – or at least that's what he said his name was. It was probably a made-up name. People often give made-up names at comedy clubs. It's very annoying, especially as they are always stupid, so-funny-they're-not-funny names. Bernardo listened to about fifteen seconds of me, leaned right back in his chair, turned to the rest of the room and shouted loudly, 'Well, this is shit.' I just laughed and continued. He soon fell asleep.

Most comics are completely sickened by hecklers. On his most recent tour Billy Connolly walked out of a gig in Blackpool because someone reportedly shouted 'Wildebeest'. At other gigs he is meant to have complained about people leaving the show to go to the bar or the toilet. How dare they? Others court hecklers. I saw Eddie Izzard at a late night show at the Soho Theatre not so long ago and you could almost sense his disappointment that he has got too 'big' to be heckled; you could feel the whole room was in awe of him and no one dared heckle in case they got it wrong. But he's there for the fun of it and the unpredictability of it – I reckon he welcomes heckles.

So far I like heckles. But that is probably only because I hardly ever get any. Heckles make it feel more like a proper gig – which, seeing as I am very rarely performing at anything that can be termed a proper gig, is only a bonus. And they keep you on your toes. Sadly heckles on the amateur circuit are fairly rare and fairly random and almost always entirely drink-fuelled and so not always comprehensible to anyone in the room, including the person who did the heckling. It's pretty rare for a performer on the amateur circuit, especially a woman, to have the sort of arrogance that will draw a heckle. More likely, the audience will heckle in the cruellest and most painful way possible: with tumbleweed. There is nothing more excruciating than polite silence. The seconds tick by like hours and your brain swells into an echo chamber. Your ego shrinks to the size of a frozen pea. The worst, most vicious, cutting heckle is a million times better than the soul-sucker that is silence.

I have seen a friendly, polite silence cause a performer to leave the stage because they just can't handle it and it makes them forget what they were going to say next. When you are performing to cold, loud silence, outwardly you're still speaking – hopefully, unless things really have gone pear-shaped. If there is silence on stage as well as silence in the auditorium, either you are a very confident performer and have balls of steel or you are about to crumble and get the hell off.

When you have silence in the room and you are still managing to continue speaking, your inner monologue goes something like this: 'They're not laughing. Try another one.' They didn't like that one either. 'Keep going.' Still nothing. 'What else do I have that they might like? How can I pep this up? How can I connect with them? Why can't I relax? I'm not relaxing and that's why they hate me.' Still nothing. If you're going to forget any of your set, this is when it will happen. So not only will you be unfunny, you will be an unfunny person who can't even remember their own bad jokes. Like a delusional amnesiac.

The monologue gets louder. 'Keep going. Whatever you do, don't stop, you'll make it worse. Don't refer to your failure.' This is around the moment when you start referring to your failure out loud. You may not even mean to do this but somehow the words just creak out of you. 'Oh dear, you don't like any of these

232

jokes do you? If you can call them jokes.' At this point (and it has only happened to me maybe three or four times that it has been this bad) I forget all my material, I forget what jokes I've already done, I repeat jokes I've already told, I repeat punchlines, the lot. It kind of doesn't matter because it's already a complete car crash.

This happened to me on an epic scale shortly before the time when I won the trophy. I did a gig at the Royal Vauxhall Tavern where my mind just went blank. I struggled to remember most of my set, at one point repeating the same line several times, trying to force the next line to come. It didn't. I just had to fast-forward to a bit that I did know. That was the worst 'memory fail' incident that has ever happened to me on stage before or since. It was like an out-of-body experience. I could feel parts of my brain asking my stomach – which was churning and screaming, 'Help me!' – 'Do you know the next bit? Because I don't.' I could feel the material I had written and learned sitting just outside the top of the back of my head, where I couldn't quite reach it. I can remember glancing down at my palms and the backs of my hands, wondering whether I might have written my set on them somewhere in biro. This is something lots of comics do. I had always vowed that I was too good for that. That night my own arrogance bit back. I swore I would never let that happen again. It gave me the kick I needed to learn my lines better.

Of course, whether you've messed up or not, there will always be someone in the audience who is happy to let you know that they didn't like you. Sometimes it's justified because you were terrible. Other times it's unjustified but your stuff is not their cup of tea and there's not much you can do about that. I don't know which is worse: these patronising non-compliments or the times when people just don't like you and they say just that. I've had this from one well-meaning older gentleman after a gig that was not that bad: 'I'm assuming you have a day job?' I almost spat out my drink. Wow – you think that was amateur? That was one of the better ones, my friend. My favourite bad review popped up on Twitter: 'Oh dear. @vivgroskop = disappointing. Didn't really get her.' The all-time winner? From an online review: 'The only blot on an otherwise brilliant evening.' What can I say? I try.

20: Gigs 88 to 96:

'You should not make jokes about Miranda.
Because she is funnier than you.'

Day 92, Gig 88: Kingston

Return to the scene of Gig 1. It's like I own this place now. I just about know how I can make it work in an unsuitable space. Felt a bit lonely there tonight, though. How much longer can I go on like this, really?

Day 93, Gig 89: Surbiton

Women's Institute with Ellie Taylor. 'We thought we'd like to try a comedy night!' Oh Christ. Extremely appreciative if bemused audience. Laughed quietly and politely. Interrupted midflow by a drunk tramp trying to storm the premises. He soon turned tail when he saw seventy members of the Surbiton Women's Institute glowering at him.

Day 94, Gig 90: Shoreditch

Competition. Humiliating. Just rubbish. That's me, apparently. A bit rubbish. Plus, one of the other (female) comics told me off for making a joke about Miranda Hart. I did a hypnosis section where I pretended to mesmerise the audience into loving women comedians. 'Don't think about Miranda. It's a man. He's admitted it and everything.' This is obviously – in my opinion, anyway – a joke and not a dig, as Miranda is hugely popular. And she makes the joke herself that she looks like a man. I am just being silly. I do not mean to offend anyone. In fact, if anything, you should get offended that I've stolen Miranda's own joke. 'You should not make jokes about Miranda,' says the other comic. 'Because she is funnier than you.'

Day 95, Gig 91: Manor House

Stage fifty feet off the ground. Audience way down below. Instrument of Truth bombed a little bit. Depressing. But used to depressing now. SOON THIS TORTURE WILL BE OVER.

Day 96, Gig 92: Kentish Town

Two gigs in one night. One notch-on-the-bedpost bad one.

Day 96, Gig 93: Kentish Town

Same. Only slightly worse.

Day 97, Gig 94: Knightsbridge

Lovely student gig with lively audience and happy people. A good gig. Tripling up tonight. GOT PAID ACTUAL MONEY (£20).

Day 97, Gig 95: Soho

The one with dodgy lemon muffins on stage. Just a bit awful.

Day 97, Gig 96: Finsbury Park

Onion rings! YES!

*

I am so close. So close. I have nearly done it. I can almost taste the sense of relief I'll feel when it's over. I'll know what it's like to stay in for the night. I won't have to dream about it any more. I can just stay in and not care. Sometimes I feel I will never go out ever, ever again. I will just live on my sofa for the rest of my life. People can bring me food and drink. I will not move. I will stay there until the end of days.

The closer it gets to Day 100, however, the more I'm realising that I'm in a sort of Stockholm syndrome. You know, when you fall in love with your captor. I'm kind of almost missing it already and it's not even over. This is the worst: realising that I don't really want it to end. It's not that I actually want to be trapped in the Directionless Comedy Binge any more. And yet I feel like I could gorge on it for ever.

I can't imagine what it will be like not to have the psychological prop of the hundred nights and the necessity of gigging to keep the numbers up. It has become what I do and it's comforting because it can be done without thinking. Put the gigs in the diary. Go to the gigs. Come home. Get ready for another gig. It's easy in some ways – as long as you ignore the fallout it creates in the rest of your life.

The progress bit is easy. Here's how you do it. You put a plan in place and you work your way through the plan. You don't have to think about anything apart from the plan. And the plan, if it's a good one, will bear fruit. You can't do a hundred gigs and not improve at comedy. You can't spend hundreds of hours at something and not see results. That's what is addictive: the investment of time and energy. It pays off. Why wouldn't you be excited about the pay-off and want to see more and more of it? The not-messing-up-your-life while enacting the plan? That's the difficult bit.

Also, I am starting to worry that this whole experiment has been a distraction: that I have used the hundred nights not as a way of finding out whether I really want to do comedy but as a way of avoiding committing to comedy properly in the long term – or giving it up completely. I thought I chose it because it was the least selfish thing. I thought it was less selfish than doing four or five gigs a week for a year. I thought I was the one who'd suffer the most from it. But I'm not sure if I've just ended up doing the most selfish thing and making everyone else suffer from that. Without properly deciding if I am in this game or not.

I can't imagine what it will be like to go back to normal life (if I have any normal life left). I can't imagine how I will start to pick apart how I feel about all of this, or where I'm going to put comedy in my life if it's not going to be right in the centre any more. I can see why people get caught up in workaholism or obsessive hobbies. I can see why – and how – people get divorced. I can see why – and how – people end up neglecting their children for years on end. I can see why most people would not put their relationship under this pressure because they would be scared it would crack.

There have been points during this experiment when I couldn't see how you really make any serious progress on something difficult without completely messing up your personal life. It has been very difficult between me and Simon but we have managed it. We've got through it because we've both known that, no matter how bad it got, we would not leave each other. And also because there was an end date.

Coming into the last few days, though, Simon is more distant than ever. He does not believe that I will be around much at all once the gigs have finished. When I told him that I had three gigs booked in for the week after I finish, he choked on his tea. 'What? You are joking, right?' 'No, I'm not joking. I have a couple of gigs. Okay, not a couple. Three. It's stuff I felt I couldn't say no to. And anyway, I can't stop just like that. It would be incredibly odd to do a hundred gigs in a row and then just do nothing for a month or something. I'm doing those three and then I'm on a break for about a fortnight. Oh, except for that one other thing I agreed to do … '. 'I can't believe you, Viv. I knew you would do this.'

The more annoyed he gets, the more I want to retreat into the gigs: 'It will be over soon, I promise.' It's like Groundhog Day. But what frightens me most is that the Groundhog Day might not be going away once this experiment is over. The Groundhog Day could become my life. Simon's right. It's not over. It's just the beginning. 'Honestly. I'm not going to do something like this again, I promise. I mean, I ought to, really. If you really want to get good, you should just do a hundred gigs in a hundred nights repeatedly. All the time.' I pause, realising what I am saying. 'Of course, I'm not going to do that again. Of course I'm not.' He looks at me sceptically.

I can't think straight about anything, though. I'm too locked into the idea that everything is going to be absolutely ruined if I don't actually get to a hundred gigs. If I only get to ninety-eight or ninety-nine in the hundred-day time frame, it's going to finish me off. Because not only will I have totally messed up my life and pushed my marriage to breaking point over the course of the past three months, but I won't even have achieved what I set out to achieve. I will have let myself down and I will have let the children down. 'Mummy, did you get to a hundred yet? Did you? Did you?'

That part of the plan, at least, worked. The children get it and they forgive me. They do not feel hugely neglected, even though I feel that I have neglected them. They know it's all going to be over soon and I will make it up to them. They are still excited about the idea of getting up to a hundred. So after everything I've put them through, I do not want to say, 'You know what? I only got to ninety-seven. But, hey, who cares, at least I gave it a go.' They have not been through the past three months of me running out of the door at 6.30 p.m. every night to have me wimp out a metre from the finishing line.

As the clock ticks I'm being dogged by disaster. I am so close to making it. I've got myself into a horrible position now where I've got five days to go and I've got to do eight gigs in those five days. If anything gets cancelled or moved, then I'm screwed and I will not hit the target. I can't stand thinking about what will happen if I don't make it.

I check Facebook several times an hour for gigs and drop-outs, desperately trying to find ways of ensuring that I can get the gigs in. I'm kicking myself for the ones I chose to miss myself over the past three months because of being ill or because I just couldn't go on. There was the gig (to make it worse, a night when I was going to double up with two gigs) when I had food poisoning, another when Simon was just going to leave me right there and then if I didn't cancel that night and another when I took a night off to go to a friend's fortieth birthday party ... why did I skip those gigs? That was stupid. Now I need to do eight in five days? Is it even possible?

Gig 92 annoys me because it's a night when I could probably have got in an extra gig but I can't because it's the first time I've been to this place, I don't know the promoter, I don't know how the bill works. So I can't double up because I can't ask to go on early or arrive late. It's a sweet little pub in north London. Although, God, how I hate having to go to north London now that I have been there so many times in the past few weeks. I have pretty much given up trying to figure out the most practical way to get to north London. There is no practical way. It can take up to two hours there and back. It would be quicker to visit my parents in Somerset.

When it comes, though, Gig 92 does offer a breakthrough. I don't have a particularly good gig. The audience don't find me that funny, although they're affable enough and I absolutely don't die. In terms of performance and nerves, it's got to the point now where sometimes I don't care how I perform or how I come across, I'm just clocking up the miles. But it turns out this is great in a way as it seems to result in better gigs. I'm also being more experimental, turning up with very little or nothing to perform and just making myself do it. I'm taking my still precariously-functioning miniature Casio keyboard everywhere I go and getting ready to improvise with it. All the high stakes and the big deal and the 'Wow, a comedy gig!' feeling have gone. That is good. This is just what I do.

The sound is hopeless where I'm performing and you can't hear the keyboard or really make out what I'm trying to do, so I move on to singing and messing around. If it sounds pretty awful, that's because it is. Thank God for five-minute spots, because if you tried to do this for longer people would lynch you, and rightly so. It's pretty shambolic but I can feel the audience relax: 'It's okay. She's just a bit of a weird one.' It's not about what you do, it's about the confidence with which you do it. I am so far down the road of 'Don't care' that it's one of the better performances I've done in a while. It's just a bit chaotic, that's all.

At least the level of the worst gigs is rising. There is some consistency. Or maybe I have just become deranged and I don't care whether I die or not. No, it's not quite that. I am listening to the audience more carefully and registering what they do and don't like instead of being focused on myself the whole time. It's not great comedy – it's not even good bad comedy – but it's a kind of progress.

The next night I have two gigs planned and I am completely geared up to power through them. But it is stressful. At one of the gigs you have to bring a friend to get on. At the other, not bringing a friend is frowned upon but it's not enforced. This is the pain you have to force yourself through: the sodding admin. All the business of bringing somebody. Stressing out when your friend is late or when they decide last minute that they don't want to go out; being ready to perform while having to prepare yourself for the fact that you might not be allowed to perform because your friend is late. All that is stressful.

I sleepwalk my way through both gigs, somehow managing to convince one MC that my friend is staying to the end of the gig (she isn't) and making it look at the second gig as if some people have turned up to see me (they absolutely haven't). I have completely run out of friends who will voluntarily come to see my act. I have even run out of friends I can bribe to see my act. I don't blame them. The one thing that has kept me going through this whole time is how lucky I am with my friends. People have turned up to the most horrible gigs in the middle of nowhere to support me. I'm constantly amazed by my friends' sense of humour at coping with surreal and unpleasant experiences.

Getting two gigs in on one night feels good but I still have a mess on my hands. Now there are four days left and seven gigs need to happen in order for me to make it to a hundred. It's a Friday. I have gigs confirmed on both Saturday and Monday. I have three gigs booked in tonight but it's a gamble as to whether I can physically make it to perform at all of them. I think I can do two gigs on Sunday night – although one of them is a shot in the dark. I have the chance of these three gigs tonight but I don't know how everyone is going to take it at any of the three places: they might be annoyed that I can't stick around and not let me on at all.

I've told the first one, a student gig in Knightsbridge, that I need to go on early as I want to go to another gig and I've told the last one, a gig in the basement of a wine bar in Finsbury Park, that I'm going to be late so they should put me on near the end. The middle one, a real dud of a gig in Soho, knows I'm going to be turning up late and that I'll be leaving to go to another gig. They must be confused that I don't want to be there early or go on last. I can't face telling them that I'm trying to triple up.

I'm stressed about transport too. I am so sick of travelling everywhere, working out how I'm going to get from place to place in the quickest and most efficient way possible. In the end I decide to drive to the Knightsbridge gig and park; this is because I'm going to be coming back from Finsbury Park and it will potentially be very late and I'm worried about missing the last train. At least if I have the car I can get back to Knightsbridge before 12.30 a.m. and then just drive home.

I also find it so much more relaxing to be in the car and in my own space rather than surrounded by drunk people on the train on the way home. On the way back from Manor House the other night I got on the wrong carriage at the wrong time and a swaying man was sick within splashing distance of my shoes. The only consolation is that this has not happened to me more often over the past three months. When I am travelling home, it is always at the optimal shoe-splash time.

The first gig with the students is a lovely one, put together by a charismatic young comic and MC. He's an affable, geeky sort who works in the Natural History Museum for his day job. You don't always get much of a chance to chat to the other acts but this is a relaxed, easy gig with a very sweet crowd so we talk beforehand. And it's paid (£20) and you get free drinks (Diet Coke ahoy). Not sure why it has got into his head but he suddenly expresses an interest in my family life: 'How do you manage to do this at your stage of life?' I look at him sideways as if to say, 'Are you saying I'm past it?' He corrects himself, 'I mean, having children and everything. And being married.'

What a good question. I reply honestly, 'It's very difficult. My husband is a total saint.' I say it and realise that I mean it, although I feel slightly sick in my stomach whenever anyone asks me this question as it's so close to the bone. I'm not far off giving up comedy because of how my husband feels about it and because of what it means for the children. And we have come so close to messing up everything because of all this. I'm afraid that if I say any more I will break down and start crying before the gig has started. I joke – although it's so obviously not a joke – 'I'm sure we'll get divorced soon anyway.' He laughs. But he is also checking my eyes to see if I'm being a bit serious.

There's a certain breed of young male comedian who obviously thinks this through a lot, has girlfriends who get fed up with all the gigging and the unpredictability and the nights away and who wonders what he is going to do about it. Maybe half a dozen young men have asked me about this. It's not a problem for them in the short term but I can see them thinking, 'It's hard for me to have a relationship now and I'm not even that successful. Imagine how difficult it would be if I had a family and responsibilities.' It's the John Bishop effect again. No one's got it easy.

Personally, I am struggling with another question: how to get out of here and to my other two gigs without looking rude and dismissive of the other acts. I want to stay at Hoopla and watch the headliner Pat Cahill. I like him very much and it would be amazing to see him in front of such a small crowd in a funny university common room (which is where we are). He has just been a finalist in the BBC's New Comedy Award 2011. He has had some films made for BBC Three. He's amazing. He does a funny rap about a dog and a song about takeaway chicken.

But there's no way I can stick around tonight. It's already 8.45 p.m. and I am supposed to be at the other gig now and it's about half an hour away. I run outside and work out the quickest way to get to Tottenham Court Road. I'm a fifteen-minute walk from the Tube and there are no buses. Black taxis whizz past. The £20 I have just earned is tucked into my bra. Sod it. I will spend it on a taxi ride – I don't have much choice. If I go by Tube, it's going to take me at least an hour and then I run the risk of not making it to the third gig and that will mess my numbers up irrevocably. Tonight is do or die.

I hail the next cab and make the twenty-minute journey to the next gig where I literally walk in the door, go downstairs and within thirty seconds am on stage. There is hardly anyone there. It's a gig in the basement of a modern-ish pub. I am in a strange mood when I get there and it gets stranger when I realise there is a discarded packet of lemon muffins on the floor right next to the microphone. I am starving. I trip over them on my way to the (non-existent) stage area. 'Excuse me, whose muffins are these?' What a great opening line. Not. I pick them up. I can see the audience – if you can call half a dozen people an audience – wondering if I will eat one, not knowing where they come from. 'Shall I eat one?' Yes, shout the six audience members. 'No, that's disgusting. You don't know where they're from.' Three of them are still shouting. The other three, having got bored, are now talking among themselves. I am really, really hungry and I can see no other way out of the situation I have created for myself. I eat one. 'Hmm. Quite nice.'

The muffins are horrible and it suddenly occurs to me that they could have come out of a bin. Or worse. Afterwards one of the comics tells me that he got them off a junkie tramp on the way there. I think he's joking. Either way, I feel sick. I have got a couple of laughs at this peculiar gig but nothing special. I wasn't focused on what I was doing, I was just thinking: 'How am I going to get to the next gig in time?'

I don't know how people do this for a living: in order to make money out of it, you need to take several gigs a night and yet be focused enough to do them all. The second I'm off the stage, I apologise to all the other comics for leaving immediately (it is not good etiquette not to support the other comics) and run out to the next gig. I am relieved to be wearing my sparkly trainers. You could not do this in heels. Maybe this is another reason stand-ups generally do not look smart: you have to run between gigs and there is no chance of remaining glamorous.

The night feels shrouded in misery and exhaustion, but there is a tinge of excitement. It's not to do with how well the gigs go. They go fine. It's do with how I am feeling and that I can barely believe I can make it to the end. I have this butterfly feeling in my stomach the whole time. I can't bear the suspense of it all. I only have to arrive at one gig too late and be told that I can't go on and the whole thing will have been a waste of time. I tell myself that it will be fine to do ninety-nine gigs in ninety-nine days or ninety-nine gigs in a hundred days. But in truth I know that it won't and I will never forgive myself. And I will never have the chance to do this again – not if Simon has anything to do with it anyway.

I take the Tube to the next gig, sending them a text to assure them I'm on my way. I'm late. I don't even know if the gig will still be going when I get there. It's one of my favourites. There's nothing special about it. In fact it's pretty awful: no stage, no proper lights, often not much audience to speak of, although sometimes it's unexpectedly packed. But somehow it's always lovely. The MC is supportive and kind and funny, especially when she tells stories about her father's disapproval of her flatulent brothers. Quite a few comics I really like turn up to this gig, people you can chat to, and it's generally run quite smoothly.

Plus it's the sort of place where I can say that I'm going to be late and they won't mind (although that's only because I've built up credit over the weeks). Usually I bring friends and I've stood here as MC before. That was the time I turned up with a pink beatbox I had bought for £15 at Sainsbury's and some CDs by Shakira and The Carpenters in case they didn't have any 'warm-up' music. (Yes. I thought 'Top of the World' by the Carpenters would be great warm-up music.) Luckily they have a sound system in the venue and my efforts were not required. It was kind of disappointing.

By this stage in the experiment I just don't care about quality or about nerves or about where I am going. You could push me onto the stage at the Apollo and I would just do my five minutes and get off and move on to the next gig without thinking about it. I'm like some kind of conveyor belt comedian: wind me up and off I go. Part of me is ecstatic; another part of me has completely lost the will to live. When I turn up, there is one comic at the gig whom I absolutely can't stand and who always sets my teeth on edge. Usually I would obsess about his presence and allow it to mess up my act a bit. But tonight I just don't care about anything. I have a good gig. Ninety-six down, four to go. On the way home I observe one of the great unwritten rules of comedy (which I have just invented now for my own purposes): you must spend cash paid for gigs on Burger King onion rings.

21: Gig 97:

'What's the worst heckle you've had?'

Day 98, Gig 97: Walton

Bonus: celebrity gig! Arthur Smith headlines! Non-bonus: the Hecklers from Hell. I also realised that I really am deep into the Stockholm syndrome now. Tonight was awful, really, but I found it hilarious. Possibly I had a better sense of humour about it than most gigs because I was close to home and knew I would get back at a reasonable hour. Possibly I have been doing this for so long that I have become completely unhinged.

*

Gigs like the Saturday night one I've just had in Walton make everything worthwhile. The evening started promisingly: very sweet MC called Gema Enseñat, who is the beautiful, hot presenter of a casino programme on cable TV, all Penelope Cruz meets Charlotte from *Sex and the City*. I like it when there is a very attractive young woman; she satisfies the audience's desire for female beauty so I don't feel I have to.

Anyway, she was funny as well as nice and so were some of the other acts. The only problem was the headliner, Arthur Smith, who had not turned up. Phone calls were made. A man was sent out in a car. Arthur Smith had been spotted in the vicinity. Once we were halfway through – battling off drunken hecklers who wanted to have a conversation with you while you were on stage and who thought they too had some jokes to tell if only they could remember them – Arthur Smith arrived, looking like a tramp. 'I got lost,' he said to me, grinning widely so that I couldn't tell if he was joking or not, 'and then I started looking for the station so that I could go home.' Genius.

It turned out he was incredibly nice, and when it was his turn to go on I was fascinated to see how he would deal with the hecklers, who were completely out of control – although to be fair they were mostly so drunk that they were incapable of speaking, let alone actually doing anything dangerous. One of them went downstairs to attempt to start a fight and was soon thrown out of the pub. Arthur Smith's tactic was interesting: he let the loons talk. And he listened. They soon ran out of steam.

The only drawback was, this all took time. He was supposed to do fifteen minutes and he ended up doing an hour. No one cared, though, because, well, he's a celebrity! There was a fascinating change of energy when he arrived. People love someone off the telly or the radio, someone they already feel a connection with. It makes it a more exciting night. Arthur let them ask questions. 'What's the worst heckle you've had?' What an ironic question from this crowd. Turned out a Danish man once tried to shout out 'I really like you' during one of Arthur Smith's gigs and this flummoxed him. (I later read that he has also had a pint of urine – 'used beer' – poured over him at a show in Edinburgh. Surely that is worse than a Danish man liking you?) I giggled at Arthur Smith all the way home. At one point he removed his trousers to reveal a pair of pants with an anatomically correct photograph on them. Maybe I needed better props.

Many bad things have happened over the last ten weeks. I have become demented and I feel like I am going to be sad when it's over. My appearance is not the worst result: that honour goes to the near collapse of any semblance of a normal home life or happy marriage. But my appearance is pretty wrecked. Over the last ninety-nine days I have become pale, spotty, smelly and put on nearly a stone in weight. So much for the healing powers of Diet Coke. (Total spend: now near £400.) My hair's lank and greasy. My skin is dry and flaky. Plus I have some kind of sinus problem which is making me snore at night. Another cross for poor Simon to bear.

I am not really getting up in the mornings at all now so he is still doing everything with the children: breakfast, school uniforms, getting them out of the door. This is on top of doing bedtime and homework most nights without me around to help. When I am up and supposedly available for maternal duties I am grouchy, exhausted and self-obsessed. It's weeks since I made pancakes. A lot of the problem is tiredness; the rest of it is the fact that overdosing on stand-up has rendered me deranged.

For days on end now I have not been home before one in the morning, often later. Sometimes when I wake up at 7 a.m. it feels like I only just fell asleep and I've often been dreaming of the gig the night before, playing it over and over in my mind, thinking of all the things I could have said which would have been so much funnier than what I did say.

It's very easy to get caught up in a cycle of self-hatred or exhilaration, depending on how your last gig went. Sarah Millican talks about this. She has a rule: you're only allowed to stay in the emotion of the gig you've just done until 11 a.m. the next morning. Then, whether it was a good gig or a bad gig, you have to let it go. It's fantastic advice from a woman who knows. I have not learned to do this yet.

It's hard to take your mind off performing generally: either you're thinking about how it went last night and wondering what you could have done to make it better, or you're thinking about what it will be like tonight. I have work to do during the day but I spend stupid amounts of time stressing about my set, booking other gigs and stalking other comics and promoters on Facebook.

I don't really like the person I've become but I can't seem to shake myself out of it. Since about Gig 60 the children have been acting as if I am no longer part of the family. There's a morning when we all end up walking to school together because I'm up and ready and Simon doesn't have to be early for work. I end up trailing back and watching them all walk ahead of me as a family. They're perfectly fine without me. They don't even notice that I'm not there. Who can blame them? They have learned to get by without me. It's upsetting. One night, as I leave for the evening, as I have done dozens of other nights in a row, as I'm closing the front door and peering back through the glass at their little faces waving goodbye, I hear Vera say, sad but resigned, 'Daddy. I think you need to get a new wife.'

Another night I have a gig I can be late for because it's local and I know the MC, so I put the children to bed myself for the first time in three months. Vera and Will have bunk beds in a shared bedroom. Usually Vera falls asleep first and Will stays awake reading with a sidelight on. As I was saying goodnight to Will and bringing him a drink, Vera suddenly woke up, sleepy and confused: 'What are you doing here, Mummy?' What indeed. Simon regularly points at Jack, who is now only fifteen months old and enjoys singing to me, 'You picked a fine time to do a hundred gigs, Lucille.'

I'm not just emotionally absent, I am a hygiene disaster zone. I have become so dirty, so sleep-deprived and so confused that I have been 'forgetting' to shower (i.e. I am too lazy to shower). I can't remember when I last washed my hair. I drag the same outfit on night after night. I despise the 'showbiz' sequinned cardigan. I just about manage to camouflage the physical wreckage at night by doing my (unwashed) hair in rollers and fixing it with loads of hairspray and by plastering on huge quantities of make-up. I have still not worked out what to wear to feel like I'm wearing the right thing. I always seem to be wearing the wrong pair of shoes and then I don't feel comfortable on stage.

After my first ever gig, one of the comics who seemed to know what he was talking about told me that I should wear a pair of shoes that I feel I can move in and that make me feel grounded. I don't think he told me this because of anything he had observed about my performance, I just think he was one of those people who likes holding fixed views on things and telling other people about his philosophies. But I convinced myself at the time that he had made this observation specifically for me and about me and that it meant that I could no longer wear high heels on stage. I did a lot of the hundred gigs Sandie Shaw-style, with no shoes on, before deciding that was really pretentious. I tried to find shoes that felt comfortable but which I was happy in. This was a problem because I hate flat shoes. I have wrecked two pairs of sparkly trainers. The sequins are falling off.

In fact, the sequins have pretty much fallen off this whole enterprise. My self-esteem is bruised. I'm having mood swings between ridiculously overconfident and neurotically depressed. I can just about get it together to look presentable for going onstage at night but in the day I'm a total mess and can't even be bothered to look after myself. It's as if it's taking all of my energy and self-respect just to get me out of the door at night and behind a microphone; I do not have any left over for everyday tasks like washing properly. It has come to my attention – slightly too late – that there is a strange infection in my belly button. I had noticed it was a bit itchy but I ignored it for a week before realising it was all red and disgusting. So that's where all the nervous sweat from the glitzy cardigan went. Nice.

I am like a junkie tramp, only one who just about managed to get up in time for the school run and to do a few hours' work in the day, only to head out in the evening for her nightly adrenaline fix. A couple of the mums on the school run know that I'm trying to get up to a hundred gigs. I've been missing the local monthly book group to do this, which has caused some consternation. As we pass on the pavement on odd mornings weighed down with buggies and school bags, another mother will shout, 'How many you up to now?' 'Another late night last night?' 'Is it over?' Or, smirking, 'How's Simon?' I have heard reports from other mothers that Simon is very proud of me. But they also keep telling me that he 'looks very tired'.

Many prices have had to be paid on this journey. The Diet Coke bill doesn't bear thinking about. Hundreds of pounds in train fares: £8.50 a day just to get to London gigs. A couple of hundred pounds on hotels. All this I can manage not to think about. I will work extra once this is over to make it all back. What I am not going to be able to recover is the marital goodwill that this experiment has cost me. That has been the biggest expense that I have run up on credit and I have no idea how I am going to pay it back. Or even if I can.

I have all these grandiose ideas of how I'm going to be the perfect wife and mother as soon as the hundred nights are over. In reality I am a husk of a person and not capable of making a bowl of Weetabix for myself, let alone cooking a five-course dinner for Simon every night for four weeks, which is what I would really like to do to show him how grateful I am. Plus, I have decided that I am going to do comedy for real now. This wasn't just an experiment; it was a decider. I have other gigs booked – not too many in the short term. But in the long term it is now looking as if this is going to become my life.

That is going to be bad news for Simon. His greatest hope was that this experiment would knock it all on the head, get it out of my system; that I'd live out my childhood dreams in these hundred nights and then go back to my old life. But my old life seems a long way away now. It's too far away to return to. And I don't want to go back there anyway. I want to gig and get better at this. The trouble is, I am not expecting to make a living out of it any time soon; that can take years.

The numbers are not really what has convinced me in the end. According to my own calculations (and this is just me measuring my own success and failure – it could be much worse or much better than I think), I've done fifty-one awful gigs and forty-eight good ones. Not many statisticians would say, 'Yes, continue!' on the basis of that. But I know it's an excellent result. The number of good gigs has doubled in the past few weeks. Maybe over time I can reduce the bad gigs completely. Or maybe you never can and you just have to accept that not everyone everywhere can like you. When I started out, I promised myself that I wouldn't continue if the bad gigs outnumbered the good, but I can see now that it's not as simple as that. What matters is to survive the bad gigs and make them useful for you (by doing new material or trying to rescue a bad situation). And to do well at the good gigs, the ones that matter. In any case, in my mind each good gig is worth about twenty bad ones. So I have done nearly a thousand good ones. (See? Demented.)

The rewards of the experiment do not take anything like as long to count as the penalties. Over the course of the past hundred days I have received the following in recompense: One KitKat, one banana and three chocolate chip cookies (taken from a back stage 'rider' platter in Brighton and stashed in my handbag, causing me nearly to crash into a traffic sign while I tried to fish out the KitKat on the journey home). Half an artisan goat's cheese pizza. £60 for MC-ing two gigs. £20 petrol money in Truro. £20 for an opening set. These are added to the payments I have received after starting performing comedy: £10 at the Royal Vauxhall Tavern, a horrible purple silk fringed scarf given to everyone who performed at a cervical cancer fundraiser, a porcelain bowl from the designer collection at Debenhams, a miniature plastic trophy, a bouquet of flowers, three bottles of supermarket cava. Spread out over two years, it's not much of a living.

At least the cost to the children has been small, I hope. They understand that things can go through phases and this has been a phase when I am not around much but another one will come when I'm home most of the time. It hasn't affected the set-up of their day. Because it's only made a difference to their bedtimes – and they are pretty easy-going about that – they're largely still supportive of the whole thing, even if I am slightly apart every time they're a family unit. All they really want is for me to win a competition and 'go through to the next round'. They have watched enough auditions for *Britain's Got Talent* to know that this is the only thing that counts. Their favourite gigs have been the competitions. 'Did you go through to the next round, Mummy? Did you? Did you?' I only did on one occasion. But they can cope with that too, partly because they see people being rejected on television who were perfectly worthy of going through. And they always tell me I was robbed and the judges are rubbish.

The children are at their best when they are helping me to recover from bad gigs. Vera just repeats her advice about the Mary Christmas joke. 'Did you tell my joke? Come on. Tell the truth, Mummy. Did you tell it?' I cannot lie to her anymore. 'No, darling, I didn't tell your joke. I didn't think they were ready for it. It's too funny for them. They might laugh so much they would do a wee.' She smacks her head as if to say, 'D'oh.'

'You need to tell that joke. That's all you need to do.'

They are used to getting into bed with me in the morning and hearing about what happened the night before. 'I wasn't very funny and nobody liked it.' 'I was quite funny and I remembered all my jokes. Most people seemed to be laughing.' 'I was really good but they didn't put me through to the next round.' They boo and cheer appropriately and always blame the audience and never blame me. (It's fine for them to do that. It's not fine for me to do that.)

I think it's really important to share with them the reality of what I'm doing: what it's like when I succeed, what it's like when I fail. I am hoping to show by example that it doesn't matter how things work out for you in the short term – win or lose – but if you keep plugging away at what you really want to do, good things will come in the end. Don't expect it to be easy. But I have also explained that what I am doing is extreme and was probably not a very good idea and I won't be doing it again. I promise.

The children are very useful, though, after the real stinkers. 'I was awful. The audience hated me. What should I do?' Will's advice: 'Run away and hide. Or find a disguise.' Vera: 'Stay at home next time.' That's not quite the idea, Vera. But I know where you're coming from.

22: Gigs 98 to 100:

It's the final countdown

Day 99, Gig 98: Borough

Triumphant Instrument of Truth gig.

Day 99, Gig 99: Whitechapel

Nice, sedate but warm gig. Good reception. Pleased. Felt like I can do this. Maybe I can do this. Although does the fact that it has taken me 99 gigs in a row to realise that I can do it and I still am not 100 per cent entirely sure that I actually can mean that really I cannot do this? I think I may finally have realised I am never going to have the answer to this question. I just have to keep going anyway.

*

Oh. My. Heavenly. Lord. I've made it. I've got to the last gig. Gig 100 is to take place at The Hob in Forest Hill, south-east London. And I love The Hob. It's just a lovely venue. Despite the permanently out-of-order toilet.

I've had an exhausting weekend but I'm running on adrenaline. After the three-gigs-in-one-night on Friday, I had the Arthur Smith gig on the Saturday (Gig 97) and then managed two low-key gigs on Sunday night, one in Borough, one in Whitechapel: 98 and 99. Sunday had been a stressful day. I had no guarantee of getting on at either gig. I was relying on knowing the MC at

Borough and then calling the MC at Whitechapel ahead and working out whether I could then get over there.

The logistics of all this have been so uncomfortable. You don't know whether you're annoying people by not staying for the whole gig. You don't know whether you'll be welcome to perform there again. But you also know that everyone appreciates that you're just trying to get as much stage time as possible in whatever way you can. No one has any illusions about that, it's what we're all trying to do. It's just that there are different ways to play the game. And it helps if you smoke and can go outside with the other acts and have a fag. And it helps if you can stay late and get drunk with the other acts. I have not been able to do either of these things.

I also spent half the day on Sunday at a workshop with some other comics. I was hoping I was going to be able to count it as a gig in an emergency, if something was cancelled on the Sunday or the Monday and left me one gig short. But it turned out to be nothing like a gig at all; it was just us talking into a hairbrush in someone's living room. (Not actual hairbrush. No, that would be too professional. Imaginary hairbrush.)

It was one of those workshops where everyone ends up analysing everyone else's appearance and performance style. That can be helpful. Or it can be hurtful. I left completely brutalised. Over the afternoon it emerged that I, apparently, physically resemble Albert Einstein. And that the audience is likely to think that I have dyed my hair with a blonde streak simply to make jokes about it – either that or my hair is 'a cry for help'. And, finally, that there is 'something about you that says "soccer mom"'. Really? Are you sure? How am I going to work with that? I am definitely not a soccer mom.

On Day 99 I don't have time to go home between the workshop and the two gigs in the evening which is, I have realised, no bad thing. I am not particularly welcome at home. Things are frosty between me and Simon. I feel we should be celebrating and feeling closer now that it's all coming to an end, but it's the opposite of that. It's almost as if he is never going to forgive me for doing this in the first place; that the end of it almost makes it worse in some way. His resentment over this whole experience is threatening to overwhelm everything. I can't blame him. It has been intensely difficult and irritating and a huge burden to him.

On the plus side, he will still watch the video footage and he has admitted that he can see a huge difference. He was watching one piece of film back the other night and started beaming with pride. 'You look so happy up there. It's like you just come alive. That is the real you.' 'You see the difference?' I said. 'That is why I needed to do this.' Then he remembered how cross he was and went back to being grumpy. It's too early for either of us to know whether it has been worth it. I've made progress and I've made the most of it. But I still regret it and I'm really not sure that I should have done it at all.

I'm puzzled that Simon's not more relieved that it's finally going to be over. That, surely, must be some consolation? That in a week's time it will all be forgotten and we can get back to our normal lives? He doesn't seem to be affected by this. He's too busy feeling aggrieved. This is understandable. It has been hellish for him. He's wary too. If we end up concluding that 'It was difficult but it was worth it' then I might do it again. He wants, as I do, to put it behind us; but he doesn't want me to sugar-coat the experience (which is entirely likely).

At Gig 99 I end up telling the audience about Albert Einstein and about the hair insult. They like it. Maybe this is the way forward for me: report back on how other people have insulted me. Everyone likes to hear that. I fell into a slightly celebratory mood once I had got over my irritation that the audience seemed to agree with my (ex) friend that I looked like Albert Einstein and I almost blurted out my secret to the audience, 'Yes! That's it! Ninety-nine down! One to go!' But I've been doing all this under the radar and it didn't seem the right moment.

Now I really don't want to be quizzed on why I've done this, how it's gone and what impact it has had on my life. Because I know I'll break down. After the success of Gig 99, I drank two gin and tonics (yes, two!) with one of the other comics and felt like telling him too but just stopped myself in time. Plus, I still had it at the back of my mind that I might never make it to a hundred gigs and I had better not tell anyone so that I could always pretend that I never wanted to do it anyway.

I am very excited that The Hob is going to be the venue for the last gig. The Hob is the place for Proper Comedy where Daniel Kitson – the 'comedians' comedian' – hosts on Monday nights and where dozens of other big comics come to perform new material and are 'friends' of the venue. It's a lovely big pub with a proper stage area and huge audience space (comparatively speaking – we are not talking the Apollo here). There's even a proper green room with sofas and jugs of water and glass bowls of boiled sweets on a cake stand. Yes. Free sweets. This the real deal. This is the big time.

Not so much tonight, though. When I arrive Emma, the promoter, is looking gloomy. 'Only four tickets booked. And they haven't turned up.' Cold terror pulses through my body. It can't be cancelled. It mustn't be cancelled. This is Gig 100. Do. Not. Cancel. Gig. 100. Imagine me doing the face from *The Scream* at this point.

No punters seem to have turned up on spec either. That is unusual: this gig can be packed. Sadly, Daniel Kitson is not hosting tonight. On the plus side, though, the MC is 'TV's James Redmond', an actor turned stand-up whom I know from when I did my very first gigs a couple of years ago. He was in the audience when I popped my stand-up cherry at the Lion's Den in King's Cross in 2009. He was the opening act at my thirty-sixth birthday gig a few weeks afterwards and lots of my friends still remember him from that night as 'the good-looking one who used to be in *Casualty*'. Unfortunately for him – or, fortunately for his comedy – this is how he is remembered everywhere. At least it gives him something to mess around with. To be doing this hundredth gig with him at The Hob feels like coming full circle. My material is not exactly box-fresh but at least I don't have anything in my set which I used in my first gig. Or do I?

The face of Emma, the promoter, falls further as the minutes tick by. I am borderline hysterical but trying to conceal it. About seven or eight comics have turned up. James starts putting a running order together, which everyone takes very seriously. This seems ridiculous to me because at the moment it looks like we have zero audience, maybe four people. And Emma is thinking about pulling the night. Still, the comics are arguing about who is going to go on first. I am starting to panic that we will hang around until 8.45 p.m. or 9 p.m. to start, waiting for people to get here, only to pull it. And then it will be too late for me to get to another gig.

This is a lovely venue and they put on great shows, but in terms of a place to gig, Forest Hill is in the middle of nowhere and I am at least an hour by car from the nearest open mic. All the same, I send a text to Gemma, the MC at Comedy Virgins in Stockwell, which is one of the most popular and well-attended new acts nights. 'Looking dead here at The Hob. Can I get a slot with you if necessary?' She replies immediately. 'Yes! Come here!' I am hoping it won't be necessary. I am ignoring the fact that if I do decide to go to Stockwell, I am somehow probably going to have to find someone to come with me because it's one of those gigs where you have to bring a friend. I try not to think about all this. Okay, at least I have a back-up plan. But I just don't think I can face a mad dash in the car to get to another gig. This gig has to go ahead.

I start agitating, trying not to sound as if I'm whining. 'Oh, come on, guys! The show must go on!' I plead with Emma. 'We're all here, we might as well go ahead, right? And there are some people who have paid ...'. There are four people who have paid. And two of them have turned up. 'They want to see comedy! We can't let them down!' Everyone is still looking doubtful and one of the comedians is muttering, 'I could do with a night off.'

I am horrified and almost on the point of bursting into tears. I am torn between flouncing off to the other gig anyway – because at least that one is guaranteed and is already happening – and screaming at them that they MUST go ahead with this gig because it is my hundredth gig in a hundred days and if we don't then my whole project will have been ruined and it will all have been a complete waste of time and I will have risked my marriage and missed countless hours with my children for nothing.

I do not tell them this, of course, because I think it will make it even less likely that the gig will go ahead if it looks like it means something to someone. But in truth I am close to an act of violence. The whole success of the past hundred days of my life, everything I've sacrificed to get to this moment, the whole mess with Simon ... it all hinges on the next fifteen minutes.

While I'm agitating about all this, the running order is being passed around, even though the gig is not yet confirmed as going ahead. I desperately want to say, 'Look, if this gig is going ahead then I should definitely headline it.' But I find that I cannot say this. I cannot find a valid reason to suggest headlining – although, to be fair, there is no valid reason why I shouldn't. I wait for someone else telepathically to pick up on this idea and propose me as the headline act.

This, it occurs to me, is yet another reason why, supposedly, women don't get anywhere in comedy: because while I am torturing myself, one of the other comics has already written his name in the last position. My last hope is the MC. 'Where should I go on, James?' I ask him, hoping that he will grin at me and say, 'Sod it, why don't you headline?' Instead he says: 'Oh, I think going on second or fourth would be a good position for you.' Thanks. These are the worst positions in the line-up.

The two other ticket-holders have arrived and it now looks as if the gig is going to go ahead. I could kiss Emma, the promoter. I buy a pint of Diet Coke to celebrate and to mark the fact that I am staying. I start to feel a little giddy. I ain't goin' nowhere, suckers. I am feeling like Muhammad Ali. If Muhammad Ali wore a very smelly Statement Cardigan and drove a Volkswagen Touran littered with Hula Hoops packets. I am going to do this gig and then, finally, it will all be over. Over. Over. Over. I am already making physical 'victory' gestures in my mind like the ones they make on *The X Factor* when they find out they are through to the next round. I text Gemma: 'Looks like gig going ahead anyway. Thanks, though. We have four audience.' They have made tonight happen and they are my favourite four people in the whole world.

I've allowed them to put me down fourth in the running order, but at this point I just really could not care less. I am flying. They could put me on first, last, 157th. I just know that the second I hit that last punchline and put that microphone back in the stand, it's done. It's over. I don't have to go out tomorrow night. Or the night after. Or the night after that. I can stay at home every night for the rest of my life. Except deep in my heart I know I'm not going to: this is what I want to do now. It's not easy, it's often cruel and it's going to be a pain in the neck for Simon for the rest of his life. This is not what he signed up for when he married me. He knew I could be quite annoying; but he did not know that I would try to become a stand-up comedian. On the plus side, I will never have to do it every single night ever again.

It's not much of a real gig with – what is it now? – six people in the audience (six people! More people have come! Walk-ins! Bless you!) but I don't care. The few genuine punters in the audience are lovely. They obviously come to The Hob often and they are comedy fans who are quite happy to entertain our foolish amateur notions and to fuel their own equally foolish hopes that one of us will become the next Michael McIntyre and they will be able to say, 'I saw him/her at The Hob when no one knew who he/she was.' (I don't know why I'm bothering to put 'she' there because it's far more likely to be 'he'. But let's not get into that here. Which reminds me, I am the only woman on tonight out of twelve acts.)

As I trot out my tired old lines, which I have now said dozens of times in a row in dozens of different places over the past hundred days, the words take on a new lease of life and feel fresh and funny and new to me. I am secretly proud of my silly jokes. They have got me through a lot. This is what I have heard from comics who know what they're doing: you fall in and out of love with your material. I'm just enjoying the fact that there are some people in the room who haven't heard my jokes and who might – just might – like them. I'm hardly going to get a standing ovation in this room tonight. Or if I did, it would just be like six people all standing up to go to the toilet at the same time. But I am going to get as much laughter out of them as I can possibly manage and I'm going to give it everything I've got.

As I'm talking away, all the costs and all the rewards of the past three months float into my mind. Before I came out tonight I did a bit of a reckoning. I have performed in venues both lovely and legendary: The Greystones in Sheffield, Relapse Theatre in Atlanta, the Marlborough Theatre in Brighton, Lincoln Performing Arts Centre, and in London the Comedy Store, Soho Theatre, The Bedford in Balham, The Hob in Forest Hill. And I have performed in horrible places that smell like they have bodies buried in them. I've stood on stage (or, sometimes, on a glorified box) in forty-nine pubs, seven theatres, five wine bars, four comedy clubs, one nightclub, one tea room, one hotel and one students' union. (That does add up to a hundred because some venues I played twice.)

In a hundred nights I've had twelve cancellations – due to food poisoning, a disgruntled husband but, mostly, promoters pulling their nights. I've had ten nights where I did two gigs and three nights where I did three. The number of friends who have attended good gigs is astonishingly high: thirty-five. The number of friends who have witnessed bad gigs is reassuringly low: eighteen. (This number amazed me. In my mind it's the other way round.)

Much of this experiment has been measured in food and drink consumed. Burger King onion rings eaten: forty-nine. Number of free drinks received over a hundred nights: ten (count them!). This includes seven bottles of Beck's Blue, two of them awarded for coming in the 'top three' comedians of the night. It also includes one Diet Coke, one cup of tea when I had lost my voice and one glass of rosé wine with the Women's Institute in Surbiton. The Diet Coke bill is now in excess of £450. The cost to my general appearance and grooming has not been insignificant. Cans of Elnett used up: three. Bottles of Prada Candy: one and a half. It has been a long road.

There's a comic in the front row who has heard my material over a dozen times and could probably deliver my set himself. He's smiling and laughing. There is James, the MC at the back, who has seen me do my first ever gig and knows what my last joke will be. He is a tough nut to crack but he still laughs hard (too hard? Is he just being nice?) on a couple of the lines. There is a woman sitting off to one side who has come here on her own, nursing what looks like a Jack Daniel's and Coke. She is shaking with laughter and wiping away a tear after one line. She is why I do this. Where was she at the bad gigs? Or maybe it's a better question to ask, where was I?

I'm the first to admit that I have not always performed as well as I am doing tonight. Finally up there for the hundredth time in a hundred nights I feel like my natural self, and that's what the audience most want to see. This is why I'm going on with this: because sometimes I can manage to be that person on stage. And I want it to be all the time.

I was worried I was going to cry at the end when I finished – and no one would know why. But instead I put the microphone back in the stand, walk off the stage and go to the bar to order a pint of Diet Coke. With extra ice. (It's now up to £452.70.) I would have something stronger but, hey, this is my drink now. Plus, I'm driving. I am so excited and relieved and devastated and amazed and happy that I could not possibly make anything other than a default drink choice. I've done it. I've done it. I've done it. It's the end. It's also only just the start. I text Simon. 'It's. Over.' He replies. 'Come. Home.'

Day 100, Gig 100: Forest Hill.

'I've been Viv Groskop. You've been an audience of six people. Thank you and good night.' Forgot to get a kebab on the way home. I will never be a proper comedian.

CURTAIN DOWN

The experiment has served its purpose. It gave me the excuse to be single-minded and to chase one objective: just do the gigs. But there is a fine line between focused and psychotic, and I think I may have crossed it at several points during the hundred nights. You have to be a particular kind of person to do something like this. And probably if you are the sort of person who would embark upon this project in the first place, it's just going to make you even more driven and obsessive in the short term. Which is not a good thing.

In some ways the experiment was genius. It was a device which allowed me to get something done. Set yourself a goal and a fixed timescale and you get somewhere. I achieved what I wanted. I got better at comedy and made the decision to continue performing. My gut feeling was right. I was meant to do this. And I can do it. But in the long term it has had a healthier effect: it has made me realise that even if I'm capable of pushing myself to some crazy extreme, this is not always necessarily the best way to proceed in life, particularly as other people's lives are impacted and it's not just about me.

In other ways, though, this whole thing has been reckless, masochistic and destructive. I'm not sure it ever really would have resulted in Simon and me splitting up, not even when I was being my most demented and childish and pig-headed. We both always focused on the temporary nature of the challenge – that was what kept us together. I came to realise that you can push someone a long way and see that they don't break, but that doesn't mean that you should keep pushing them. More likely it teaches you that you were wrong to push them that far in the first place.

One major benefit is how much I appreciate my husband now. I did before, but I took his support for granted. Now I've seen that he will support me even when he doesn't want to. He will stand by me even when he is completely exasperated. He will walk out to clear his head, but he will not walk out completely, however crazy and annoying I am. This makes me want to be less crazy and annoying, not more so. The only thing that stopped this interlude from being a complete disaster was that our marriage turned out to be strong enough to withstand it. Do I regret doing it? I don't think so. Would I do it again? No.

One important thing has changed. In a strange way the hundred days have taught me to be more patient. If you binge on something productive, you will get results; but you would get the same results if you worked steadily over a year or eighteen months, or, as Richard Herring would have it, five years. And would that really be so bad? The hundred gigs was not a magic pill. It made me a slightly better performer at the expense of being a significantly worse wife and mother. It didn't make me a brilliant performer. That is the work of a lifetime. You can't get around the work of a lifetime, you just have to do it.

On the other hand, I feel curiously protective towards the idea of the hundred days. It is immensely powerful. Much better than any New Year's resolution. It really makes you do something and propels you forward. If you have a painful change that you need to make in your life, if you need to shake things up, if you want to see fast results and are not too scared of the fallout, then I would recommend it. The problem is, I became scared of the fallout.

I do have a new-found respect for the loons who have made comedy their life. They have done the equivalent of this experiment dozens of times for years. It's not unusual for people to do a hundred gigs in a month just at the Edinburgh Festival. To be fair, most of the people who have done something like this were not at the same stage of life as I am. But still. They may not have had spouses and offspring waiting at home, disgruntled. But it's still admirable to go out there and force yourself to get better. Some people would argue it's just a form of addiction: you get hooked on the buzz and the adrenaline and you keep going back for more.

That's a part of it, but I no longer think that's the whole picture. The best stand-up comedians are committed, focused and ridiculously hard-working. They're not unlike athletes, really, training for a big race. Or, say, competitors getting ready for the World Professional Darts Championship. It's like the motto of the US Olympic team: 'Not every four years. Every day.'

I tell Simon this. 'Yes,' he answers, 'but that is an appropriate motto for an Olympic athlete. It is not an appropriate motto for you.' He's right. He's right. I know he's right.

AFTERWORD

One Year Later

Six months after Gig 100, Julia Chamberlain, the judge from the Reading New Act of the Year competition, found herself making a phone call: 'Viv? Congratulations. You're in the semi-finals of "So You Think You're Funny?".' This is the biggest new act competition. It was Viv's first gig in Edinburgh, attended by her friend Dawn. Viv did not go through to the next round, which meant that she did not perform in front of Ruby Wax and did not win £5,000. On the way back from Edinburgh, Viv received a text from Simon quoting Vera: 'I hope you have a safe journey home. You tried your best. THOUGH YOU HAVEN'T WINNED.' Dawn's mother Rosemary has not expressed a desire to see Viv's comedy.

One year to the day after she first started the Directionless Comedy Binge, Viv heard she was through to the finals of Funny Women 2012 at Leicester Square Theatre. She did not win.

Valerie Landsburg (Doris in *Fame*) continues to work as an actress, director, singer and on-set coach. Viv recently joined her online fan club at www.valerielandsburg.com and has tried repeatedly to connect with her via LinkedIn and other social media channels, so far unsuccessfully.

In August 2012 the clown–comic Dr Brown won the Foster's Edinburgh Comedy Award (formerly the Perrier). Viv has still not taken her children to see his show.

Viv never returned to the club where she met Orgasm Man. She has yet to impersonate herself having an orgasm on stage.

Viv has still not performed at Touching Cloth.

Latvian comic Gatis Kandis, who won the Gong at the Comedy Store the night Viv managed to get to fifty-two seconds, appeared in the audition rounds of *Britain's Got Talent*, where Simon Cowell called him 'the world's funniest unfunny comedian'.

Oprah Winfrey continues to be one of the most successful women in the world. She says: 'When you're aligned with your heart's desire, when you're in sync with who you're meant to be and how you're supposed to contribute to our magnificent Earth, you feel a shift in perception.' Viv has still not met her and does not expect to.

Stephen Fry never seems to mention the fact that he performed with Viv in Cambridge in 1992. It's like it means nothing to him.

Simon and Viv celebrated their thirteenth wedding anniversary in February 2013.

Viv no longer drinks Diet Coke.

Acknowledgements

This book only exists because of Marcel Theroux, John Mitchinson and Dawn Isaac's mother, Rosemary. Without them laughing in my face at the turn my life had taken, it would never have occurred to me that there was a story here. Also, without necessarily meaning to, these people all made this happen: Logan Murray, Phil Burgers, Rachel Brushfield and Prue Harrison. But I would most like to thank this man for his endless tolerance, support and inspiration: Andrew Gordon.

Thank you to all the incredible team at Orion, especially editor Jane Sturrock, publicist Jess Gulliver and marketing guru Mark Rusher, who 'got' this book from the start. Thanks to Nicola Crossley and Abi Hartsthorne for putting up with my demented emails and general control freakery. Thanks to photographer Pal Hansen who shot the cover. And to Pete Avery and Susie McConnell for their brilliant creative ideas.

I could not have done any of this without the unexpected kindness, surprising generosity and mammoth disorganisation that is the amateur comedy circuit. Thanks to everyone on Comedy Collective on Facebook and all the comics and promoters who unwittingly enabled this ill-advised experiment including Tom Webb, Thom Tuck, Sara Pascoe, Danielle Ward, Rosie Wilby, Helen Rutter, Kerry Shale and True Stories Told

Live, Daisy Leitch and Eleanor O'Keeffe at 5 X 15, Barry Ferns, Katerina Vrana, Eden Rivers, Emma at The Hob, Richard Rogers, Liam at Walk the Plank, Martin Besserman, Gemma Beagley, Janet Bettesworth, Oli Bettesworth and Jayde Adams at The Painted Grin, Michael Kossew, Linus Lee, Ellie Taylor, Mr Soundbytz, Catia Ciarico and everyone at the RVT, Jay at Comedy Bin, Xave Fernandez, Dan Green, Julia Chamberlain, Sarma Woolf, Richard Ryszynski, Steve Bowditch, Junior Booker, Daphna Baram, Adam Larter, Zoe Grisedale, Tiernan Douieb and Comedy Club 4 Kids.

Huge thanks and a cake vodka toast to Wes Kennemore, Shellie Schmals and everyone at Relapse in Atlanta. I owe a huge debt of gratitude to Lucy Porter which can never be repaid. She was supportive and encouraging at a time when I really didn't deserve it. To anyone offended I have missed them out: it's not intentional and anyway you can use your anger for material.

These people are to be thanked for their friendship, support and the best loud, false laughs: Mako Abashidze, Chas and Jane Awdry, Sam Baker, Simon Booker, Lucie-Anne Brailsford, Alex Brewer, Maura Brickell, Claire Cozens, Adam Chase, Kira Cochrane, Hana Downing, Sarah Franklin, Eleanor Garland, Tania Glyde, Rosie Hallam, Birna Helgadottir, Christie Hickman, Dawn Isaac, Jo Kuenssberg, Ruth Lee, Gareth Llewellyn, Tim Moore, Fin O'Sullivan, Carla and Michael Maroussas, Jen Mathias, Sue Matthias, Melanie McGrath, Zoe and Ed Millington-Jones, Rebecca Mitchell, Susan Pollock, Lucy Rock, Tamsin Stanley, Antonia and Duncan Taylor, Will Tillotson, Hanne Tuomisto-Inch, Sian Walters and Naomi West.

For support and inspiration after the 100 gigs and during the period when I was writing up, thank you to Lynne Parker and everyone at Funny Women, Maggie Tibble at Dead Parrot Society, Suzanne Azzopardi, Sean and Renata Brightman at We

Heart Comedy, Simon Lukacs at Gits and Shiggles at the Half Moon and everyone in Upstairs Downton. For reading stuff that no one should have had to read and innumerable other selfless acts: Alex Clark and Hannah Droy. For being amazing: Ola Majerz. For emergency childcare and a lifetime's patience: my wonderful sister Trudy and my long-suffering parents Ivor and Anna.

But the biggest thank you has to go to Will, Vera and Jack, to whom I owe everything. Even more so to Simon who now says, 'I don't hate stand-up comedy. I just hate bad stand-up comedy.' And who can blame him?